PRINT AND POPULAR CULTURE IN IRELAND, 1750–1850

EARLY MODERN HISTORY: Society and Culture
General Editors: **Rab Houston,** *Professor of Early Modern History,
University of St Andrews, Scotland,* **Edward Muir,** *Professor of History,
Northwestern University, Illinois,* and **Bob Scribner,** *Professor for the
History of Western Christianity, Harvard Divinity School, Cambridge,
Massachusetts*

This series encompasses all aspects of early modern history from 1400 to
1800. Broadly conceived to emphasize innovative work in social and
cultural history, it includes not only the traditional venues of British and
European history but also the Americas and other cultures around the
globe. The editors seek fresh and adventurous monographs, especially
those with a comparative and theoretical approach, from both
new and established scholars.

Titles include:

Niall Ó Ciosáin
PRINT AND POPULAR CULTURE IN IRELAND, 1750–1850

Samantha A. Meigs
THE REFORMATIONS IN IRELAND: Tradition and Confessionalism,
1400–1690

Early Modern History: Society and Culture
Series Standing Order ISBN 0–333–71194–7
(*outside North America only*)

You can receive future titles in this series as they are published by placing a standing order.
Please contact your bookseller or, in case of difficulty, write to us at the address below with
your name and address, the title of the series and the ISBN quoted above.

Customer Services Department, Macmillan Distribution Ltd
Houndmills, Basingstoke, Hampshire RG21 6XS, England

Charles Seale-Hayne Library
University of Plymouth
(01752) 588 588
LibraryandITenquiries@plymouth.ac.uk

Print and Popular Culture in Ireland, 1750–1850

Niall Ó Ciosáin
Lecturer, Department of History
University College, Galway
Ireland

First published in Great Britain 1997 by
MACMILLAN PRESS LTD
Houndmills, Basingstoke, Hampshire RG21 6XS and London
Companies and representatives throughout the world

A catalogue record for this book is available from the British Library.

ISBN 0–333–66684–4

First published in the United States of America 1997 by
ST. MARTIN'S PRESS, INC.,
Scholarly and Reference Division,
175 Fifth Avenue, New York, N.Y. 10010

ISBN 0–312–17455–1

Library of Congress Cataloging-in-Publication Data
Ó Ciosáin, Niall, 1960–
Print and popular culture in Ireland, 1750–1850 / Niall Ó Ciosáin.
p. cm. — (Early modern history series)
Includes bibliographical references and index.
ISBN 0–312–17455–1 (cloth)
1. Ireland—Civilization—18th century. 2. Popular literature–
–Publishing—Ireland—History—18th century. 3. Popular literature–
–Publishing—Ireland—History—19th century. 4. Popular culture–
–Ireland—History—18th century. 5. Popular culture—Ireland–
–History—19th century. 6. Printing—Ireland—History—18th
century. 7. Printing—Ireland—History—19th century. 8. Ireland–
–Civilization—19th century. I. Title. II. Series.
DA947.3.O29 1997
941.5—dc21   97–5891
                                                              CIP

This book is printed on paper suitable for recycling and made from fully managed and
sustained forest sources.

10 9 8 7 6 5 4 3 2
06 05 04 03 02 01 00 99 98

Printed and bound in Great Britain by
Antony Rowe Ltd, Chippenham, Wiltshire

Contents

List of Tables

List of Figures

Acknowledgements

So many people have given help and advice during the writing of this book that it would be impossible to list them all. However, I wish to express a special thanks to David Dickson and Daniel Roche who supervised the dissertation on which it is based. Thanks are also due to those who read and commented on the whole or part of the text: Thomas Bartlett, Martin Burke, Brian Earls, Rab Houston, Tanya Kiang, Ed Muir, Éamon Ó Ciosáin, Séamus Ó Ciosáin, Cormac Ó Gráda, Gearóid Ó Tuathaigh, Larry Taylor, Chris Wheatley.

1 Approaches and Methods

This book is intended as a contribution to the reconstruction of the local and popular cultures of eighteenth- and nineteenth-century Ireland, of beliefs, attitudes and practices among the majority of the population. The problems of documenting such cultures in the past are well known. The words and beliefs of the majority are rarely, if ever, available in forms which are not heavily mediated. Most of the archives and material objects which survive were produced by rich and powerful minorities, and deal with their immediate concerns. When the majority are described, it is usually by hostile or uncomprehending observers. It is easy in these cases to mistake the categories of interpretation of an educated observer for those of the people being described. There are some archives, particularly judicial and inquisitorial, which transcribe statements made by ordinary witnesses, but these are witnesses who find themselves in unusual and often intimidating circumstances.

The case of Ireland presents additional problems, since there is a relative lack of even these unsatisfactory sources. Institutional archives in Ireland have little of the type of material used in studies of popular culture elsewhere in western Europe, such as ecclesiastical visitations and court proceedings. The destruction of much of the Irish public records in the wars of 1919–22 entailed the loss of most of the legal material, as well as many of the records of the state church, the Protestant Church of Ireland. Because of the semi-clandestine nature of its existence in the eighteenth century, Catholic church material, such as pastoral visitations, is scarce also, and parish registers are rare before 1800.

One way of beginning to resolve the general problems of documentation is to study cultural objects which survive, in this case cheap printed books, and to attempt to reconstruct their production, circulation, use and interpretation. Studies of cheap print in early modern Europe have proliferated in recent decades, and there is now a substantial historiography devoted to the *Bibliothèque Bleue* in France and chapbooks in England.[1] The subject remains relatively neglected in Ireland, although given the shortage of other sources, a study of popular print culture assumes greater importance than usual in the Irish context.

In studying the printed popular literature which circulated in rural Ireland between the middle of the eighteenth century and the middle of the nineteenth century, the aim of this book is therefore to reconstruct

1

the dynamics of popular print literacy as a guide to the wider cultures of the time. In particular, cheap print gives an initial hold on popular cultural practice during a period of transition from a predominantly oral culture to a predominantly literate one. There is therefore an interaction between print and previous cultural forms, producing a range of possible uses and interpretations. The texts examined are not taken to be a straightforward reflection of popular cultures; an ethnography of their use, however, offers an opportunity to see those cultures at work, to see them as dynamic processes as well as sets of fixed ideas.

The aim, in other words, is not simply to study texts, but the circulation, possession and reading of popular print more generally. For a readership in the past, however, and particularly for a popular readership, this can rarely be documented in detail.[2] The subject remains underdeveloped, and many contributions are in the form of proposals rather than syntheses.[3] In Ireland, moreover, there are again problems of documentation, and even within the field of popular reading, resources used elsewhere are scarce. Probate inventories, for example, have been fundamental to studies of material culture and the possession of books in England and France; in Ireland, inventories for any but the rich are almost unknown.[4] Similarly, working-class autobiographies have been collected and used by Vincent to construct a rich and nuanced account of popular reading in eighteenth- and nineteenth-century England; such a corpus has not been collected yet in Ireland, although there are of course a few well-known examples of the genre.[5]

Some impression of the styles of reading can be inferred from the way a text is presented in printed form, from the 'implied reader' envisaged by the writer or, more usually, printer. The printer was also a mediator between cultures, however, and the readings envisaged by him or her were not necessarily those of the purchaser. We need, therefore, to take account of a broader social and cultural context from which may be inferred a range of possible readings of popular printed texts.

IRELAND 1750–1850

For the majority of the rural population in Ireland, the period from the mid-eighteenth to the mid-nineteenth century can be treated as a single, fairly coherent, unit. It ends with the Famine of the late 1840s, probably the great cultural break in modern Irish history. The Famine marks a discontinuity, not so much for psychological reasons as for material and demographic ones. The quarter of the population which died or emigrated in those years consisted largely of the rural poor, labourers and small farmers, whose previously vibrant culture was shattered in most areas, and whose language, religion and world-view were increasingly confined to the west coast.

The population of Ireland, which peaked at over eight million immediately before the Famine, had begun to increase about a century before. This increase was of course shared with most of western Europe, but the rate of growth in Ireland was unusually high: the population quadrupled in little over a century. The economic stimuli which partly underlay this growth also began to produce broad cultural change, in particular a rise in demand for literacy skills, with a consequent expansion in educational facilities and printed production. These developments make the middle of the eighteenth century an obvious point of departure for a study of popular print and its reception.

These stimuli were part of what can be characterised as a double economic cycle which encompassed the century in question. This cycle can be broadly allotted to two regions. In the south and east, there was a shift from the traditional pastoral farming towards tillage, responding to demand for grain in Britain. In the north and west, there was rapid growth in domestic textile production, particularly of linen, also largely aimed at export to Britain. The buoyancy of both sectors was reinforced by the Revolutionary and Napoleonic wars which gave Ireland a privileged position in the British market.

After about 1820, however, the economic context was less favourable. The linen industry made a successful transition to factory production in Belfast and the north-east. this however produced massive deindustrialisation in the rest of the textile area from the 1820s onwards. In the south and east, tillage prices declined relative to cattle prices in the same period, and the sector began to reach the limits of its productive capacity. Large farmers with access to capital turned back to livestock; smaller farmers and labourers, whose numbers continued to increase, suffered severe underemployment and impoverishment. In the north and west, therefore, poverty was evenly spread, social structure relatively homogeneous, and farm sizes relatively uniform. In the south and east, on the other hand, the growth in the number of poor was accompanied by the emergence of a prosperous commercial farming class, and the distribution of farm sizes was bimodal.[6]

The social tensions which accompanied the economic fluctuations of this period were articulated through large and frequently violent oath-bound agrarian organisations. These organisations, under such names as Whiteboys and Ribbonmen, attempted, through communal sanctions and violence, to regulate economic and social transactions. They may be crudely characterised by reference to the two economic areas already mentioned.

In the tillage and cattle areas, the issues at stake were of two kinds. Conflict over rent and declining harvest labour, as well as the evictions through which large cattle farms were created, pitted small farmers and labourers against the larger commercial farmers who were their employers and immediate landlords. Conflict over the tithe payable to the established Church of Ireland united the predominantly Catholic rural population, producing violent campaigns of immense size and duration.

In many of the textile areas, the demographic balance between religious denominations was more even, and agrarian societies there were more frequently divided on sectarian or kin-group lines, attempting to gain or control access to land and employment. Protestant–Catholic conflict was by 1800 institutionalised, with the emergence of the Orange Order on the Protestant side and the Defenders and Ribbonmen on the Catholic. The Ribbonmen, who like the agrarian societies of the south were illegal, and the Orange Order, who were suppressed in 1836, engaged in sporadic conflict throughout the nineteenth century, both in the countryside and later in the growing industrial town of Belfast.[7]

The historiography of these societies, influenced by studies of popular protest and collective action elsewhere in Europe, emphasises the strong sense of legitimacy, different to that of state law, which underlay their activity and organisation. This sense of legitimacy, whether derived from custom or from communal agreement, found symbolic expression in Ireland in a number of ways. Many agrarian societies claimed the authority of a mythical figure, a 'Captain Right' whose name permeated their actions. Perhaps the strongest expression of alternative legitimacy was the administering of an oath of secrecy to members, often using a printed text for its quasi-magical powers. This oath took precedence over legal oaths and over the confessional, and was consequently a source of great alarm to both state and churches. Questions of legitimacy were particularly acute in Ireland, and questions of authority and legitimacy are prominent in popular literature in Ireland.

At a national level, political activity and innovation were concentrated in two decades, the 1790s and the 1820s. The 1790s witnessed the confluence of campaigns for reform of the parliamentary system by the radical, mainly urban, United Irishmen, and for civic equality for Catholics by the Catholic Committee. When combined with the influence of the French Revolution and a strong reaction by government and conservatives, this produced a high level of political mobilisation and later of military activity, culminating in a brief but bloody rebellion in the summer of 1798 in the counties of the eastern seaboard, notably in Antrim and Wexford.

The 1820s saw the mobilisation of a very large section of the Catholic population of the south and east of Ireland, particularly in east Munster and south Leinster, in an organisation directed mainly at parliamentary elections, the Catholic Association. Its principal innovations included using the local structures of the Catholic church to achieve unanimity in the Catholic vote. The Association, headed by Daniel O'Connell, was based in the towns of the tillage areas, drew much of its funding from the Catholic merchants and large farmers of the area, and successfully used the personnel and discipline of the agrarian societies of the surrounding countryside.

As regards religious affiliation, most of the population, particularly in the southern part of the country, was Catholic. In the eighteenth century, Catholics had certain legal disabilities, including restrictions on the ownership and leasing of land and entry to some occupations. These were removed towards the end of the eighteenth century. Protestants, consisting essentially of Anglicans and Presbyterians, were concentrated in particular areas, and were a majority only in the north-east.

In terms of popular religious belief and practice, it appears that the Protestant population, and particularly the Presbyterian, was as a whole more evangelised and orthodox. The profile of female religious literacy shows a strong religious base in Protestant areas which is lacking in Catholic ones. Another indicator would be accusations of demonic witchcraft, which at a popular level would indicate the impact of reform. The two principal accusations recorded in Ireland were both within Protestant communities, in Youghal, Co. Cork, in 1661, and in Larne, Co. Antrim, in 1711. Popular Catholic conceptions of witchcraft were still largely concerned with individual, non-demonic magic. Peasant cosmologies, in the eighteenth century at least, remained little affected by official church doctrine, and the widespread printing and possession of catechisms, for example, was a development of the late eighteenth century. Most of the rural Catholic population, therefore, and particularly the lower class, participated in what can be described as a traditional peasant culture. Its sense of time was regulated by seasonal and calendar rituals; its cosmology was deeply local and supernatural, emphasising the powers inherent in places, objects and people.[8]

A comprehensive Catholic Tridentine reform began in the mid to late eighteenth century, sponsored by the large farmers and urban merchants of the tillage area. It was consolidated in the aftermath of the Great Famine, which decimated the least orthodox classes. Parallel to the Catholic mission was a revival of activity among the Catholic peasantry by Protestant churches and lay groups. This 'second reformation', partly influenced by the revival of evangelicalism in Britain and partly in reaction to the radical political activity of the 1790s, was at its height in the early nineteenth century. The reaction to these efforts by the Catholic church led to a rapid rise in inter-denominational competition, with the result that the first half of the nineteenth century was, in most of Ireland, a period of high sectarian tension, most evident in a protracted struggle over control of primary education during the 1820s.

Alongside the religious divide, but not coinciding with it, was the other great cultural divide, that of language. Ireland was at all points between 1750 and 1850, an intensely bilingual and diglossic society. English was the language of the elite, the state, law and print. Its economic and social benefits were clear, and by the late nineteenth century, Ireland had undergone one of the most rapid and total language shifts in modern European history. Because of the rise in population, however, the absolute numbers speaking Irish did not decline between 1750 and 1850. They may even have been increasing in the decades around 1800, and remained high until the Famine. Printed popular texts in English were therefore frequently entering a community which was partly if not wholly Irish-speaking, or which had recently become English-speaking.

This has been a very general sketch of a context of reception for popular print, and particular local contexts and cultures will emerge in the course of this study. In this regard, the lack of sources mentioned should not be exaggerated, and there is much material which can be exploited, making, of course, due allowance for its biases and omissions. Voluminous state inquiries into Irish conditions, preoccupied and shaped by perceptions of economic crisis and popular disorder, were published in the early nineteenth century. Many of them, such as the decennial censuses beginning in 1821, and more than twenty reports on education, constitute rich social description. A substantial police and central administrative archive remains, which has been extensively used in studies of popular politics and protest. There is also a rich avowedly ethnographic literature, ranging from commentators on social and economic conditions to early folklorists.

This study has also used Irish language material, looking for traces of what was overwhelmingly an English-language print literature. A large body of manuscripts was produced in the eighteenth and nineteenth centuries, constituting a tradition which ultimately stemmed from the learned classes of pre-seventeenth century Gaelic Ireland. Although relatively democratised by 1800, manuscript culture was still an educated culture, transmitting many technical legal and historical texts. The scribes and poets of the nineteenth century were generally poor. Particularly useful for a study of popular attitudes is the work of such 'public poets' as Tomás Ruadh Ó Súilleabháin of Kerry, or Antaine Ó Raiftearaí (Raftery) from Mayo, who composed verses on current affairs, notably the political campaigns of O'Connell in the 1820s.[9]

The principal source of oral material is the large state folklore archive which was collected by the Irish Folklore Commission in the 1930s and 1940s. This archive, containing material in both Irish and English, while immense, presents a number of difficulties for the present study. In the first place, it dates from the early twentieth century and is more accurately regarded as a reflection of attitudes and practices in that later period. Secondly, the Commission directed its attention principally to the west coast, where Irish was still spoken and which was felt to be more 'authentic', and sent fewer collectors elsewhere. Finally, the material collected was influenced by the interests of both the Commission and individual collectors, some of whom condensed it in transcription.[10]

Like all transcriptions of oral sources, therefore, this archive is not a direct approach to a popular culture, but is substantially mediated through the working assumptions of its collectors. Nevertheless, much can be learned from oral archives. Narratives and other material were collected which clearly derive from chapbook originals. Such survival is not necessarily a guide to the relative appeal of printed texts in an earlier period, since other items deriving from print may simply not have been collected. It can, however, offer a guide to the styles of reading employed, and to the ways in which some printed material was appropriated and transmitted, some of which can appear quite radical to a literate observer.[11]

THE HISTORIOGRAPHY OF POPULAR LITERATURE

As with popular cultures in general, most descriptions of popular printed literature come from outsiders and mediators, and are formed by the attitudes and interests of those observers. A study of the history of representations of popular literature, down to the present day, is consequently a necessary prelude to a study of that literature itself.

At the beginning of the early modern period, as cultural practices changed within an elite which was increasingly acquiring education and literacy, popular cultures began to be differentiated from those of the elite. In the field of literature, texts which had previously been located among the elite, or had formed part of a common culture, came to be located exclusively in popular milieux and produced in exclusively popular formats. These included for example romances of chivalry, which were originally medieval courtly literature but by the eighteenth century were only found in chapbook form. Ireland was no exception: romances had been written and translated for the aristocracy, particularly in the later Middle Ages, and had become folk tales and folk literature by the eighteenth century.

There was a continuous tradition of elite commentary on this popular literature, both in Ireland and Europe. It was not homogeneous, however, and descriptions varied with time and with the cultural outlook of the commentator. Three types of attitude are visible within this tradition. They are disdain and ridicule, suspicion and a desire to control, and finally antiquarian and folkloric interest. They emerge roughly in that order, although examples of all three can be found during most periods.

An elite perception of popular literature as debased had emerged by the late sixteenth century in England. According to George Puttenham's *Arte of English Poesie* of 1598, 'poets should rise above the common taste of tavern minstrels reciting such stories as *Bevis of Southampton*, *Guy of Warwick* and their kind, made purposely for the recreation of the common people', while the poet Thomas Nashe asked 'Who is it that reading *Bevis* can forbear laughing?' A London bookseller's catalogue of 1657 condemned those who:

> idly sit down in the chair of ignorance, travelling by the fireside, with the wandering knight John Mandevil, or it may be Bevis of Southampton, whilst the laws of nations, admirable foundations of commonwealths, pass undiscovered or dived into.[12]

A more hostile Irish example comes from the English commentator Barnaby Rich who, while criticising Catholics, contrasts 'the lettered sort of papists' with those who:

> scarcely understand what they themselves do read, but are better practiced in Gesta Romanorum, in The Seven Wise Masters, in Bevis

of Hampton ... than they be in the Bible or Testament, or in any other book that doth concern true godliness ...[13]

These attitudes persisted throughout the seventeenth and eighteenth centuries. A Dublin Catholic bookseller in 1735 condemned 'the reading of old immoral, ridiculous romances', while a similar contrast to that of Rich was put into the mouth of a priest by the Ulster poet Aodh Mac Gabhráin in about 1700:

> Tráth bhínn-se ag an bpápa ag staidéar na ngrásta
> 'S ag glacadh na ngradhamh thall ins an Róimh
> 'Sé an *Seven Wise Masters* bhí agat ar do tháirr
> 'S tú ag rósta na bprátaí láimh leis an tSídh Mhóir.[14]

[When I was studying the graces with the pope and being ordained in Rome, you had the *Seven Wise Masters* on your belly while you roasted potatoes beside Sheemore.]

By the middle of the eighteenth century, aesthetic or religious condemnation had been joined, and even superseded, by suspicion of the politics of popular literature. Progressive sections of the elite saw it as perpetuating archaic values, while conservative elements blamed it for political unrest and rebellion; elements in both sections attempted to replace it with material of their own. In revolutionary France, a questionnaire about the language and customs of rural areas was circulated by the National Assembly in 1790, and when cheap popular literature, known as the *Bibliothèque Bleue*, was mentioned, it was in negative terms, such as 'ces misères'.[15]

In Ireland both the radical United Irishmen and various conservative organisations attempted to infiltrate and control the channels of popular print. Examples of conservative suspicion in particular are numerous after the 1790s. The chapbook literature was frequently referred to in pamphlets and reports on political and social conditions, and held to be subversive in content. Robert Bell in 1804 referred to:

> Romances describing the manners of barbarous and superstitious ages (such as the Seven Champions of Christendom, Guy Earl of Warwick, Valentine and Orson, Don Belianis of Greece etc.) [which] were not calculated to inspire youth with correct notions of law or government, especially when unaccompanied with any other kind of reading that might do away with the bad impressions they had made.[16]

After 1850, elite interest became more antiquarian, though a great deal of suspicion and condescension remained. France under the Second

Empire saw a comprehensive attempt to suppress the *Bibliothèque Bleue* through a system of state censorship and licensing. One by-product of this process was the first full description of the corpus of texts, published by Charles Nisard, the head of the commission of investigation. *Histoire des Livres populaires ou de la Littérature de Colportage*, with lengthy extracts from a selection of texts, appeared in 1854.[17]

Nisard's book found echoes in Britain, where Cardinal Wiseman chose it as a model in a lecture at an education exhibition in London in 1855. Cheap printed literature was, according to Wiseman, 'a mass of trash' and some of it was 'absolutely intolerable, and cannot be mentioned with propriety'. In passing, however, he pointed to the emerging antiquarian interest:

> I might have added that some of the books which have been published, and up to a very late period circulated, are in their character so curious, and will become in a few years so rare, that they are already being snatched up by collectors and placed in their libraries.[18]

By the late nineteenth and early twentieth century, when different political and moral dangers were preoccupying elites, discussion of the chapbook literature became nostalgic, the province of antiquarians, folklorists and bibliophiles.

Antiquarian journals in England had regular articles on the subject, and there were some collections of facsimile reprints such as John Ashton's *Chap-books of the Eighteenth Century*, printed in 1882. These characterise the texts as quaint and unusual objects for collectors. Ashton's preface describes the books as 'very curious . . . bear[ing] strange testimony to the ignorance and credulity of their purchasers', but they are 'prized by book collectors and fetch high prices'.[19]

In Ireland, the second printing of Nisard's book was noted and its contents summarised in the *Dublin University Magazine* in 1865. The following year, the magazine carried a similar article on Irish popular literature. The anonymous articles were written by the bookseller and folklorist Patrick Kennedy. Although the *DUM* could be described as politically conservative, Kennedy did not share Nisard's alarm, saying that perhaps only half of the French books were in any way pernicious, and that few of those who read them would be affected. He also pointed to the contradiction involved in publishing extracts from these supposedly dangerous books. Kennedy described having read many of the Irish texts while young, and dismissed the idea that they might be harmful.

The absence of alarm can also be seen in the fact that the second article was called 'Irish folk books of the last century', although the article itself mentions that most of the texts discussed were still being printed. The only disdain which accompanies this antiquarianism is aesthetic: 'the narrative [of chivalric romance] has scarcely more continuity and consistence than a dream.'[20] The principal further examples of antiquarian interest in Ireland are a history of Irish almanacs by Evans, published in 1897, and a series of short articles in the principal bibliographic periodical, *The Irish Book Lover,* in 1910–12.[21]

By 1900, therefore, the chapbook literature was seen as distant, as a relic of another culture which had disappeared or was disappearing, along with folk tales and folk song. The texts are presented as curious and slightly grotesque, not conforming to the artistic canons of the time. This was due in part to the fact that they contain strong residues of oral tradition and were probably intended to be read aloud. During the early modern period, they had come to be located exclusively among those social groups where reading aloud continued to be practised.

This helps explain a parallel and contemporaneous process, by which the texts of chapbook literature, like fairy and folk tales, became a part of children's literature within the elite. In other words, where silent, individual reading had become the norm for adults, oral texts gravitated to the only place where reading aloud survived, and where adults read to children. Spufford cites examples of nostalgia for youthful reading of chivalric romances and other texts among non-popular readers: James Boswell, for example, bought two dozen chapbooks in London in 1763 because they reminded him of his childhood reading.[22] Similar examples can be found in early nineteenth-century Ireland. Like Patrick Kennedy, the barrister Edward Vaughan Kenealy recalled in his autobiography reading fairy tales and *The Seven Champions of Christendom* when growing up in a middle-class home in Cork in the 1820.[23]

This study will not consider the chapbooks as children's literature, however, except to the extent that they were used as reading books in primary schools. In any case, they were read in schools not because they were thought of as children's books, but because they were the easiest books to find in the countryside for a pupil who had finished with elementary reading primers.

RECENT DISCUSSION AND METHODOLOGY

Within modern historiography, attention began to be focused again on early modern popular literature in the 1960s, in the context of social and cultural history, particularly in France. The first large-scale treatment was that of Robert Mandrou, whose *De la Culture Populaire* appeared in 1964. This work took the corpus of the *Bibliothèque Bleue*, printed in Troyes in the seventeenth and eighteenth centuries and mainly preserved in the municipal library there, and subjected it to a global analysis. The corpus was ideal for the quantitative and serial approach taken by Mandrou: it consisted of a limited number of texts in a small number of locations, and could be analysed diachronically over a medium duration as well as synchronically. The texts were allotted to a number of genres, and conclusions drawn about popular mentalities based on characterisations of those genres and their relative quantitative importance. A similar approach is found in the work of Spufford on seventeenth-century England, again based on the study of a single library holding, which compares the importance of genres in England and France.[24]

An alternative approach, which developed simultaneously with the first, was to select one well-defined genre within popular literature, and to subject both its content and its use in practice to a close analysis. Almanacs, for example, were treated by Bollème for France and by Capp for England. The most substantial manifestation of this approach was the publication of a series of genre-based collections of original *Bibliothèque Bleue* texts in the early 1980s, each with a lengthy introduction discussing the genre, the origins of the texts and their uses. The featured genres were criminal biography, rogue literature, tales, cookery books, books about women and books about death.[25]

More recently, particularly in the work of Chartier, this genre-based approach has moved towards a history of popular styles of reading, similar to the 'aesthetics of reception' practised within literary criticism. Due to the relative lack of sources with which to document possible styles of 'popular' reading in the early modern period, and particularly the absence of direct testimony from lower-class readers themselves, the approach is necessarily broader. It focuses not only on the reading implied by the authorial voice, but also on that implied by the interventions of publisher and printer. This leads to a greater consideration of the book as a material object, of publishing strategies, of the ways in which texts were adapted from elite or learned sources, and attempts to infer popular styles of reading from the physical layout of the texts in popular editions. A more ethnographic approach is possible for nineteenth-century readers, and Vincent has used principally working-class autobiographies to provide rich documentation of the impact of printed material in general on people's lives.[26]

These different approaches have produced different interpretations of the cultural role of popular literature. Mandrou was struck by the absence of realism, whether social or scientific, in the corpus as a whole, and concluded that its effect was escapist and retrograde, distracting attention from social and political questions. A milder version of this thesis was adopted by Spufford, who saw the chapbook literature as escapist but harmless, and a more extreme version by Robert Muchembled, who in 1978 presented the *Bibliothèque Bleue* as a form of ideological domination of the people by the elites, to whose advantage such escapism operated.[27]

The conclusions of those who adopt the genre-based approach tend to be more positive. Bollème, for example, presents the almanac as a transitional form of literacy, in which the reader is helped by pictures and diagrams to make sense of the text; moreover, the use of almanacs is indicative of a methodical and proto-scientific approach to time and the agricultural year. For other genres, conclusions tend to vary. Lusebrink, for example, takes the opposite attitude to Mandrou and Muchembled in arguing that criminal biography contained the possibility of a critique of state institutions, and therefore addressed very concrete social and political issues.[28]

Within Irish historiography, only one work has been devoted exclusively to the chapbook literature, Adams's *The Printed Word and the Common Man*. This deals with Belfast printing and adopts the totalising approach, surveying the entire popular output of Belfast presses up until the early nineteenth century, and allotting titles to genres. Eighteenth-century Dublin chapbook printing has also been briefly discussed in the context of the print trade as a whole by both Phillipps and Pollard.[29]

This study will broadly follow the genre approach, for a number of reasons. From a practical point of view, in Ireland there is no library holding, such as those in Troyes or Cambridge, or series of printers' inventories, which presents itself for quantitative or serial treatment. Concentration on a limited number of genres also permits a closer examination of the genesis and reception of particular texts, and consequently a more nuanced view of the dynamics of print culture. Finally, the genre approach allows for a flexible comparative framework, looking at groups of similar texts elsewhere.

To determine these groups, two strategies are used. The first begins with consumption, and uses contemporary elite descriptions of popular reading. These descriptions are found principally in pamphlets on the state of Ireland in the late eighteenth and early nineteenth centuries, occasionally in travellers' accounts (notably in Thackeray's *Irish Sketch Book* of 1843) and less frequently in the testimony of popular readers themselves, such as the autobiography of William Carleton (1794–1869), a novelist who came from a peasant family in Co. Tyrone.[30]

The second strategy focuses on the production end of the market, mainly on printers' lists and similar documentation. From a material analysis of these data a number of genres emerge; not all were susceptible of treatment, however, since in some cases insufficient texts had survived.

CONTEMPORARY DESCRIPTIONS

From the pamphlet literature on Irish conditions in the early nineteenth century referred to above emerges a strikingly unanimous picture of what the ordinary people in rural areas were reading. An early example from Whitley Stokes in 1799 is representative both in content and tone, and lists some of the most frequent genres:

> The lower classes in Ireland, until within these few years, confined their purchases of books to a particular kind, called Burtons, which they got for sixpence apiece ... of these there were about eighty, and they might be divided into the following classes: histories of robbers and pirates; books of chivalry; books of witchcraft and gross superstition; indecent books; these classes constituted about two thirds of the whole number, the remaining third consisting of useful or innocent books of voyages, travel, history or novels ... Some will think romances innocent, but these works contribute greatly to keep alive a false admiration of courage, a spirit of war and revenge, and a love of adventure so incompatible with the happiness of mankind.[31]

Very similar lists are found in some of the early nineteenth-century statistical surveys and descriptions, usually in their sections on education;[32] and this list-type attained official status in a parliamentary report on education in 1825:

> The character of the books formerly in use in the common pay schools of Ireland is described by the Reverend Mr. Cooke, Moderator of the Synod of Ulster, who states that when he was a boy, in the five schools through which he passed in the course of his education, the works which formed the subject of his studies were the *Seven Champions of Christendom*, the *Destruction of Troy*, *Hero and Leander*, *Gesta Romanorum*, the *Seven Wise Masters*, the *Chinese Tales*,

Parismos and Parismenos, Don Belianis of Greece, the *History of Captain Freney,* a robber, *Valentine and Orson, the Irish Rogues and Rappar*ees, and the *History of Redmond O'Hanlon,* a notorious Highwayman.[33]

Commentators seem agreed, therefore, on the broad outlines of a corpus of popular literature, a corpus which strongly features chivalric romance and criminal biography. How reliable are these descriptions as evidence?

An initial difficulty concerns the fact that many, if not most, of these writers are referring to the reading material of rural schools, and that therefore these books were read by children rather than adults. Most of these texts, however, would have been too difficult for children who were only learning to read. When they were used in schools, they were probably read by older pupils. This impression is borne out by a list of pupils, together with the books they used, in a school in Valentia, Co. Kerry, in 1795. All the pupils under ten years of age used reading primers, while *The Seven Champions of Christendom* was being read by a 17-year-old, *Captain Freney* by a 16-year-old, and *The Irish Rogues* (also known as *Irish Highwaymen*) by a 14-year-old. Secondly, the books used in schools were usually those which had a more general circulation in the countryside, given that graded readers did not exist. As the 1825 report put it, 'The selection of the book in which each child is to learn to read has been left to the child itself, or to its parents . . . the books which were easily and cheaply to be procured, were thus naturally preferred.' In practice, these would have been the books sold by pedlars, and in this way school reading is a reliable, if indirect, guide to popular texts.[34]

The second problem arises from the very obvious bias of most of these sources, which is clear in the extracts from Stokes and that from Robert Bell quoted earlier. These commentators were suspicious of popular literature and wished to suppress or replace it. They saw it as a contributory factor to the political unrest of the 1790s and the 'disturbed' state of Ireland in the late eighteenth and early nineteenth centuries. They pointed to the existence of unofficial, uncontrolled channels of communication, and to the listed books as the content of a dangerous counter-culture. This has clear implications for their selection and presentation of popular reading. It is possible that the type of book which best fitted this thesis, such as crime literature, was taken as most representative, regardless of whether it was the most read.

This was not quite what happened, however. The texts were presented as subversive, but the reasoning of the writers was different.

They took the books which were in fact being read, and interpreted them as being dangerous. In other words, the bias of these authors affects the presentation and interpretation of the titles, rather than their selection. This is clear in the attitude of Stokes to chivalric romance, or in the comment of Richard Edgeworth in 1809:

> I have been told that in some schools the Greek and Roman histories have been forbidden; such abridgements of these as I have seen are certainly improper; to inculcate democracy and a foolish hankering for liberty is not necessary in Ireland.

In the same period, it was precisely these classical texts which were becoming the basis of a newly institutionalised gentry education in Britain and Ireland.[35]

The final reservation one might have concerning these commentators comes from precisely the unanimity of their descriptions. In fact, many of the later writers were quoting or paraphrasing earlier lists: that of Hely Dutton (1808) was reproduced by Wakefield (1812) and by two correspondents of the Parochial Survey (1814–19), and that of the 1825 Education Report was quoted by pamphleteers and even by travellers throughout the 1820s and 1830s. Therefore, instead of having many sources all apparently corroborating each other, we have in fact two or three original observations being repeated. These observations are, however, supported by the testimony of a few writers who were themselves the product of Irish peasant society, and who had attended hedge schools. That of Henry Cooke is quoted above, and William Carleton in his autobiography gives a very similar list of the books which were circulating in Co. Tyrone during his youth in the 1780s and 1790s.

Overall, therefore, it seems reasonable to accept the testimony of these commentators. Chivalric romance, criminal biography and so on were popular lower-class reading material. They were not, of course, the only works which circulated, but a part of the total: the 1825 Education Report contains a list of books which were in use as readers in schools in only four counties, Donegal, Galway, Kildare and Kerry, and it contains over 300 titles.[36]

QUANTITATIVE SOURCES

Although contemporary testimony is valuable, it clearly needs to be corroborated with other types of source. The most obviously useful is bibliographical, the quantitative analysis of printers' records, printers' advertisements or library holdings and, as we have seen, many studies of popular literature begin from such a quantitative base. Mandrou's work is based on an analysis of the collection of *Bibliothèque Bleue* imprints in the municipal library of Troyes and on the inventories of printers' stocks, while Spufford counted titles in Samuel Pepys' collection of chapbooks and in London printers' records from the 1690s.

The initial form of quantitative analysis divides the material into categories such as 'religion' and 'everyday life', counts the number of titles in each category, and draws conclusions from the proportions of material in the different categories. This procedure structures Mandrou's book, each category providing a chapter. Spufford adopts Mandrou's categories for counting purposes, in order to facilitate comparison between England and France, although in her description of the chapbooks' contents, she adopts the classification of late seventeenth-century London printers themselves, as found in their trade lists and advertisements.[37]

The advantage of such an analysis is that it gives a good initial hold on the subject – if over half of the titles are religious, then it seems safe to assume that religion occupies an important place in the lives of peasant readers, and that their religious practice is text-based to some extent. It also seems to offer a good basis for initial comparison between countries or regions of the sort undertaken by Spufford. For it to be successful, however, it is necessary to have a strictly delimited, fairly representative sample of surviving books. For late eighteenth- and early nineteenth-century Ireland no such sample immediately presents itself. Too many titles seem not to have survived, library holdings are patchy and there is no suitable private collection. A similar problem exists with reference to printers' records. There are very few surviving lists or catalogues of the printers in Dublin who dominated the rural chapbook market in the eighteenth century, and it is impossible to be certain about matters such as the size of print runs and numbers of editions.

In any case, apart from such practical considerations, an approach which derives its initial orientation entirely from this sort of quantification presents many theoretical and methodological problems. Two related questions in particular can be distinguished initially: how are the categories into which the material is to be divided chosen or determined; and, having determined categories, by what criteria are the books allotted to them?

The initial classification schema was that of Mandrou, who distinguished five categories in the seventeenth- and eighteenth-century *Bibliothèque Bleue*: 'pious works', 'popular culture', 'portraits of society', 'everyday life' and 'fairy mythology'. Similarly Martin divides the titles in three parts, 'religion', 'imaginative literature' and 'information and educational'. In both cases, the divisions are introduced without comment and without explaining their origins, although they subsequently structure the discussion of the corpus as a whole.[38]

There are a number of problems with the use of such categories. In the first place, they are vague and imprecise, needing to be subdivided in order to distribute texts satisfactorily. Even these subcategories can be fairly broad: 'popular culture' contains two subsections, 'songs' and 'theatre', which in themselves could contain aspects of most other categories. Secondly, no changes are envisaged in the categories over time: some evolution is possible within them and in their relative weight (such as a decline in religious material, for example) but the overall world-view implicit in them is taken to be fairly static. Finally, the categories are open to the accusation of arbitrariness. Queniart, among others, has sketched alternative ways of dividing and counting books listed in personal inventories, such as distinguishing between those pertaining to the owner's occupation and those not, or between traditional material and modern material. Ultimately, there are no 'objective' taxonomies, and the categories adopted depend on what information is desired from a list.[39]

A further difficulty arises when decisions have to be made allotting individual texts to the categories which have been created. The résumé of one section of *The Seven Champions of Christendom*, for example, is as follows:

> How St. Anthony slew a giant, and released many ladies out of captivity; how St. Andrew travelled through a vale of walking spirits; how St. Patrick redeemed six Thracian ladies from thirty satyrs; how St. David slew the Count Palatine, and how he was sent to the enchanted garden of Ormondine, where he slept seven years.

This can be classified as 'fairy mythology', but its heroes are Christian saints whose non-Christian enemies occasionally attempt to kill them for religious reasons. Similarly, Mandrou and Spufford both place criminal biography as part of 'popular culture' rather than under 'portraits of society', although it can frequently permit a questioning of social rules or demonstrate the consequences of breaking those rules.

These examples show the difficulties of any such attempt at hard and fast division into categories, since it tends to impose the judgement of a cultivated twentieth-century observer on material to which it is not necessarily appropriate. To treat religion as a category separate from society or the supernatural can prejudge the issue of how the books were approached by their readers and indeed conceived by their authors. As De Certeau put it, 'The terms "fairy tale", "supernatural", "pagan", "scientific" and "occult" define less the content of a popular culture than the historian's gaze itself.'[40]

These taxonomic problems are indicative of broader difficulties faced by attempts to quantify and characterise large bodies of printed texts over long periods in a unitary way, attempting to infer a single overall mentality from its constituent parts. Not surprisingly, this mentality turns out to lack coherence, or at least to be tolerant of contradictions. It may well be true that, as Mandrou argues, these contradictions were less apparent (or less worrying) to readers in the past than to the historian in the present; but it seems equally likely that different books were intended for, and read by, different sorts of reader. Very few peasant readers, for example, would have read even a fraction of the amount of books examined by the modern historian (Mandrou looked at 450 *Bibliothèque Bleue* texts), and few would have come close to being presented with this supposed incoherence.[41]

In any case, the incoherence discerned by Mandrou and others resides principally in the texts and not in the readers. This is a key to the problems involved in this sort of approach. It concentrates on production, and needs to be supplemented or even corrected by an examination of consumption, that is, on the reading and interpretation of individual texts. Examination of a large corpus assumes the extensive reading practice of a later age, or of a prosperous educated reader and collector such as Pepys, instead of the intensive and repeated reading of a small number of texts characteristic of a lower-class audience in the early modern period.

In contrast, analysing the reading or use which is made of a text has a number of advantages.[42] It allows the possibility of multiple signification rather than the single meaning usually alloted to a text in most quantification schemes. A text such as *The Seven Champions* might be read as pious, magical and mythical at the same time. Other texts could be read either in a straightforward way or as parodies, and indeed it is occasionally difficult to decide whether certain works are parodies or not. There is also the linked possibility of an interpretation radically different from that which is apparently obvious. An example of this would be the cookery books of the *Bibliothèque Bleue*. One of them, *Le Cuisinier François*, diffused a particular style of cuisine down the social scale. However, it has also been suggested that for some readers, those who could not afford the rich ingredients specified, the book was 'a fairy tale rather than a practical manual', describing feasts they could only dream of.[43]

Despite all these problems, both methodological and, in the case of Ireland, practical, there is clearly a role for quantification and for some sort of initial categorisation of texts. The approach adopted here consists of selecting genres of texts which were remarked on by contemporaries, are a substantial presence in printers' catalogues and indeed in the popular literature of other countries; determining which titles within these categories had the greatest circulation, both in terms of numbers of editions and over time;[44] and working towards some consideration of the ways in which these might have been read at the time. Particular attention will be paid to those genres which were singled out by commentators as being influential, and each genre is the subject of one chapter. The genres are chivalric romance, criminal biography, historical works and religious song.

This study also attempts to follow the study of reading implied by authorial and editorial strategies. The latter differ somewhat from those discerned by Chartier and others in the *Bibliothèque Bleue*. There are of course definite similarities, such as the discontinuous presentation of narrative in the chivalric romances. By and large, however, the texts of Irish origin change very little in their adaptation to chapbook form; it seems that printers and publishers picked those texts which were most susceptible to transfer, and whose original form was short and small. This is the case, for example, with the criminal biographies and with the historical texts of Irish origin. This is not to say that editorial interventions do not occur, and additions and subtractions to different texts will be taken to imply certain interpretations of those texts. The locally specific case of printing in the Irish language, the editorial decisions involved in the presentation of texts in Irish, and the styles of reading which they embody, will also be examined.

MATERIAL CHARACTERISTICS

In selecting a manageable group of texts for analysis, therefore, both contemporary comment and some type of quantification have been taken into account. However, the corpus under discussion is defined not simply in terms of content and genre; equally important are its material appearance and distribution.

In the first place, the books are fairly small in format. They are duodecimo, and usually about three inches by two (7.5 cm by 5 cm).

Most consist of 48, 72, 120 or 144 pages. This makes them longer than the chapbooks considered by Spufford, which are 12 or 24 pages long; on the other hand, many of those in the Troyes collections analysed by Mandrou are even longer than the Irish books, some containing over 200 pages. Shorter Irish texts are much rarer, at least in surviving collections, than the 72- or 144-page volumes. The texts considered, therefore, are relatively lengthy, and imply a public which has achieved a certain facility in reading. At the same time, however, they are capable of being read in short sections, and may have been chosen for that reason. Some of the lives in *Irish Highwaymen*, for example, are two pages long, while longer texts, such as romances, are episodic in structure.

Another feature of the books which implies some fluency in reading is the relative absence of visual illustration in the form of woodcuts within the text, although there was often a single illustration on or inside the front cover. This again means that they bear more resemblance to the Troyes books than to the English chapbooks. Images could act as a transitional form of literacy, and there were various printed forms which embodied different relationships between image and text. Single sheet pictures usually contained some form of text, while short chapbooks such as those discussed by Spufford let a narrative be carried by a series of pictures as much as by the written word. Longer texts without illustration were therefore aimed at a relatively accomplished reader.

This is not to say that popular print culture in Ireland did not contain a visual element, and there was certainly a market for religious prints, sold in single sheets during this period. The Cork printer, Henry Denmead in 1814, for example, printed five reams (some 2500 sheets) of various religious pictures. A traveller visiting a bookshop in Tralee, Co. Kerry, in 1835 saw an old man buying religious prints at one penny each: he took three dozen and sold them quickly at a penny-halfpenny each. Single-sheet ballads, particularly in the nineteenth century, usually had a picture at the top of the page.[45]

A possible reason for the absence of such illustration in the chapbooks is cost. Woodcuts were relatively expensive and scarce, and were frequently borrowed from other printing houses. It might be difficult under these circumstances to procure a reasonably continuous series of cuts which might even loosely illustrate a text of 72 or 144 pages.[46] If on the other hand a printer went to the expense of commissioning a woodcut, it would be more attractive to have a larger picture which could be sold by itself as a print, at a relatively high profit per sheet, rather than a smaller cut in a cheap book, whose profit margin was low. A sheet printed with four religious pictures would retail at sixpence altogether, whereas a sheet used as part of a chapbook of six sheets sold for threepence would work out at only a halfpenny a sheet retail.

Of course, similar considerations would apply to English chapbooks, which did contain woodcuts. Here the difference may be one of scale, since the large English firms were much bigger than the Irish. They might therefore have a larger stock of cuts, as well as a bigger print run which would justify the use of cuts. On the other hand, the *Bibliothèque Bleue* texts rarely had illustrations, although the firms which printed them were as large as the English firms.

If cost to the printer was an important feature of the books, so also was cost to the purchaser. In the early nineteenth century, these books were sold at threepence or sixpence each. Whitley Stokes in 1799 mentioned a price of sixpence, while Thackeray bought six chapbooks in Ennis in 1841 for threepence each. Taking these prices relative to income, they would have made such books an infrequent purchase for unskilled labourers, who might earn between sixpence and one shilling (12 pence) per day, and perhaps as much as two shillings at harvest time. They would have been more within the reach of skilled labourers and artisans, earning three to four shillings a day, and small farmers.[47]

Setting these prices relative to expenditure is more difficult. When studies of consumption patterns in late eighteenth- and early nineteenth-century Ireland have discussed the poor, they have focused on their lack of consumer goods relative to other countries. Nevertheless, there were few who did not make regular cash purchases. The most frequent purchase was probably tobacco, the principal article of mass consumption. In the 1790s, Ireland imported over a pound of tobacco per head of the population every year, enough for a pipeful a day for half the population.[48] Tobacco was 'considered quite indispensable in this country', according to the poor inquiry of the 1830s, and 'cannot be had except for money'. It is not clear how much would be bought at a time. The Galway farmer-poet Marcas Ó Callanáin wrote of buying one ounce for threepence, but smaller sums were probably more frequent.[49]

More substantial purchases, such as furniture, household goods or clothes, would have been seasonal. Humphrey O'Sullivan, a schoolteacher in Co. Kilkenny in the 1820s, referred disparagingly to August as 'mí na n-óinseach', 'the month of the foolish women', since this was when clothes would be bought with harvest earnings. The cost of clothing was substantial. The 'clothing of the lower orders', as described in a survey of Donegal in 1801, cost 40 shillings or more for men (a wool suit), and 30 shillings or more for women (flannel suit).[50]

A threepenny book, therefore, while perhaps a luxury, was not an impossible one. It was cheaper than a single issue of a newspaper, which in the early nineteenth century cost four or five pence, mainly due to Stamp Tax. The prices were extremely low compared to larger, elite books, and even to some formats considered 'popular'. In 1830, the Catholic Bishop of Kildare and Leighlin, John Doyle, who was as familiar as anyone with the condition of the poorer classes, considered that a Bible selling at 16 shillings was cheap and 'accessible to persons of very limited means'.[51]

The fourth material characteristic of the books was their mode of distribution. They were produced mainly for a rural readership, as is clear from the printers' advertisements which are addressed to 'country dealers and chapmen'. The books were sold in small grocery shops or general stores, or by travelling pedlars, rather than in town or city bookshops. The occasions for buying such books were therefore infrequent, and an individual family or group might have bought a book or two in a year.

The fifth characteristic is length of availability. Most of the texts under discussion were reprinted regularly over the century 1750–1850, and were therefore continuously in circulation during that period. (I have included some exceptions: O'Sullivan's *Pious Miscellany* was first printed in 1802, but then had some 20 editions by 1850.) Nearly all of the texts under discussion were still in print in 1866. This is in line with a concern for the underlying elements of popular print culture over a long period. This criterion will exclude texts which had a large number of editions in a short space of time, such as Paine's *Rights of Man*, which had a number of printings in the 1790s, but few afterwards.[52]

Finally, this study will concentrate on genres and texts which had equivalents in the popular literature of Britain and France, in order to facilitate comparison and see what local variations existed in Irish texts. This is particularly the case with reference to the genres of chivalric romance and criminal biography, the latter of which has been especially well researched in recent years.

A number of texts which fit these criteria have not been considered. These are of two types.

First, there are what one might call 'universal texts', such as school reading primers, catechisms and almanacs. These are excluded partly due to considerations of space: they exist in large numbers and would merit a study in themselves. It is also because of questions of content, since these books tend to be uniform over such large areas. The purpose of catechisms, for example, was to achieve conformity of basic belief in all places. Irish Catholic catechisms would therefore differ little from those in France, nor Irish Protestant catechisms from those in Britain. Indeed, Irish Catholic catechisms are usually translations of French or English texts.[53] School primers were also frequently reprints of English schoolbooks, with very slight adaptation: in the case of arithmetic texts, containing appendices giving equivalents in Irish measures.[54] To set these texts in a western European, or even an Anglo-Irish, context would require a large amount of extremely fine comparative analysis.

The second type of text which is not dealt with is that which has not survived. Certain types of text are not available in sufficient quantities to discuss with confidence. One example would be the manuals of courtesy, courtship, conversation and letter-writing which were advertised in printers' lists in Ireland as well as England and France, and which would be relevant to the questions of orality and print culture under discussion. *The Academy of Compliments* is one such frequently advertised title, but no Irish edition appears to have survived. A book of the same name was often printed in London, and the text may well have been identical; but to rely entirely on London editions would defeat the purpose of a comparative study.

Broadly, then, this study will consider four genres of cheap and popular books which had a non-elite readership over a century or more (Chapters 4–7). These are as far as possible Irish versions of types found in Britain and Europe: romances of chivalry, criminal biography, historical works and religious texts. They constitute different genres not only by virtue of their subject matter, but also because of their form. Chivalric romances and criminal biographies are episodic narratives of a kind which approximated to oral storytelling, one of the principal historical texts was in fact a frequently performed folk play, and the principal religious text discussed is a collection of songs in the Irish language.

The books are first set in a material, cultural and educational context (Chapters 2 and 3), and elite attempts to intervene and direct the content of popular literature are discussed (Chapter 8). Some of the features of reception, political and linguistic, specific to Ireland are outlined (Chapters 9 and 10), and finally a few cultural and ideological conclusions are suggested (Chapters 10 and 11).

2 Literacy and Education

The purpose of this chapter is to investigate levels of reading ability in late eighteenth- and early nineteenth-century Ireland, providing an initial context for the reception of the cheap printed books. To begin, however, two fundamental distinctions need to be made. In the first place, there is a difference between the history of literacy on the one hand, and the history of educational institutions on the other. In the second place, within the broad category of literacy itself we need to distinguish between reading ability, which is our primary concern, and writing ability.

Within the recent historiography of literacy, it has become normal to distinguish between schooling and the acquisition of literacy. Literacy existed independently of schooling and pre-dated the establishment of large-scale educational projects in many countries. As Furet and Ozouf put it, 'literacy is not schooling', while in England, according to Laqueur, 'over several centuries, the literate popular culture of England largely made itself'. By the eighteenth century, of course, schools were the principal response to a demand for literacy. That demand could also be met independently, however, particularly in areas where a low density of population might rule out the permanent employment of a teacher. People were taught by their parents, neighbours, itinerant teachers or others. Evidence of such teaching in eighteenth- and nineteenth-century Ireland, even quite low on the social scale, is discussed by Logan. He found the correlation between literacy and schooling in mid-nineteenth-century Ireland to be weaker than that between literacy and other variables, such as occupation or language.[1]

This chapter therefore treats schooling separately from literacy. It will discuss first the factors in the demand for literacy, and then look at the earliest comprehensive figures for reading ability, those of the 1841 census. Nevertheless, schooling remained the principal mechanism for the achievement of literacy, examples of chapbook literature were used in many schools, and the debates over schools give an indication of the political importance of literacy. A section on schooling is therefore included at the end of the chapter.

The second distinction to be made concerns the nature of the literacy in question. Literacy is not a dichotomous variable, but encompasses a whole range of abilities, ranging from repeated rudimentary reading of a single text (such as a catechism), to fully fluent reading and writing. In particular, reading and writing were clearly separate skills, and some areas had a large proportion of people who could read only, often for religious reasons discussed below. Even among those who could both read and write, the two skills were usually acquired at different times, as pedagogic practice and the census figures make clear.

Since this study is concerned with reading, no use will be made of one of the standard measures of literacy in the past, the ability to sign documents such as marriage registers. Signature data have many advantages, being easily calculable and comparable over time and between different areas. What they tell us about the writing and reading ability of individuals is not clear, however. There is a wide range of opinion among historians with regard to French eighteenth-century marriage registers, for example. Some have seen them as underestimating writing ability, since higher figures were recorded in other sources such as wills or notarial marriage contracts.[2] Others have pointed to the possibility of being able to sign one's name only. People might learn to sign their names with the help of a model signature, without being able to write anything else, since to have been unable to sign an important document would have involved loss of face. In Brittany, parish registers sometimes recorded witnesses or spouses as 'knowing how to sign, but not being able to, not having their model with them'; or 'knowing neither how to write nor to sign'. Queniart has even attempted to class signatures on a scale of facility, reflecting the signatories' familiarity with writing.[3] As regards reading, there is a fairly general consensus that signature data would probably significantly underestimate reading literacy, though some have cast doubt even on this.[4]

Instead of signature data, therefore, this study uses the figures for reported reading ability in the first national census to include them, that of 1841, to provide an initial sketch of the distribution of literacy. One disadvantage of this source is that it comes from the end of the period under discussion. The census itself provides a means of partially overcoming his difficulty in its analysis of literacy according to ten-year age cohorts. First, however, we need to look at the circumstances which, over the previous century or more, produced the levels of reading and writing ability described by the census.

DEMAND FOR LITERACY

By the second half of the eighteenth century, the greater frequency and regularity of market transactions within the Irish rural economy set a far higher premium on literacy than before. In the south and east, this was the result of the rapid expansion of the tillage economy in response to demand in urbanising and industrialising Britain. In the north and north-west, it was due to the growth of a household-based textile production, mainly of linen. These two developments, which underlay the massive rise in Irish population in the same period, increased the demand for literacy in two related ways.

First of all, printed and hand-written commercial documents had become ubiquitous, and an ability to read was essential to the success of even small-scale farmers or weavers. This was particularly true during the Revolutionary and Napoleonic wars, which gave Irish produce, grain in particular, a virtual monopoly of the British market. Moreover, a shortage of metal during the wars led to a reliance on paper currency for sums as small as three shillings, and the consequent spur to literacy was commented on by contemporaries. In Londonderry in about 1812, 'we may note the influence of paper currency in promoting education among the lower class', in Queen's County in 1800, 'paper money is the only currency'. Moreover, not only were notes used for quite small transactions, but they were issued by a wide variety of banks, some of which were sounder than others. In King's County in 1800, 'Clonmel, Limerick and Waterford notes are current for 3 shillings and ninepence, 6 shillings, 9 shillings and upwards', but in Kilkenny in 1818, a clergyman noted that 'our paper currency makes it necessary for [the people] to read English, especially as they have suffered so severely by the failures of country banks.'[5] Such failures could be traumatic in a partly commercialised economy. Oral tradition in mid-twentieth century west Kerry remembered that pre-Famine emigrants to America took gold with them in preference to paper, which was considered worthless. Paper money was known as 'Billí an Róistigh', 'Roche's bills', after a Cork and Limerick bank which failed in 1820.[6]

The second way in which increased commercialisation stimulated literacy relates to the provision of education for children. The frequency of paper transactions was, in the immediate sense, a motivation for adult literacy, particularly for males, since they were the main market agents, and it is likely that some learnt to read or write in adulthood as a result. However, the increasing desirability of literacy, coupled with the rise in rural incomes consequent on commercialisation, meant

that parents were both more willing and more able than before to invest in education for their children. In the eighteenth and early nineteenth centuries, this meant an increasing tendency for rural communities
in particular to hire schoolteachers.

The general downturn in the Irish economy, which was acute by the
1820s and which continued until the Famine in both the tillage and
textile sectors, did not decrease the demand for literacy or education,
as one might expect. Indeed demand probably increased, since they
were seen to gain in importance as economic opportunities narrowed,
while the declining demand for child labour freed more children to
attend school.[7]

Alongside participation in a commercial economy, contact with politics
and civic affairs was also widening in the late eighteenth century. It is
tempting, for example, to point to the extraordinary burst of political
activity of every sort in the 1790s as producing intense pressure to
become literate. Many accounts of the 1790s stress the role played by
print for the first time in popular agitation. In their attempts to mobil-
ise the populace in the countryside, the United Irishmen, along with
the conservative tract societies which opposed them, distributed unprecedented amounts of printed propaganda. According to Donnelly's
account, for example, the countryside was flooded with posters, fliers,
newspapers and books. People in both town and country, particularly
in the eastern half of Ireland, were seeing more printed material than
ever before, at a time of intense political debate.[8]

The precise causal link between political turbulence and advance in
literacy is not clear, however. The widespread involvement of schoolmasters in radical political activity may have disrupted the activity of
schools in many areas, and similar periods of ferment, such as the
1640s in England and the 1790s in France, were periods of declining
literacy.[9] On balance, it is more likely that the widespread use of printed
propaganda was a sign of a pre-existing literate public rather than a
spur to further literacy.

Literacy also had a part to play in the less conventional political
activity of the late eighteenth and early nineteenth centuries, that of
agrarian secret societies. One of the commonest preliminary weapons
used by these societies was the anonymous threatening letter. This weapon
implies the established presence of literacy in the society – the sender
can write and the recipient can read. For our purposes, we can note
that the members of these societies, and frequently their victims as
well, were from the rural lower classes; moreover, the often rudimentary spelling and grammar of these letters would indicate that they

were written by people whose education had been partial.[10]

A good example of the pervasiveness of literacy in these organisations is a description of the establishment of branches of the Rightboys, an anti-tithe secret society in Munster in the 1780s:

> The method of swearing was this. A letter signed by *Captain Right* was sent to some respectable Farmer in the Parish commanding him to carry a Book to the Chapel on the following Sunday where *Captain Right's* rules (as they were call'd) were shewn fairly written, and every Person swore to the voluntary Observation of them..

Most of those charged with Rightboy activities were small farmers and labourers.[11]

Much of this political activity can be defined as opposition to state structures or a desire to change those structures, and a growing contact at a local or individual level with a state which functioned with written documents was another reason why literacy might be desirable. Two examples will illustrate this growing contact.

An early form of involvement with state agencies was the very large number of Irish recruits in British armies between the 1760s and the 1820s. It has been estimated that up to one in six of Irish adult males spent time in uniform in that period, mostly in the regular army, and after the 1790s also in local militias. While serving in the army, they would be in constant contact with written documentation such as daily company reports, and be made aware of the advantages of reading and writing. According to Neuburg 'in order to be promoted, the ability to write was virtually a necessity'.[12]

Another example was the judicial system, in which a large proportion of the population regularly participated by the early nineteenth century. In Maghera, Co. Londonderry, in about 1810, according to the Anglican curate:

> [the] peasantry are in general very litigious ... The sessions of the district usually continue for a week, and the town in which they are held is crowded during the whole time.

The addition of petty sessions in the 1820s significantly reduced the cost of litigation, and by the 1840s, there was an audience for small booklets of advice on going to law. One such 24-page pamphlet commented that 'quarter sessions litigation, among the peasantry of Ireland, has superseded quarreling and fighting at fairs'. In a study of Co. Mayo, McCabe estimates that perhaps a quarter of all families in the county were involved in litigation in 1839 alone, and that almost

70 per cent of cases were taken by the peasantry. Bearing in mind that Mayo was one of the counties furthest removed from the administrative centre of Dublin, such a rate of participation is remarkable.[13]

A third type of motivation for the achievement of literacy in Early Modern Europe, along with the economic and the political, was religious. Both Protestant and Catholic Reformations placed great emphasis on the reading of scripture, catechism or other religious books as part of their ideal of Christian behaviour, and as being necessary to individual salvation. The type of literacy which ensued was heavily weighted towards reading, and contained a large proportion who could read but not write; it was also less gender-specific than a literacy based on commercialisation or politicisation, since men and women were equally to be saved, though this resulted in less imbalance rather than equality.[14]

If in the sixteenth century Protestantism was a religion of the word to a greater extent than Catholicism, by the eighteenth century they were closer ideologically and in practice. Where social and geographic conditions were similar, there was little difference between the literacy levels of groups belonging to different churches. What accounted for variations in religiously-based literacy was organisation: it was higher in areas where the churches were firmly established or had succeeded in mobilising the state in their support.[15]

In Ireland there were at first sight large differences in this respect. Protestant communities in general were catechised sooner and more intensely than Catholic, and in the relatively Protestant north-east, literacy levels were the highest in Ireland. Moreover, the character of that literacy suggests a religious motivation, since the north-east contained a high proportion of women who could read but not write. It is difficult to be precise about the role of religion in producing these levels, compared for example to economic factors, since north-east Ulster was also highly commercialised and industrialised. As Akenson has pointed out, moreover, even within the north-east it is difficult to distinguish between the effects of religion and those of wealth. Presbyterians were the most literate because they were concentrated in the middle class, Anglicans had a broader social base, and consequently a lower literacy rate, and Catholics, being disproportionately represented among labourers and smallholders, had the lowest rates. Census data, discussed below, can offer a preliminary way of disaggregating these factors.[16]

As regards signature data, Kirkham has examined leases in north-west Ulster in the eighteenth century and found that religious affiliation was a better indicator of the ability to sign than wealth (defined as the value of the holding). The proportion of (male) Protestants signing was already high in the early eighteenth century. That of Catholics was low, and did not begin to increase substantially until the economic context improved late in the century. Kirkham is sceptical of a purely religious explanation, however, and points to other possible reasons for this difference. Many of the Protestants were immigrants from areas of England or Scotland which would have had high levels of literacy; Catholics tended to live in more remote areas; and Catholics were monoglot Irish speakers to a far greater extent than Protestants, whereas literacy was usually acquired in English.[17]

Protestantism, therefore, although not crucial as regards writing, provided a motivation for a high level of reading ability, particularly among women, which was not exclusively linked to social status, and which would have predated the intense commercialisation of the mid to late eighteenth century. This pattern would be similar to that described by Lacqueur for seventeenth- and eighteenth-century England, where religious motivations were more influential than economic before literacy became absolutely necessary for economic activity, or by Furet and Ozouf, who describe in France a 'very widespread semi-literacy based on reading, organised by the [Catholic] Church and in the home, and chiefly intended for girls' which they distinguish from 'modern' literacy which included writing.[18]

Kirkham's observations on language point to another influence on the chronology of literacy in Ireland. Literacy usually meant literacy in English, and the geography and chronology of English speaking in the eighteenth and nineteenth centuries corresponded closely to those of literacy. In the nineteenth-century censuses, areas of high illiteracy were also areas of high Irish speaking. There is a fairly clear relationship, therefore, between the acquisition of English and of literacy, though the precise causal nature of that relationship is not obvious. This is discussed below in Chapter 9.

THE CENSUS OF 1841

The earliest source of comprehensive national figures for literacy in Ireland is the census of 1841. It contains figures for overall literacy, divided into 'read and write', 'read only' and 'neither read nor write'; these figures are further divided by gender and by age cohort of ten years. There is also a four-fold classification of house size, which can be used as a rough indicator of wealth or social class.

The individual household forms from the census, with minor exceptions, have not survived, making precise study of the social or occupational distribution of literacy impossible. In any case, where some forms have survived, they do not contain data on literacy. These were collected separately on a larger abstract by the census enumerators. The printed census reproduces the data from these abstracts at the levels of townland, parish, barony and county respectively. For the purposes of this study, the data have been analysed initially at a county level. Like the French *département*, the Irish county often includes a number of regions with distinct characteristics, leading to aggregate figures which can conceal local differences. For the very general conclusions drawn here, however, county figures are sufficient; the next subdivision, the barony, is used where necessary.

The principal difficulty with census data of this sort is that what they report is a subjective measure, a declared ability to read or write, rather than a test which is objective and uniform such as a signature. The concepts of reading and writing ability, unlike age or family size for example, are not absolute, and cover a wide spectrum of possibilities. What did people mean when they declared themselves able to read? Historians and statisticians have usually been loath to give too much credence to this type of subjective information. Among historians of literacy, Cipolla states that self-evaluation results in 'a higher percentage of literacy [being] recorded than the actual conditions warrant', while Schofield maintains that 'if literacy is associated with high status, the dangers of misrepresentation are considerable'.[19]

On the other hand, where comparison between census figures for literacy and other measures is possible, censuses are found to be fairly reliable. Logan has compared marriage signatures with ability to write as declared in the census of 1871, and found a strong correspondence. In three counties, the proportion of those signing is actually greater than the census figure; and for 15 counties, the census figure is less than 5 per cent higher than the figure for marriage registers. It is fair to assume, therefore, that reported reading ability, which would have been easier for a busy enumerator to verify if necessary, corresponds closely to actual reading ability. Overall, as Graff has noted, self-assessment is 'surprisingly reliable'.[20]

In 1841, then, 47 per cent of the population over five years of age were able to read. Traditionally, historians have interpreted these figures in negative terms, a standard historical geography presenting them under the heading 'illiteracy' rather than 'literacy', and within a chapter called 'Social Problems'. However, in Cipolla's tables of literacy in European countries in the mid-nineteenth century, which offer a rough guide,

Ireland is in the middle division of three, described as having 'average adult illiteracy', along with England and France. This placing is remarkable when two further points are considered. First, Ireland was an intensely rural society, whereas literacy was usually higher in urban areas, since the professions associated with literacy were urban, and ordinary people in towns were more likely to have frequent contact with written and printed material. Secondly, the literacy being estimated is literacy in English, and since the Irish and English languages were roughly equal in the early nineteenth century (Irish was, if anything, dominant in 1800), this literacy was being achieved in a new language to a greater extent than in England and perhaps France.[21]

Within the global figure, there are the variations one might expect between town and country, male and female. In rural areas, 45 per cent could read, in urban, 64 per cent; of males, 54 per cent could read, of females, 44 per cent. Regional differences were more marked, literacy in general declining as one moved westward, along with the cash economy, contact with state structures and participation in political organisations. In parts of Ulster 85–90 per cent of the population could read, in parts of Connaught only 10–15 per cent. However, these were extremes. Most of the country had a substantial partial literacy – most of Leinster between 50 per cent and 75 per cent and most of Munster between 25 per cent and 50 per cent (Figure 2.1).

As regards Ulster, a role for religion is suggested by the profile of female literacy. In Antrim, Down and Londonderry the number of women who could read only (RO) was higher than for those who could read and write (RW), in some cases by a ratio of 3:1. In Leinster and Munster, on the other hand, the overall figures show more women able to read and write than able to read only. Moreover, the numbers in the north-east are strikingly regular in all age cohorts, indicating that this literacy was already strongly established by the mid-eighteenth century. In Antrim, for example, the number of women who could read only was between 48 per cent and 52 per cent in every age cohort above the age of 16, whereas the numbers who could read and write rose from 22 per cent in the 56–65 age group to 36 per cent in the 16–25 age group (Table 2.1). In other words, female RO literacy was established at about 50 per cent by the 1770s.

Relating these figures to religious affiliation is not straightforward, as the census of 1841 did not include religion as a category. The earliest comparable data come from the census of 1861. Correlating these with the literacy data from 1841 shows a strong relationship between Protestantism (Anglicanism and Presbyterianism together) and female

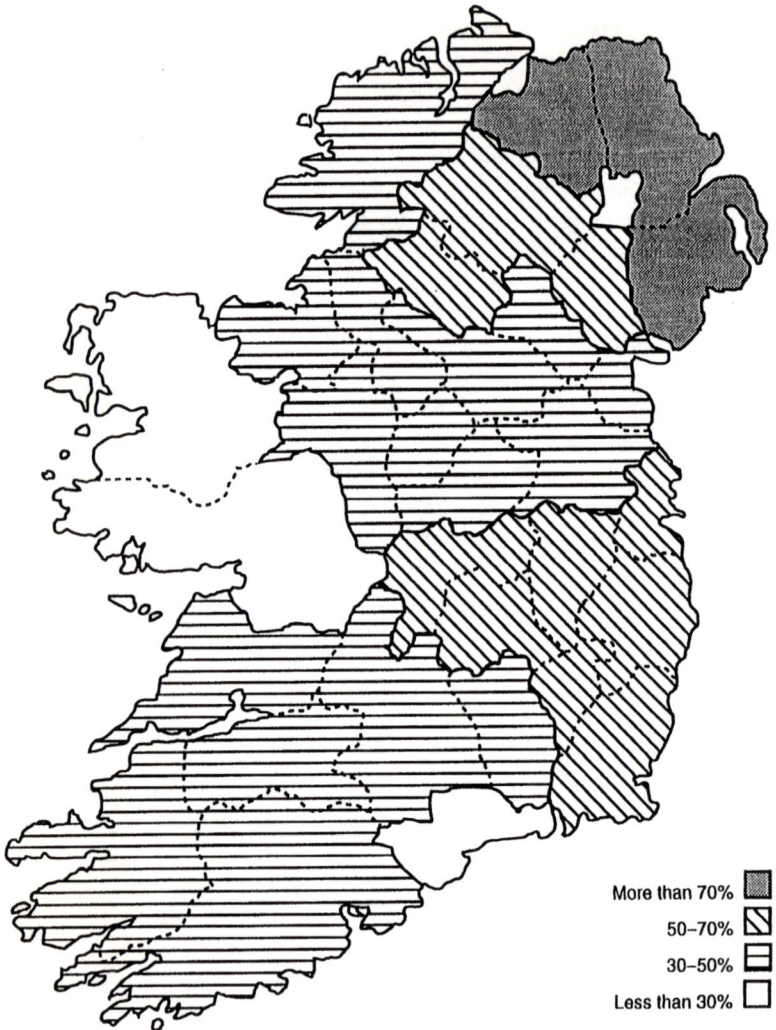

More than 70%

50–70%

30–50%

Less than 30%

Figure 2.1   Reading ability in Ireland, 1841

Table 2.1 Literacy by age, 1841 (%)

		11–15	16–25	26–35	36–45	46–55	56–65	66–75	76–85
Antrim	MRW	42	61	64	65	63	63	60	58
	MRO	40	27	24	22	23	22	24	25
	FRW	27	36	31	28	26	22	23	19
	FRO	53	48	50	51	51	51	51	50
Down	MRW	44	63	66	65	63	61	62	58
	MRO	35	23	20	19	20	20	20	22
	FRW	28	38	33	30	28	24	24	19
	FRO	46	42	43	43	42	43	45	46
L'derry	MRW	38	57	58	55	53	50	49	47
	MRO	42	29	25	26	24	25	27	23
	FRW	24	30	23	20	17	15	13	12
	FRO	53	50	50	48	46	45	47	47
Leinster	MRW	40	53	54	53	50	48	46	43
	MRO	23	21	19	17	15	14	13	12
	FRW	29	36	30	27	24	21	22	20
	FRO	29	31	29	25	21	17	16	13
Munster	MRW	37	46	43	43	41	36	39	34
	MRO	17	13	10	9	7	7	6	5
	FRW	23	26	18	17	14	11	13	10
	FRO	19	18	15	12	10	7	7	6

MRW: Male read and write FRW: Female read and write
MRO: Male read only FRO: Female read only

RO ability, and a much weaker one between Protestantism and female RW ability.[22] This is partly, of course, a consequence of the regional and social distribution of religious affiliation, since Protestants were disproportionately concentrated in Ulster, and Catholics were over-represented in lower social classes throughout the country. Taking the population of Ulster in isolation, both Protestant and Catholic, an attempt can be made to distinguish between the effects of wealth and those of religious affiliation by means of a multiple regression, using baronies as units of analysis. The result suggests that the influence of religion on female reading-only levels was relatively strong, whereas that of wealth was negligible.[23]

More fundamental to the study of a popular readership is variation between social classes. Unfortunately, the census data of 1841 do not allow this to be precisely calculated. However, given that in many parts of rural Ireland, the middle and upper classes were not numerically very strong, the figures would seem to suggest a fairly firm lower-class reading ability. To be any more useful, these figures need to take social stratification into account, to determine as far as possible the extent to which the global figures for reading ability are influenced by the relative wealth of an area.

Some indication of wealth and social class is offered by house size. Houses were divided into four classes in the 1841 census: class 4 consisted of houses with one room only; class 3 had two to four rooms; class 2 had five to nine; and class 1 ten or more. The inhabitants of houses in classes 3 and 4, along with cases of multiple family occupancy of larger houses (a small minority), have been taken to be lower class, to constitute a 'popular' audience.

As might be expected, the relationship between reading ability and the proportion of houses in the top two classes is a strong one. The county totals are plotted on a scatter diagram in Figure 2.2, along with the regression line which shows the hypothetical relationship between wealth and reading.[24] This line suggests two features of lower-class or popular literacy. Firstly, it shows a theoretical minimum for lower-class literacy of 19 per cent, that is that a county with no houses of class 1 and 2 would still have a typical literacy rate of 19 per cent. This is close to the case of Mayo, for example, which has a literacy rate of 21 per cent but in which only 7 per cent of houses are in class 1 and 2. Secondly, the slope of the line shows that the literacy rate increases proportionately faster than the percentage of larger houses. There would theoretically be universal literacy in 1841 in a county just over half of whose houses were in classes 1 and 2. A map of lower-class literacy, therefore, would have the same geographic distribution as the map of global literacy, but the regional contrasts would be more marked.

In 1841, therefore, a substantial potential reading public existed for popular literature. However, we are also concerned with the century before 1841, and it is difficult to get any reliable estimates for this period. Neither the 1821 nor the 1831 censuses measured literacy. We can project backwards from the 1841 census to a certain extent by using the age cohort figures for global literacy. These give male and female literacy rates for decennial groups starting from the age of 5, and these can be used to get an indication of the growth of literacy

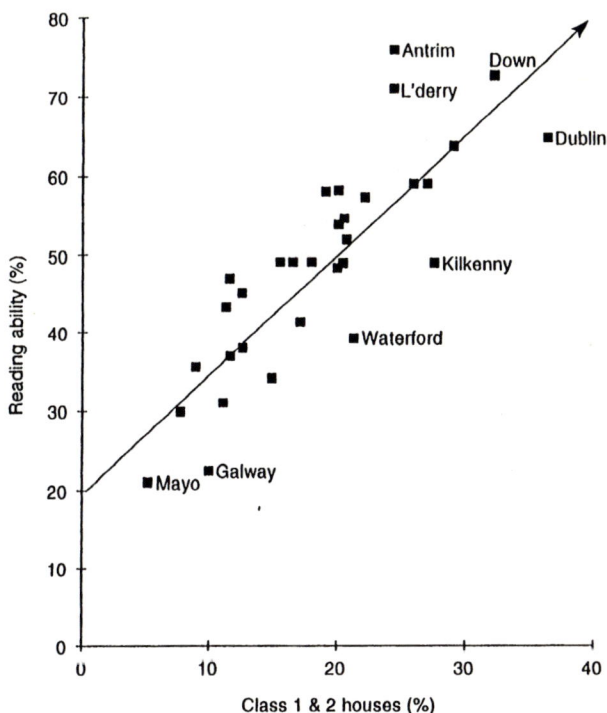

Figure 2.2   Reading ability and house size in Ireland, 1841

since the late eighteenth century (which was why the census compilers included them).

Using age cohort data in this way is subject to two types of qualification, educational ones which are specific to literacy figures, and demographic ones which apply to such use in general. As regards education, it is possible that some older people in 1841 may have learnt to read and write later in life, and that these skills cannot be projected back to their earlier life. Some of the efforts of the educational and bible societies of the early nineteenth century were directed at adults, for example, although it is doubtful whether they had an impact on sufficiently large a scale to affect the figures substantially. On the other hand, people who had learnt to read and write in their youth may have forgotten in later life, something which is quite conceivable for writing, which needs regular practice.[25]

Table 2.2   Male literacy by age cohort, 1841

Age	Born	Leinster %	Munster %	Ulster %	Conn. %
16–25	1816–25	74	59	77	46
46–55	1786–95	65	48	70	37
66–75	1766–75	59	45	67	32

Table 2.3   Female literacy by age cohort, 1841

Age	Born	Leinster %	Munster %	Ulster %	Conn. %
16–25	1816–25	67	44	68	30
46–55	1786–95	45	24	52	15
66–75	1766–75	38	20	51	12

The principal demographic qualification would be the influence of socially differentiated mortality, that the better-off, and consequently more literate, would live longer and consequently be over-represented in older age groups. Backward projection would therefore produce some overestimation of literacy levels in previous decades.

With these qualifications in mind, we can compare the literacy rates of three age cohorts in the four provinces. The result shows a remarkably gentle increase in male literacy (Table 2.2) and a rather more rapid one for female literacy (Table 2.3).

Working backwards from 1841, therefore, we can postulate the presence of substantial literacy among males from the late eighteenth century and probably before, slowly increasing (as a proportion) until the mid-nineteenth century. There was also a later but more rapid growth of female literacy from a lower base.

It might be objected that the levels of literacy proposed are not sufficient to justify the study of a 'popular' printed literature, particularly if the reception of that literature is to be a guide to Irish peasant culture. However, printed texts entered and circulated in what was still a predominantly oral culture via those members of the community who were literate – that there were cultural intermediaries, frequently, but by no means always, priests or schoolmasters, who provided the link between print and oral culture. The clearest way in which this process took place was through the practice of reading aloud, the classic interface between written and oral. This was a common cultural and interpretive practice in both the late eighteenth and early nineteenth centuries, and is discussed further in Chapter 11. It was these literate groups and literate individuals which were the intended market of those Dublin printers who from the early eighteenth century began to produce cheap popular books for a lower-class, mainly rural market. The fact that this sector of the trade survived and prospered throughout the century is itself a demonstration of the establishment of a popular literacy by the mid-eighteenth century.

SCHOOLING

This account of literacy has treated it as a demand-led phenomenon, and the same was true of the principal mechanism through which that literacy was attained, the school. Most primary schools in rural Ireland in the eighteenth and early nineteenth centuries were the result of local initiative: parents in a village or district employed a schoolteacher for their children by collectively guaranteeing the teacher's livelihood. Contemporary observers frequently commented on the strength of desire for education among the poorer classes in Ireland, and it seems that employing a teacher was a sign of prestige for a community. (This is well caught, for example, in Carleton's fictional account of the kidnapping of a particularly good teacher by one village from another.)[26] Spontaneous employment of teachers was by no means a purely Irish phenomenon, of course: in eighteenth-century rural France, it was also the most frequent way in which a primary school was established.[27]

The provision of education by institutional intervention, whether by church or state, was usually reacting to this pre-existing system of schools, and aimed either at displacing it or bringing it under closer supervision. The pattern of growth of schooling was therefore largely independent of political or administrative innovation. In France, for example, the actions of government during the Revolutionary period 'wrought no lasting change in the traditional school system'; in Ireland, although it used to be customary to point to the establishment of a state-sponsored national school system in 1831 as a turning point, more recent writing has tended to stress the continuity of structures in place before and after that date.[28]

The different types of school which existed before 1831, together with the numbers of pupils attending them, are summarised in the largest government report on education of the period, that of 1825.[29] By far the largest category was that of the pay schools, sometimes known as hedge schools, which contained about 400 000 pupils, over 70 per cent of the total. The second type, Catholic day schools, were organised as part of the Catholic parish structure, and accounted for 33 500 pupils. The third type were the Protestant Charter Schools and the Erasmus Smith schools, which had been established in the early eighteenth century, mainly as proselytising agencies. In 1825, they accounted for 11 000 pupils. Finally, there were the schools run by, or associated with, the various educational societies which dated from the late eighteenth and early nineteenth centuries. These were the same societies which distributed bibles and moral and religious tracts, many of which were used in their schools. Altogether, there were nearly 120 000 pupils in these schools.

This classification is not entirely satisfactory, since, as Logan points out, the commissioners' definition of a pay school was a school which charged fees, and that many schools charged fees while at the same time being supervised by the parish clergy, whether Catholic or Anglican, the former accounting for perhaps half the total of pay schools. Bearing this in mind, the relationship between the categories may be understood by considering their history.[30]

The pay schools were the schools established by local initiative. Although these had no official church backing, they were predominantly Catholic, both in pupils and teachers. During most of the eighteenth century, Catholics were forbidden by law to teach schools. Like much of the penal code, however, the laws against teachers were not strictly enforced, and the pay school system was tolerated or ignored after about the 1730s. By mid-century, many of these schools were informally linked with the Catholic parish structure, and taught a catechism in association with the parish priest. In some dioceses from the 1750s, the schoolmaster was an object of episcopal visitation along with the priest, and in the second half of the century, according to Corish, there was in effect a Catholic parish school system over much of the country.[31]

This makes it difficult to differentiate these schools with precision from the second category used in the 1825 report, Catholic parish schools. These were schools established on the initiative of the Catholic church and under a more strict supervision, since the church did not always approve of the atmosphere of the pay schools. In this sense, official Catholic church involvement in schooling, like that of the state, was reactive, bringing pay schools under its supervision or establishing its own alternatives. There were two related reasons behind this policy, both of which were very much in evidence by the end of the eighteenth century. In the first place, schools were to be an instrument of the belated Tridentine reform which got under way in Ireland from the mid-eighteenth century. Secondly, the Catholic church, like the government and the Protestant churches, was concerned at what it saw as a mounting problem of social order, and saw schooling as a solution. According to a Catholic priest in Cloyne in 1809:

> The influence which the clergy formerly possessed over their flocks . . . was considerably diminished by the relaxation of the popery laws; it thenceforth continued gradually to decline and received at length the *coup de grace* by the [anti-clerical] Whiteboy disturbances in 1786 . . . [Clerical influence] is still inconsiderable . . . though never perhaps (at least in this diocese) were the powers and energies of the clergy more forcibly and uniformly exerted in instructing, and particularly in catechising, and attending to the minds and morals of the rising generation.[32]

Before 1800, however, the pay school system was far less Catholic in tone than was the case for example in France, where the schoolteacher has been described as a 'sous-clerc', with specified church duties outside school hours. Most pay school teachers in Ireland were fairly independent of church structures. Their later perception of the conditions of employment in national schools as onerous would seem to bear this out.[33]

Protestant church involvement in primary education was also largely reactive, but in contrast to the Catholic strategy, aimed to displace the pay schools rather than to absorb them. The Charter schools and the Erasmus Smith schools were set up in the wake of a Church of Ireland report in 1731 on 'Popish schoolmasters', which revealed the existence of a clandestine network of pay schools with Catholic teachers. They were restricted in their impact by poor funding and administration, however, and were condemned by a series of government reports in the early nineteenth century.

Later Protestant initiative took the form of educational societies established in the early nineteenth century and, to an even greater extent than the Catholic or Charter schools, were the result of mounting elite concern with popular education. The idea that popular education was a means of promoting social harmony was commonplace by the late eighteenth century, in Ireland and elsewhere. At an official level, the matter received little attention between the founding of the Charter schools and the social and political upheavals of the 1790s. An exception was the introduction of a plan for state provision of primary education into the Irish Parliament by the Chief Secretary, Thomas Orde, in 1786, but this plan was never put into effect.[34]

The 1790s changed this situation in two ways. Firstly, the political mobilisation of large sections of the people by the United Irishmen, and that organisation's links with Revolutionary France, made the problem of disorder more acute than ever for the government. Secondly, the effective use of printed propaganda by the United Irishmen made it clear that there was a substantial literate element in the population. In the context of the debate on popular education, this changed the underlying suppositions: previously it had been assumed by advocates of popular education that disorder was the product of ignorance and lack of education; now it was clear that there was a system of education in operation, but one which was outside the control of the authorities.

The state therefore turned its attention to the subject of education, and a commission produced 14 reports between 1809 and 1814, the last of which summarised the new perception:

> Such education as has been objected to under the idea of its leading to evil rather than to good, they are actually obtaining for themselves; and though we conceive it practicable to correct it, to check its progress appears impossible – it may be improved, but it cannot be impeded.

And as for the pay school teachers:

> a more disloyal and bigotted set of men does not exist than the hedge [i.e. pay] schoolmasters of the adjoining country.

The commissioners therefore recommended the creation of a supervised national system of education for the lower classes.[35]

Initially, however, the task was left to voluntary societies such as the Society for the Education of the Poor of Ireland, known as the Kildare Place Society. These were the same societies which produced the tracts discussed in Chapter 8, for the same reasons of social improvement, and the tracts were used in their schools. These societies were subsidised by the state, either directly or through the Church of Ireland. The Kildare Place Society, for example, received a state grant from 1816 onwards, reaching a peak of £22 000 in 1824.[36]

By the 1820s, however, the scriptural flavour of the curriculum in the schools of the Kildare Place and other societies, and their association with the Protestant evangelical impulse of the 'Second Reformation', along with the revival of Catholic political mobilisation, meant that they began to be perceived by Catholics as proselytising and sectarian. When agrarian violence in the early 1820s was directed against tithes, and was therefore sectarian in tone, the educational societies could even be represented as adding to social disorder rather than easing it.

In this context of sectarian unrest, a series of large-scale state reports on education between 1825 and 1828 therefore gave great attention to the question of denominational education and the avoidance of sectarian disputes.[37] The commissions of the 1820s ensured the adoption of a radical solution to the problems of sectarian tension and disorder. This was the establishment of a national state system of primary schools, proposed in the report of 1828, and put into operation in 1831. The state would directly endow individual schools, supervise them through a national board, and supply them with approved textbooks. There were also elaborate arrangements for separate religious instruction for different denominations within the same school.

The activities of the educational societies began to decline after 1831, since their state financing was severely reduced or even withdrawn. On the other hand, Catholic schools and many pay schools entered the system, and were in effect endowed by the state. For them, this was an enormous advantage, since educational resources, particularly in the Catholic church, were being seriously stretched by the 1820s under the pressure of population increase. This was recognised by Bishop Doyle of Kildare, for example, who told a state Poor Enquiry in 1830 that:

the expenses attendant upon those [Catholic] schools are such that we cannot well bear them with our other burdens; they require very much to be aided in some way by the government.[38]

In the longer term, therefore, attempts to promote social order through control of education had fallen foul of religious divisions among the elite in Ireland. State sponsorship of one section of this elite, the Protestant, had only increased disorder by provoking a response from the Catholic section. The school statistics of the 1825 report show this tension at its highest. The 1831 solution of a non-denominational national system, while on the surface an attempt to bypass both groups, in fact recognised and cooperated with them. Given the religious demography of Ireland, the result was a state-subsidised denominational system of primary education. In most of Ireland, this represented a tacit recognition by the state of the Catholic church as a civilising agency with control of education (and a victory for the Catholic strategy of taking over the pay schools against the Protestant one of supplanting them).

The chronology of growth of schooling probably coincides roughly with that of the growth of literacy, with the late eighteenth century the period of 'take-off', particularly in the east and south of the country. Firm data are notoriously lacking in the eighteenth century, particularly for pay and Catholic schools, which were the majority outside the north-east. Some idea of developments can be got from the diocese of Cloyne in east Co. Cork. The *Report on Popery* compiled by the Church of Ireland in 1731 shows only 17 Catholic schools; the low figure is probably due to the fact that the report was not comprehensive, and that penal laws against Catholic teachers were applied more strictly in 1731 than later. A Catholic diocesan visitation in 1775 found a more credible total of 117 Catholic schools; by 1809 there were 259, and the 1826 Report on Education counted 421 schools described as 'Pay schools', out of a grand total of 496. (There were 33 Church of Ireland parish schools, 18 supported by private patrons, and 24 attached to educational societies.) The late eighteenth-century take-off was pronounced in Co. Meath, where the number of schools more than doubled between the 1780s and the 1820s.[39]

Broader figures for the eighteenth century are scant, however, and the first fairly comprehensive figures which exist for school attendance are from the early nineteenth century. A state commission in 1813 estimated that a total of 4600 primary schools had been operating in 1808, with over 200 000 pupils attending.[40] For the early 1820s there are two estimates available. The first is the census of 1821, which counted 394 000 attending all schools during the summer of 1821. This figure is an underestimate due to the seriously incomplete nature of the coverage. The second is the systematic enumeration of the Education Commissioners in 1824, which found 560 000 pupils attending 11 800 primary schools. Assuming a population total of 6.8 million as given in the census, this gives a schoolgoing population equivalent to 8 per cent of the total population, representing roughly 40 per cent of the children of schoolgoing age.[41]

As with the figures on literacy, these do not bear out the image of a severely under-educated country. They are of course much lower than the highest European totals of perhaps 80 per cent of children of schoolgoing age, but compare favourably with many areas which are usually seen as more advanced than Ireland. Early nineteenth-century Baden, for example, had 10 per cent of the total population in school, say 50 per cent of the schoolgoing age. Ireland's figures are also incomparably higher than Europe's worst, such as Russia, where in 1807 it was estimated that less than 0.5 per cent of children of schoolgoing age attended. As regards numbers of teachers, Ó Gráda has calculated that between the 1820s and 1840s Ireland had 17 teachers per thousand population, higher than Prussia (14) and roughly equivalent to Holland (18).[42]

More detailed figures are available in the census of 1841, which categorised pupils by gender, by age and by whether they were attending a primary or superior school. However, it counted attendance in only one week in June of 1841, and since attendance was erratic, particularly in rural areas where child labour was frequently in demand, the figures represent varying underestimates of longer-term attendance. As Mokyr notes, they give an attendance relative to total population which is only about 70 per cent that of 1824.[43]

Looking at school attendance among 6–10 year olds as a proportion of that age cohort (Table 2.4), the 1841 figures show a relative uniformity. Outside Connaught, where the figures are very low, and the cities in the south, where they are very high (Cork city reaching 62 per cent), most counties fall between 20 per cent and 35 per cent. The highest county figures are in the south-east, in Wexford, Wicklow and Carlow.

The superiority of east Ulster in literacy rates in the census, therefore, is not reflected in its figures on school attendance. Whether calculated as part of total population or of 6–10 year olds, the figures for Antrim, Down and Londonderry are not higher than other areas, and indeed are lower than those for the south-east. One reason for this is the nature of school attendance. The profile of attendance overall in Ulster shows pupils to be somewhat younger than average, more concentrated in the 6–10 year age group and less in the 11–15 group than in other provinces (Table 2.5). At the same time, comparison of the 11–15 year olds with 16–25 year olds shows that writing was learnt slightly later in Ulster, for both males and females. This indicates a more irregular attendance, probably due to a higher demand for child labour in the textile industry in Ulster.

Differences in the age distribution of pupils do not entirely explain the disjunction between literacy figures and school attendance in Ulster. Another factor is that the older age groups in the north-east were more uniformly literate than elsewhere, suggesting a superiority in schooling in earlier decades. The very consistent pattern of writing ability among males in Antrim and Down, over 60 per cent in all groups from 16 years to 75 years, as well as the uniformity of reading ability among female cohorts, would bear this out.

Primary school attendance figures as a whole show a high proportion

Table 2.4 School attendance 6–10 years as % of cohort 6–10 years, 1841

	Total	M	F
Carlow	38.5	42	35
Drogheda	27	43	11
Dublin city	27	33	22
Co. Dublin	37	41	33
Kildare	32	32	31
Kilkenny city	32	41	22
Co. Kilkenny	31	35	28
King's	25	25	24
Longford	22	23	21
Louth	24	24	23
Meath	24	26	22
Queen's	27	29	24
Westmeath	26	29	23
Wexford	36	41	30
Wicklow	37	39	35
Clare	21	24	17
Cork city	62	64	61
Co. Cork	26	30	22
Kerry	19	22	16
Limerick city	47	48	45
Co. Limerick	31	36	25
Tipperary	26	29	22
Waterford city	27	35	19
Co. Waterford	29	32	26
Antrim	30	34	27
Armagh	23	25	20
Belfast	33	36	30
Cavan	21	22	19
Donegal	20	21	18
Down	31	35	27
Fermanagh	22	23	20
Co. L'derry	34	35	33
Monaghan	18	20	16
Tyrone	23	24	21
Galway town	56	60	52
Co. Galway	14	17	11
Mayo	10	12	8
Roscommon	18	20	15
Sligo	17	20	15

Table 2.5 Primary school attendance by age, 1841

	Leinster	Munster	Ulster	Connaught
Male				
4–5	6 040	5 442	8 631	1 821
	8%	6%	12%	6%
6–10	39 656	47 936	44 175	17 754
	54%	51%	61%	58%
11–15	24 797	35 672	17 685	9 443
	43%	38%	245	31%
16+	1 898	4 453	1 372	866
	2.5%	5%	2%	3%
Unspecified	818	378	893	484
Total	73 209	93 881	72 756	30 368
Female				
4–5	5 641	4 925	8 188	1 678
	10%	7%	14%	8%
6–10	31 680	34 184	36 243	12 147
	55%	52%	61%	58%
11–15	18 565	24 369	13 719	6 488
	32%	37%	23%	31%
16+	1 084	2 437	1 102	400
	2%	4%	2%	2%
Unspecified	705	175	689	346
Total	57 675	66 720	59 891	21 059

of pupils to be older than might perhaps be expected (Table 2.5). In Munster, 38 per cent of male pupils were aged 11–15 and 5 per cent were over 16.[44] Leinster and Connaught show similar distribution; Ulster is different, with fewer 11–15 year olds, but more 4–5 year olds (12 per cent, as opposed to 6 per cent in Munster and Connaught). Moreover, the provincial figures are almost identical for male and female, with at most two percentage points in the difference. The number of older pupils reflects the non-continuous nature of primary education: poorer pupils in particular might attend for a few months a year as family labour demands and finances permitted, and elementary education might be spread over a much longer period than nowadays. The skills of reading and writing were therefore acquired consecutively at different times, and must be considered separately from each other. This is reflected in the age cohort literacy figures: in most counties, comparison of the 11–15 year olds and the 16–25 year olds shows an increase in those able to read and write, and a decrease in those able to read only. Writing was therefore frequently acquired quite late in life, and after reading.[45]

The equal gender distribution of 11–15 year-olds suggests that increasing priority was being given to female education, since traditionally boys had been kept in school longer than girls, and one might expect therefore a lower proportion of girls to have continued in school after the age of 10. Finally, from the point of view of popular literature, the high number of 11–15 year olds is significant, since, as we shall see, it was the older pupils who used chapbooks as reading material in schools.

As far as concerns social class, the parliamentary reports on poverty in the 1830s give the impression that even the very poor in most areas had access to some sort of schooling, and that it was given priority within overall family strategies. The two parliamentary commissioners who visited Corofin, Co. Clare, in 1834 spoke to the town beggars, who traded in manure:

> So anxious were these mendicants to show how attentive they were to the education of the younger class of the family, that frequently the commissioners were prevailed upon by their solicitation to sit down and hear the children read, and inspect their copybooks, which evidenced a regular attendance at school, and a laudable thirst for learning.

Potential access did not always become attendance, however, and often extreme poverty kept children away from school. The same commissioners were told by the Anglican curate of Corofin that more children would attend if they had any decent clothing, while in nearby Ennistymon, an unemployed weaver's children 'were so badly clothed that it would be considered indecent for them to appear in school in that state.' While those particular children could not go to school, the assumption behind such a statement is that such poor children would normally attend.[46]

They would probably have done so through a system such as that in the diocese of Kildare described by Bishop Doyle in 1830:

> In each of the towns there is a free school. In the country parishes the children generally pay, but paupers are sent to school by the priest who pays privately to the master a certain sum for them, and they pass among the other scholars, not as paupers, but as persons paying.

This was the sort of system which was becoming a severe financial strain on Catholic church structures as poverty in parts of rural Ireland reached crisis proportions after 1820. Without state intervention, it is conceivable that the proportion of children in education might have declined in the pre-Famine decades, as indeed it may well have in practice in parts of Connaught.[47]

The relationship between poverty and basic education is not always an inverse one, however, particularly in nineteenth-century Ireland. In industry and in agriculture, one of the principal obstacles to attendance was the demand at home for the child's labour. It has been suggested that one of the principal causes of poverty in this period, deindustrialisation in domestic textile production, may in some cases have encouraged school attendance by diminishing the importance of child labour in the household economy.[48]

POPULAR LITERATURE IN SCHOOLS

Among the different types of school which existed before 1831, the pay schools are of most interest, since not only were they the majority, but they represent the clearest form of 'spontaneous' education. However, since they were independent of one another, it is impossible to generalise about their curriculum. The vast majority taught reading, writing and arithmetic, consecutively in that order, and the fees for reading were lower than those for writing or arithmetic. The poorer pupils, attending for a shorter period and paying less, would therefore have learnt to read, but probably not to write or count.[49]

The most frequent books in use would therefore have been reading primers, and after that basic arithmetic texts and catechisms. The best known of the primers was *Reading Made Easy*, which was already proverbial by the late eighteenth century, appearing for example in a ballad printed in Monaghan in 1788:

> It happened in spring when the small birds did sing
> And fields were enamelled with daisies,
> I met with my jewel a-going to school
> With her turf and her *Reading Made Easy*.

For older pupils who had learnt to read, further reading material had to be found or supplied by themselves, and here the Irish schools were influenced by their relative lack of contact with church or state. Whereas in France primary school reading was almost entirely religious (with perhaps the addition of Erasmus's *Civility*), Irish pupils read a more heterogeneous sort of work, frequently examples of popular literature.[50] The novelist William Carleton, who was educated in pay schools in Co. Tyrone, recalled 'hunting through the neighbours' houses for books of some or any description to read'. As the 1825 education report put it, 'the books which were easily and cheaply to be procured, were those naturally preferred', that is, the books sold by pedlars and grocers. In practice, this meant that an extraordinary variety of books was used, and even within a single school, each pupil might have a different book. The 1825 report lists over 400 different texts used in schools in counties Donegal, Kildare, Galway and Kerry. These were catechisms (16), religious works (97) and 'works of entertainment, histories, tales etc.' (301). This last category contains all of the best known titles in popular literature, such as *The Seven Champions of Christendom* and *Irish Highwaymen*. These texts had a higher circulation than most of the others in the list (Guicciardini's *History of Italy*, and *The History of Tythes: their influence on agriculture and population* were two) and their use in schools must have been very frequent.[51]

This is borne out by the descriptions of pay schools in early nineteenth-century social and economic literature quoted in the introduction. Although these writers were engaged in the debate on popular education, pointing to the reading of the chapbooks in pay schools as part of an explanation of social disorder in Ireland, this is not to discount their testimony. As noted previously, they seem to have been concerned with construing as seditious the books which were in fact used, rather than claiming that seditious books were read when in fact they were not.[52]

In any case, supporting evidence can be found in the recollections of those who had been educated in pay schools. One of the witnesses before the 1825 Commissioners was Henry Cooke, at that time Moderator of the Presbyterian Synod of Ulster, who had been educated in hedge schools in Co. Tyrone until the age of 14:

> I recollect reading a book, called *The Seven Champions of Christendom and Destruction of Troy*; I recollect reading *Hero and Leander, Gesta Romanorum* and *The Seven Wise Masters . . . Don Belianis of Greece*; another extravagant tale I recollect having read, *The History of Captain Freney*, a robber . . . *Valentine and Orson . . . Irish Rogues and Rapparees . . .*

The logistical problems of obtaining cheap books in remote areas, at least during the eighteenth century, meant that chapbook texts might be used even in church schools. In an Erasmus Smith school in Co. Kerry in 1795, 25 texts are listed, including *Reading Made Easy*. Three of the older pupils, however, were reading *Irish Highwaymen, The Life and Adventures of James Freney* and *The Seven Champions of Christendom*.[53]

The establishment of the national system and the diffusion of its specially commissioned textbooks produced some alteration in the primary curriculum. A *First Book of Lessons* was published in 1831, a *Second* in the same year, and a *Third* and *Fourth* in 1835. While the chapbook literature was probably used less than before, the change was not as sweeping as might be expected. In the first place, there was a substantial continuity in teaching personnel and buildings, and many of the more advanced pupils no doubt continued to supply their own books. Secondly, in some areas the pay school system survived independently of the national system and its funding. A study of Co. Roscommon shows that only one third of pupils in that county in 1841 were attending a national school, and even as late as 1851 there were still more pay schools than national schools. This was partly due to opposition to the national system on the part of the Catholic Archbishop of Tuam, John McHale, whose archdiocese contained part of Roscommon, partly to a perception of the inferiority of national schools among parents, and partly to the unwillingness of many teachers to enter the national system, since employment by the national board placed strict restrictions on a teacher's professional behaviour and social life.[54]

In practice, then, chapbooks and other popular literature continued to be used in primary schools in Ireland, at least until the Great Famine, and in some places even afterwards. Patrick Keenan, the Chief Inspector of National Schools, told a parliamentary inquiry in 1868 that:

the circulation of such books has not ceased, for the Inspectors inform me that they frequently meet hawkers through the country with their knapsacks well charged with such books.[55]

3 Production and Distribution

PRINTING

Research on the printing and production of popular literature in Ireland is hampered by a comparative shortage of primary sources. The most recent survey of the Dublin trade before 1800 remarks that 'surviving primary documents connected with the book trade are particularly rare' and the principal article on provincial printing begins by pointing out that 'substantial primary sources for the history of Irish printing are regrettably few, and for provincial printing almost non-existent'. These observations apply to the Irish book trade as a whole; the shortage is even more pronounced at the lower end of that trade.[1]

In France, Mandrou used a series of probate inventories of the goods and stock of *Bibliothèque Bleue* publishers in Troyes and elsewhere. For late seventeenth-century England, Spufford also used probate inventories, as well as records of the licensing system for publications in the Guild of Stationers. The Irish printing trade was subject to even less state surveillance and control than those of England and France, and there are few official documents referring to it. Most eighteenth-century wills were lost in the early twentieth century; and the records of the Guild of St Luke, to which most Irish printers belonged, are useful for following the careers of some individual printers, but give no idea of the workings and economies of the trade. The only inventory-type document for Ireland is the 1735 will of Samuel Fuller, a Quaker bookseller in Dublin who produced schoolbooks and other small texts; there is also the job book of Henry Denmead, an early nineteenth-century Cork printer, which lists the work undertaken in a small provincial printing house. For the rest, this account is based mainly on secondary sources, impressionistic evidence and some features of the surviving books themselves, such as advertisements and booklists, frequently printed on the back covers.[2]

THE EIGHTEENTH CENTURY

The printing and selling of popular literature in Dublin was inspired by similar enterprises in London which have been described by Spufford.

This is evident in the advertising formula for these books used by the trade, which replicates the London form: 'by wholesale or retail, to country chapmen and others' or 'where country booksellers, chapmen and others may be furnished'. ('Chapmen' were pedlars, and 'chapbooks' the small books they sold.) Moreover, it is likely that until about 1700, the Irish market was supplied from Britain. Some of the chapmen who operated in Ireland were based in London, travelling to Dublin via Chester. Dublin booksellers may also have imported chapbook stock from Britain. The names of Dublin chapbook publishers occur as importers in the Chester port books in the late seventeenth and early eighteenth centuries: James Malone in 1681, for example, and Luke Dowling in 1702.[3]

By the early eighteenth century, chapbook publishing had become established in Dublin, and formed a small section of a very prosperous general printing trade. This prosperity was due partly to the expanding domestic market, and partly to the absence in Ireland of a copyright control such as the British Copyright Act of 1709, which created a profitable market in early reprints of books published in London. The Irish book trade was centred in Dublin in the eighteenth century, and catered principally for the 'English-speaking, Protestant establishment' who were the main customers and commissioners of books. The trade itself was dominated by Anglicans, while Catholics and non-conformists could not for example become full members of the Guild of St Luke. For Catholic printers and booksellers, there was the added disadvantage of a legal ban on the production of devotional literature, although in practice there was a degree of toleration.[4]

Because of this marginalisation, Catholic and Quaker printers dominated the chapbook market for much of the eighteenth century. Catholics naturally concentrated on the 'country' market, since that was where their co-religionists were mainly to be found, while Quakers produced a lot of schoolbooks along with the chapbooks.

The chapbook market was already well-established by 1719, when James Malone, the principal Catholic bookseller in Dublin, died. Malone had been operating since at least the 1680s, and seems, exceptionally, to have been a full guild member at his death. His stock, which included standard chapbook titles such as *Valentine and Orson* and *The Seven Wise Masters*, was bought by Luke Dowling, another Catholic bookseller, who had been indentured to Malone. In the 1720s and 1730s the main Catholic country dealers were Dowling and Luke Dillon, followed in the 1740s and 1750s by John Fleming and Thomas Browne. Brown had taken over Dillon's premises and stock, giving a continuous line of business since Malone, producing the classic titles of the popular book market, and underlining the stability of the trade.[5]

The earliest large Quaker bookseller was Samuel Fuller, who was listed as a bookseller in 1720 and died in 1735. Fuller had been a schoolmaster and he wrote some of the schoolbooks which he later printed, becoming the first specialist supplier of schoolbooks in Ireland. (He was the official printer to the Society of Friends and wrote a catechism and a number of pamphlets on religious subjects.) Fuller advertised to chapmen from 1724 onwards, and reprinted texts which had been produced specifically for that market in seventeenth-century England, particularly those by Nathaniel Crouch, who wrote under the pseudonym 'Robert Burton'. It seems probable that the 'Burton book', commonly used in Ireland for chapbook, comes from these books, and indicates the success of Fuller in penetrating the market, a success evident in the valuation of his stock and equipment at his death at over £1300.[6]

A certain amount of cooperation between the Catholic and Quaker printers is suggested by Fuller's will, in which one of the larger debts owed by Fuller at his death, eight pounds twelve shillings, was to Luke Dillon. Fuller was followed in the 1740s by Isaac Jackson, who took over Fuller's business on the death of Fuller's widow Mary in 1737. In 1746 Jackson was advertising to 'country chapmen and others' a list that included some of the titles contained in Fuller's 1736 stock, as well as Fuller's own catechism. Jackson was still active in 1770, and the Fuller–Jackson line forms a Quaker parallel to the continuity among Catholic printers of chapbooks.[7]

The country trade continued particularly among Catholic booksellers in the late eighteenth century. Among those whose advertising was directed towards chapmen were Patrick Wogan, James Byrne, Richard Cross, Fitzsimons and Bartholomew Corcoran, who was one of the principal ballad printers of the time. One non-Catholic firm which also supplied the chapbook market was the Rein-Deer, Mountrath Street, run in the 1750s and after by Anne Law. This firm was one of the main producers of songs and broadsheets for Dublin city hawkers, and its trade list of 1759 featured regular chapbook titles such as *Reynard the Fox*, *Valentine and Orson* and *The Seven Champions of Christendom*, and was directed at 'country booksellers, chapmen and others'.

All these printers and booksellers tended to reprint the older classics of the genre, or texts produced for the London trade in the seventeenth century. Texts of Irish origin appeared quite slowly, the most notable early example being *Irish Highwaymen*, which was being advertised as a 'country book' by Anne Law in 1759. The fairly static condition this implies reflects the position of chapbooks in the book trade as a whole. There was no firm in Dublin which produced chapbooks exclusively, or even principally, as was the case with some of the firms in London or Troyes. Dublin printers used the chapbooks as a steady seller, a part of the stock which could be held permanently, and which brought in a slow but steady income. Cheap books could be printed during slack periods in business, using old paper and type, and stored unbound in sheets for slow but steady sale. Moreover, the advertising formulas directed at pedlars and 'country dealers' frequently do not specify what titles were available, but give the impression of an unchanging and familiar list: 'where country booksellers, chapmen and others, may be furnished with all kinds of books in their way' or 'may be furnished with a variety of histories not here set down'.[8]

In 1749, for instance, when Thomas Brown was retiring from business, he sold most of his stock, but retained his 'country chapbooks and histories', which he continued to sell in his retirement. Fuller's will, similarly, shows that he had some 700 chapbooks in stock in their bound form, but had 26 000 unbound in sheets, which constituted about 10 per cent of his stock by value. It was worth printing a lot of the books, therefore, but they were going to sell slowly.

In terms of scale, Fuller's stock of chapbooks is modest compared to that of Tias in London in the 1690s (70–90 000) or to that of the Oudots in Troyes in 1722 (500 000). The comparison is not straightforward, however, since chapbooks represent only 10 per cent of Fuller's business, whereas Tias and Oudot were mainly publishers of chapbooks. In the case of Tias, 93 per cent of his list had a retail price under sixpence. Taking into account the structure of the trade in Dublin, as well as the far smaller population of Ireland, Fuller's business is substantial. Moreover, it seems reasonable to assume that some of the Catholic printers held stock on a similar scale.

The fact that in the eighteenth century cheap books were initially imported through Dublin, and later largely produced there, reflected Dublin's dominance of Irish trade. Most imports came through the port of Dublin and manufacture was also largely located in the city. Pedlars would have bought their goods, including books, in Dublin, and travelled along a national road system which radiated from Dublin. For the eighteenth century, therefore, the Irish cheap print trade resembled that of England, which was dominated by London, rather than that of France, where the printing of the *Bibliothèque Bleue* was essentially a provincial phenomenon.[9]

The dominance of Dublin Catholic printers in the 'country trade' in the eighteenth century influenced the texts that were printed. The printers were English speakers in an anglophone environment, and were therefore not able or inclined to supply a chapbook literature in the Irish language (assuming there to have been a demand for it). In any case, their readers were probably concentrated in the more anglophone eastern half of the country in the eighteenth century. The printers were Catholic, very aware of their secondary status as quarter-members of the guild, and involved in the early campaigns of the Catholic committees.[10] These campaigns were based in Dublin, which by the late eighteenth century had moved from having a Protestant majority to having a Catholic one. Dublin Catholic printers were therefore more aware of and involved in Catholic politics than their country readership, and were instrumental in the politicisation of this readership. This is most evident in the printings of Reily's *Impartial History*, which in its chapbook version contained a Catholic petition to Parliament of 1720.[11] The supply of the country market from Dublin in the eighteenth century was therefore culturally anglicising and politically Catholicising.

THE NINETEENTH CENTURY

By the early nineteenth century, the picture is somewhat different. The continuing integration of Ireland into the larger British economy led to the weakening of Dublin's position as an economic centre, and the relative emergence of provincial towns. A significant beneficiary of this process was Belfast, as the important linen export trade from Ulster began to be conducted there rather than through Dublin. Administratively and politically, Dublin also lost many of its functions with the passing of the Act of Union in 1800. The Union is traditionally held to have affected the Dublin printing trade adversely in two ways. The extension of the copyright law to Ireland meant the end of the reprint trade, and the end of the Irish Parliament meant the decline of printing for the administration. The early nineteenth century was therefore a period of slack demand and low wages within the printing trade as a whole. The effect on a low-level, fairly static and secure business like the chapbook trade was less than on elite printing, however, and it prospered perhaps more than other sectors. The Catholic booksellers, for example, moved their offices gradually to better areas of the city. After 1810, the activities of the tract societies in the chapbook and schoolbook market added further to business.[12] Not only did these societies publish numerous titles, but their editions were large, runs of 10 000 being common.[13]

In any case, Dublin was less the centre of the trade in Ireland as a whole after 1800, as the early nineteenth century was a period of greater printing activity in provincial towns. Belfast had become increasingly active in the later eighteenth century and in the early nineteenth century was joined by Cork and Limerick, as well as by smaller centres such as Monaghan, Newry and Clonmel. Trade frequently developed in tandem with regional newspapers from about the 1760s: the production of a newspaper was a printer's first line of business, and the printing of books followed. For provincial printers, as for those in Dublin, a steady source of income was possible from chapbooks, and they began to publish advertisements directed at pedlars in the late eighteenth century. In Limerick, for example, a song book probably printed in the 1780s by J. Gloster announced that 'chapmen may be supplied with histories, manuals, primmers, ballads' at Gloster's premises. Similar notices are found from the printers J. and T. McAuliffe, W. Goggin and other printers in Limerick in the early nineteenth century.[14]

The rise of the provincial printers increased the variety within the chapbook corpus, in particular by adding more texts of Irish origin. The most popular chapbook text in the Irish language, the *Pious Miscellany*, was printed in Cork, Limerick and Clonmel. The early nineteenth century was the great period of printing of Irish language catechisms, particularly in Munster towns, and what appears to be an attempt to provide a native equivalent to international chivalric romances, *The Battle of Ventry*, a translation of a medieval Irish legend, was printed in Cork in 1824 and in Limerick in 1835. For Belfast, Adams's survey features many Presbyterian works and texts of Scottish origin for both the eighteenth and nineteenth centuries.[15]

After 1850, the Irish print trade shifted back towards being centralised in Dublin. Developments in printing technology such as steam printing demanded greater capital investment of a size which favoured larger firms in Dublin and London. Moreover, improvements in communications, particularly the spread of railways, enabled the Irish rural market to be centrally supplied.

In the early nineteenth century, to judge from surviving copies in libraries, two printers in particular seem to have been the principal suppliers of the traditional titles, with the addition of some post-1750 texts. These were C.M. Warren in Dublin, active from about 1815, and Joseph Smyth in Belfast who had been in business from a few years earlier. The two seem to have cooperated to some extent, binding and reselling each other's productions and advertising almost identical lists in similar typographical layout on the back covers of their books. They both advertised *The Seven Champions of Christendom* and other romances, *Irish Highwaymen* and *Captain Freney*, *The Battle of Aughrim* and *The Siege of Londonderry*, some of the more successful items from the lists of the tract societies, along with more recent entries into the chapbook literature such as *Paul and Virginia*.[16]

Like the eighteenth-century printers whose trade they were continuing, neither Warren nor Smyth was exclusively (or perhaps even mainly) a publisher of chapbooks, but found them a steady sideline. Both had institutional customers. Smyth did some local state work, and is recorded in the Co. Down Grand Jury Presentments as having been paid £20 for printing. Warren was printer to a number of Catholic institutions such as the Carmelite Order, produced in 1836 a volume for the Catholic Book Society, and in 1832 printed a book of rules of the Purgatorian Society 'with the approbation of superiors'.[17]

Also like the eighteenth-century printing houses, Smyth and Warren's chapbook business was stable and continuous. A succession of Warrens continued to print the standard titles until the early twentieth century. Smyth was succeeded by Alexander Mayne in about 1850. Mayne inherited many ballads in standing type from Smyth, and may well have inherited chapbooks also.[18]

THE ECONOMICS OF THE TRADE

As regards the everyday economics of the cheap book trade, the lack of documentation makes it nearly impossible to know about most aspects of printers' and booksellers' activities: the size of the printing houses, their dealings with country shopkeepers and pedlars, their relationship with authority and their social origin all remain obscure.

A few observations can be made. Print runs were relatively large, probably about 2000, since the sale was steady and sure. Henry Denmead in Cork, for example, who did not run a large enterprise, printed 1500 copies of Challoner's *Think Well On't*, a popular Catholic devotional work, for his own sale, his Protestant catechisms had runs of 2000, and the *Universal Spelling Book* had a run of 4000. Fuller's inventory of 1736 contains large unbound editions of Burton's small books: 2020 copies of *The Lives of Pirates*, 2050 of *Moll Flanders* and 3500 of *The History of America*.

Both retail prices and profit margins seem to have declined in the century between Fuller and Warren, indicating a pattern of lower social diffusion over time. In 1736 Fuller's unbound Burtons were valued at a penny farthing, the bound Burtons at twopence, with an advertised retail price of tenpence.

In the 1840s Thackeray bought cheap books, probably printed by Warren, at a cost of threepence each. However, the cost of production was probably not correspondingly lower in the 1840s, despite the use of stereotype. The Kildare Place Society Book Sub-Committee in 1814 estimated the cost of production of their books (which were intended to supplant chapbooks and therefore made to look like them) at £40 per thousand bound, or about tenpence each. They were then heavily subsidised and sold at two shillings a dozen (twopence each). If book society productions needed such heavy subsidies to compete, then the producers of cheap books must have been operating on very low overheads indeed. The consequent low wages are consistent with the picture of labour surplus and misery among printing workers in the 1820s and 1830s.[19]

PEDLARS

It is evident that there was a potential readership for cheap popular literature in the Irish countryside, both among adults and children, and that there was a profitable trade in printing this literature in Dublin and in other towns. How were production and consumption connected?

In the absence of bookshops in the countryside, a rural customer had three options: firstly, a book could be bought from a bookseller in a large town. However, due to the probable rarity of visits to towns large enough to have a bookshop, this was most likely a marginal possibility.[20] Secondly, it was frequently possible to buy small books in general stores in smaller towns or villages. According to Thomas Parnell in 1822:

> The common mode of getting books in Ireland, the kind of books the peasantry buy for their children, is through the means of grocers and hardwaremen; they keep a shelf of what they call Burtons, and spelling books and almanacks, and books of that kind. They cannot of course be considered booksellers.[21]

Finally, and most frequently, small books were bought from travelling pedlars, who carried them along with clothes and hardware. This form of distribution of books is noted in government reports and by observers in the early nineteenth century:

> Books for reading are very few in number, and of that description well known to those who examine the books which pedlars and petty shopkeepers sell to the country people. (Co. Kilkenny)
> In the schools, the books for those advanced to reading are generally those sold by pedlars. (Co. Tyrone)[22]

Peddling was a common form of retail distribution in Europe before the arrival of shops in the countryside. Pedlars sold mainly clothes and hardware; they usually carried their goods in a backpack, but a minority possessed a horse or two, and consequently operated on a fairly large scale. One in six had horses in late seventeenth century England, for example, and in the early nineteenth century the figure was one in five.[23]

Many or most of these pedlars carried some books as part of a wider range of goods. Occasionally, pedlars sold only books: this was particularly the case in France, where in the mid-nineteenth century a special licence existed for book pedlars, as part of the censorship mechanism of the Second Empire.[24] These book pedlars were in effect travelling booksellers, selling far more than small cheap books. In Ireland also, pedlars occasionally carried more expensive items: in Co. Roscommon, one travelling bookseller in 1757 was selling a selection of relatively expensive history books and travelling with a horse and cart.[25]

Book pedlars were an accepted part of the book trade, and some made a successful transition from peddling to bookselling and printing. One was Luke White, who began life as a book pedlar in the eighteenth century. He had accumulated enough capital to set up as a bookseller by the 1780s, and his was the only Dublin shop to order copies of the *Encyclopédie*. James Duffy was a book pedlar in the 1830s, travelling not only in Ireland but also to the Irish quarters of Liverpool and Manchester, before becoming a successful publisher for a mass readership from the 1840s onwards.[26]

The pedlar is a difficult figure to describe with precision, being usually very mobile and often not a person of substance. In the most complete survey of the subject, Fontaine distinguishes four types of source, all of which see the peddling system from the outside, and consequently denigrate or misrepresent the occupation to some extent. These are administrative records, interested in controlling and taxing; complaints of shopkeepers against competition from pedlars; police and

judicial records of exceptional cases; and fictions, comprising literature, iconography and oral history.[27]

Using documents internal to the peddling network, such as inventories, wills and business correspondence of pedlars and their suppliers,
a picture emerges of a trade which, in contrast to the image of
vagabondage and semi-illegality presented by outside sources, was stable,
long-lasting and resourceful. Fontaine classifies pedlars not according
to type of goods sold or distances travelled, but by method of financing and credit. What she terms 'Faméliques' had little access to credit,
dealt in small amounts, and existed at the margins of trade; family
pedlars, by contrast, were allowed large amounts of credit by their
suppliers and equally allowed it to their customers. Finally, shopkeeper
pedlars travelled with very large amounts of goods and opened temporary shops.

All these types existed within extensive family business networks
whose centre was in a specific small area. A group of villages in the
French Alps, for example, fostered a book peddling trade in the sixteenth century, which by the eighteenth century had become a network
of 51 booksellers in France, Italy, Spain, Portugal and Brazil, with
associated pedlars, still run as a family business centered on the Alpine villages where its members owned land and practised endogamy
in marriage. A similar pattern may well underlie the distribution of
licensed pedlars in England in the 1780s. By far the largest number
(outside London) were settled in Staffordshire, and 'the hamlet of
Holinsclough . . . was, it appears, almost entirely inhabited by them'.[28]

Pedlars functioned, therefore, within larger enterprises, opening up
rural areas to market goods and establishing extensive credit networks.
Supporters of pedlars in the British Parliament in the 1780s all stressed
the very large amounts of money tied up in the trade and the length of
the lines of credit.

PEDLARS IN IRELAND

For Ireland, unfortunately, the materials for such a picture do not exist.
Very few of the wills, inventories or business correspondence that might
have constructed a picture of regional origins and commercial contacts
in Ireland have survived. We are dependent to varying degrees, therefore, on the 'outsider' sources listed above, from which some idea of
a peddling network in eighteenth- and nineteenth-century Ireland can
be derived.

Pedlars were well known since the seventeenth century in Ireland. Shopkeepers in Derry were complaining about the activities of pedlars as early as the 1630s, an early system of licensing was proposed in 1664, and a traveller in 1681 described Irish cabins as:

> abounding with children which, with the man, maid and wife, sometimes a travelling stranger, or pack-carrier, or pedlar or two; nine or ten of them [sleep] together, naked heads and points.[29]

The commercialisation of the agricultural economy, along with the growth of domestic industry, particularly linen, in the eighteenth and early nineteenth centuries would have given a boost to the peddling trade. Not only did this produce a rise in cash income in rural areas, thus increasing the pedlar's market, but in addition, peddling seems also to have carried the products of domestic industry from the countryside into the towns and cities, or even to Britain. Pedlar families in Co. Armagh in the twentieth century accounted for the origins of their trade in this way – originally bringing linen from Ulster to England to sell in markets, and later hawking finished linen articles from house to house.[30]

How many of these pedlars carried books is not clear, although Spufford describes pedlars buying books in London to sell in Ireland in the 1690s, and Phillipps considers that the 'country trade' in books, supplied by pedlars, was established in Ireland by the late seventeenth century. Certainly by the 1720s, to judge from printers' and booksellers' advertisements discussed above, a solid book-peddling trade had evolved.[31] Some idea of numbers and distribution of pedlars can be derived from administrative sources, which in Ireland are either records of licencing systems in the eighteenth and early nineteenth centuries, or population censuses in the nineteenth century, particularly those of 1831 and 1851.[32]

Much of the early information on pedlars comes from attempts to regulate or suppress the trade, as a result of the strong suspicion of pedlars which existed since at least the early seventeenth century, and which will be discussed below. From this time, therefore, there was strong lobbying of parliaments to act against them. In the 1690s, some ten bills were introduced in the London Parliament to suppress them completely. The measure ultimately preferred, however, was to license them, a procedure adopted in Britain in the early 1690s and in Ireland in 1746.[33] This continued in Ireland until the 1830s.

The licence records give an idea of the number of pedlars (an underestimate), trends over time, and geographic distribution. Thus Spufford can give a picture of England in the late seventeenth century, and Darmon of France in the 1850s, both from fairly full licence records.[34] Although the Irish licence records are far less complete, a few tentative guesses can be made.

From 1746, pedlars in Ireland had, by law, to register and buy a licence, which cost one pound per year, plus one pound for every animal used. The money raised was to go to the Protestant Charter Schools, which had been founded in the 1730s: control of a disapproved system of communication was to provide financial support for an approved system of education. The fee was doubled in 1786 and continued through to the 1830s, after which it fell into disuse.[35] The same measure discontinued the appropriation to the Charter Schools. The number of pedlars shown by such a licensing system is almost certainly a significant underestimate, since avoidance must have been possible by those unwilling or unable to pay. The figures are, however, useful as a minimum indication.

There was clearly a well-established network of substantial pedlars in existence by the 1740s, since only four years after its introduction the annual revenue from the licences reached £2258, corresponding to some 1800 pedlars. The revenue later stabilised at about £1300–£1500 between the 1750s and the 1780s. This compares with about 2500 pedlars in England in the 1690s, about one per two thousand people. However, the Irish licence was much cheaper, £1 compared with £4 in England. In the late 1780s (at £2 p.a.) the duty brought in £3000, about 1200 pedlars. In 1817–23 the reported number of licences varied between 506 and 863, but the lower figures were due to a decline in the system of collection: by 1840 only three licences were issued, and in 1843 none. In the rest of the United Kingdom, by contrast, there was no such decline in the system of collection.[36]

Direct comparison of the Irish figures with those for England and Wales given by the Muis is made difficult by the fact that some of the revenue would be from licences for horses, and that most of the figures give total revenue only. In 1782–5 in England and Wales, three-quarters of the licences issued were for foot pedlars only, and the Muis use this proportion for their calculations. Assuming a similar proportion in Ireland, the schematic calculation shown in Table 3.1 can be made.[37]

The figures for England and Wales may be artificially low in 1751 and 1781 due to widespread evasion of what was an expensive tax, a possibility pointed out by Shammas. The drop in the overall Irish figures, however, suggests a similar phenomenon, as was also the case for

Table 3.1   Pedlars in the eighteenth century

Year	Pedlars	Population	Pop./pedlar
England and Wales			
1720s	2321	5.6 m	2412
1751	1523	6.2 m	4070
1781	1343	7.57 m	5636
Ireland			
1750	1808	2.4 m	1327
1780s	1200	4.2 m	3500

the hearth tax in Ireland in the same period.[38] The coverage of Ireland by pedlars during the eighteenth century was therefore on a par with, or even more dense than, that of England and Wales.

Comparison is not possible for the early nineteenth century, since the types of information vary. Licences were issued to 7479 pedlars in England in 1830, one for every 1752 people.[39] The 1831 census of Ireland, however, lists a total of 7569 people under the occupational heading 'hawkers, pedlars and duffers', approximately one for every thousand of the population. This is clearly due to a far less restrictive definition than that of the licences: some of these pedlars were probably operating on a very small scale indeed and over short distances. Nevertheless, they represent an intensive covering of the entire country, and only two counties, Clare and Tyrone, had more than 2500 people per pedlar. Even if only a small minority of these carried books, many areas, particularly in Leinster, were very well served.

Figure 3.1 shows the density of pedlars per population in 1831, and shows a trade network which was centred on Dublin. The city itself had the second highest proportion (after Drogheda), and the county was one of three with a ratio of one pedlar for less than 600 people. Apart from Tipperary, the counties with densities of between 1:600 and 1:900 were in Leinster and within easy reach of Dublin by main roads. Those with densities of 1:900–1200 form a ring around Dublin, and those with the lowest densities were farthest from Dublin, in the north-west and south-west. (The only exception to this pattern was Antrim, and while there was undoubtedly a peddling trade from Belfast, many Antrim pedlars may have travelled to and from Scotland.[40])

By the time of the census of 1851, the density of pedlars seems to have dropped significantly.[41] The census lists 4147 pedlars, or one to approximately 1500 people. The reported distribution had also changed

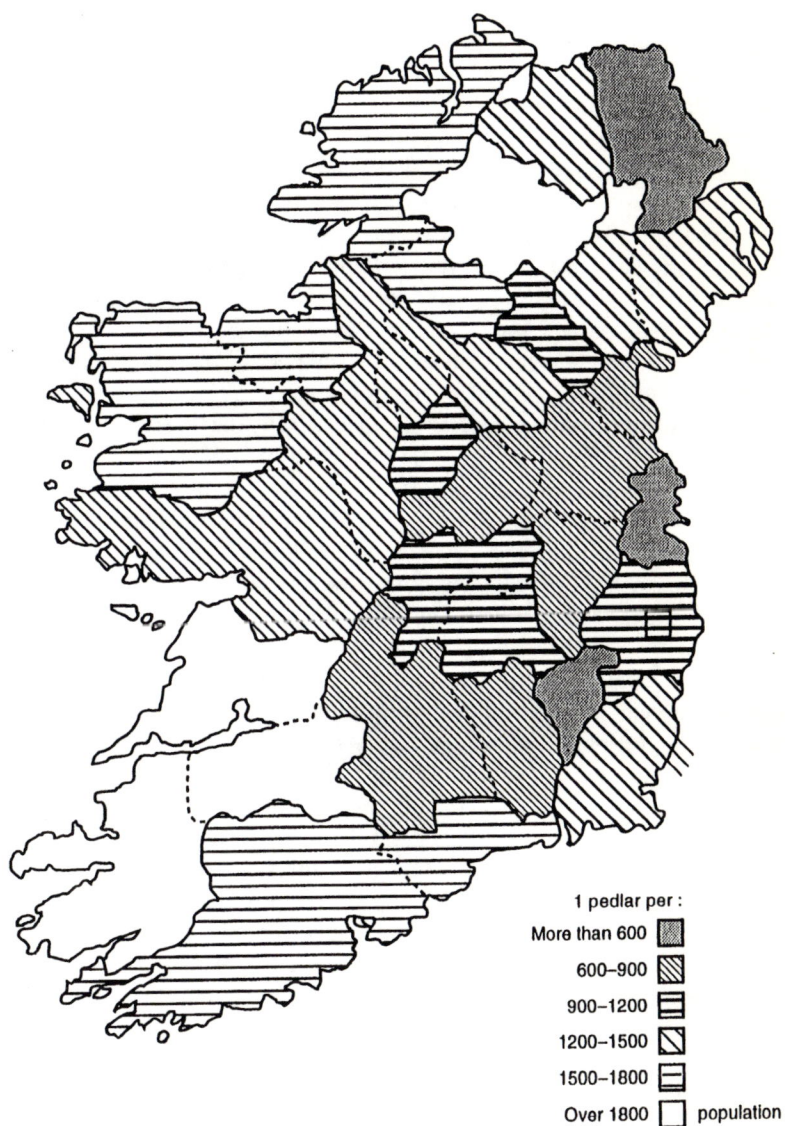

Figure 3.1 Pedlar density in Ireland, 1831

since 1831, and pedlars were now concentrated in a belt from Galway to Wexford, with Ulster relatively better served than before as well. (Figure 3.2). The counties with least pedlars formed another belt from Mayo to Louth. This may well be due to the collapse of the domestic linen industries in this area in the 1830s and 1840s, and the consequent shrinking of the cash economy.

It is doubtful whether any definite conclusions can be drawn from a comparison of 1831 and 1851. On the one hand, the drop in the density of coverage in most counties (particularly Co. Dublin) may reflect the spread of a retail system of small shopkeepers. On the other hand, much of the decline is probably due to differences between the organisation of the two censuses. Peddling was frequently a seasonal occupation, a trade carried on in summer, when the weather was fine and when, if you had a patch of land or a small shop, it could be left to someone else to take care of. (The only remaining revenue collectors' accounts which mention pedlars' licences, from the 1780s, show that the great majority of licences were taken between March and June.[42]) The 1851 census was taken on the 31st of March, probably well before the beginning of the summer circuit for many pedlars, whereas the 1831 census was taken in June, probably the high point of trade. Moreover, the 1831 census was spread over a number of weeks, which in itself would tend to swell somewhat the reported size of a mobile population.

It is not easy to discern an overall pattern for the eighteenth and nineteenth century in Ireland. In England, the Muis point to the fact that the proportion of licensed pedlars with a horse drops continuously from the 1780s on. A similar impoverishment of the average pedlar may well have happened in Ireland, contributing to the winding down of the licensing system. In France, on the other hand, Barbier sees the early nineteenth century as the apogee of the small-scale book pedlar in the countryside, when a growing readership was not yet served by mass communications; and Darmon sees the final decline as taking place after 1850, when the spread of railways was accompanied by the development of permanent migration, instead of temporary migration such as peddling, after the agricultural crises of the 1840s. This pattern is also found in Ireland, where the early nineteenth century was the high point of production of peddled cheap printed forms as chapbooks and single sheet ballads, and where permanent migration began to replace temporary (mainly harvest) migration from the west and northwest around 1880.[43]

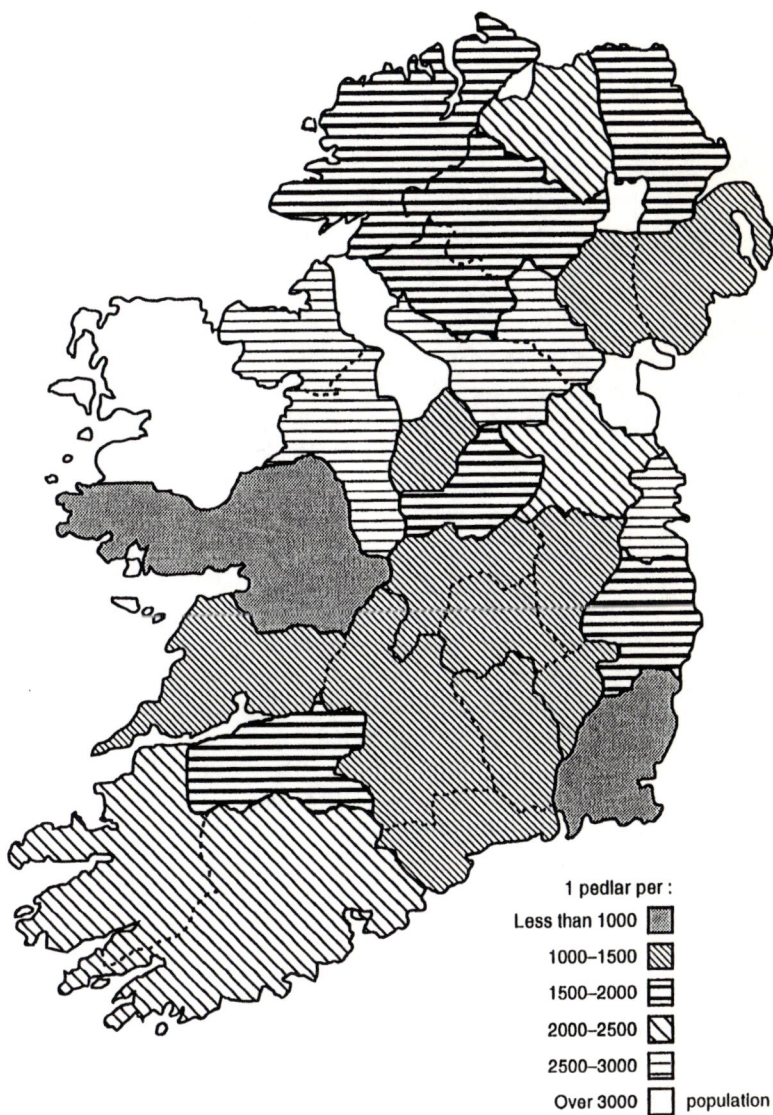

Figure 3.2 Pedlar density in Ireland, 1851

ATTITUDES TOWARDS PEDLARS

As regards the other types of source listed by Fontaine, the complaints of shopkeepers and police records, in Ireland as elsewhere, tend to give a negative picture of the pedlar.

Shopkeepers' disapproval of pedlars was strictly commercial, since pedlars were in competition with the retail system. In particular, retailers disliked pedlars because they cut out the trader and shopkeeper, and because they did not pay local rates, as fixed traders did. This sort of criticism is found from the early seventeenth century onwards, and retailers mounted frequent campaigns against pedlars. One such campaign took place in the late 1720s, and the arguments can be illustrated from this.

The campaign was organised from London, and a petition was presented to parliament stating 'The Case of the Shopkeepers, Manufacturers and Fair Traders of England against the hawkers and pedlars'. The shopkeepers were also supported by Daniel Defoe in a pamphlet of 1727. 'Trade', wrote Defoe, 'run[s] on in a happy round of buying and selling, importing and exporting . . . and all the way as it passes, tho' through a multitude of hands, it leaves something of gain everywhere behind it.' The pedlar, however, 'projects to cut off the progress of things from their natural course . . . and thinks to put the gain of five or six stages of the trade into his own pocket.' Due to his 'avarice and envy', he 'acts like a thief and destroyer'. This campaign of the 1720s also sought support in Ireland, publishing an appeal to Dublin shopkeepers in 1730 to sign their petition.[44]

Pedlars were disliked by the law principally because of their mobility, which was thought to facilitate smuggling and receiving stolen goods. According to two English magistrates in 1808, they were 'the medium through which stolen and smuggled goods are introduced into the country, and counterfeit money is circulated to a great extent.'[45] Similarly, a manual for Justices of the Peace in Ireland in 1812 described them as 'deceitful fellows who go from place to place selling goods which ought to be sold in open market'.[46]

In Irish language sources, the terminology for pedlars, although usually neutral, was sometimes tinged with a similar disapproval. McCurtin and Begley's English–Irish dictionary of 1732 translated 'pedlar' in a straightforward way as 'ceannuidhe seachráin', 'a travelling merchant', and 'to peddle' as 'mionearradh do dhíol', 'to sell small goods'. 'A hawker', on the other hand, was defined as 'neach do bhíos ag imtheacht síos suas ag díol earraidhe beaga, cneamhaire', 'someone who travels up and down selling small goods, a rogue or crook'.

Disapproval of pedlars reached its height in Ireland in the politically disturbed conditions of the 1790s, when fears of conspiracy made any traveller suspect. This political suspicion had been evident as early as 1790, when magistrates in Limerick were 'very much alarmed [about] the conduct of two pedlars in this place'. The pedlars were arrested, but nothing seems to have been found against them. The fear was perhaps more justified in the case of the pedlar arrested at the fair of Gortin, Co. Tyrone, in 1797 'who was hawking about and selling ballads and other books and papers' including an eight-page booklet, *Christ in Triumph coming to Judgement*. This forecast an egalitarian millennium, preceded by 'great wars and commotions' after which 'happy times will succeed to many people, and the poor will be had in equal (or perhaps superior) estimation to the rich'. The magistrate not surprisingly found these ideas 'very dangerous at this time'.[47]

Finally, pedlars were distrusted because they were mobile and did not fit easily into a social hierarchy. They were included with beggars and gypsies in the 'rogue' literature of the sixteenth and seventeenth centuries which, as Chartier and Sorbier note, was a 'portrait of society's outcasts', and an attempt (mainly by urban dwellers) to make sense of the new poor and vagrant. Thus as early as the sixteenth century, there were laws against pedlars as part of the new displaced population. Under the English Vagrancy Act of 1597, pedlars were to be 'whipped until bloody' and sent home.[48]

The figure of 'the pedlar', therefore, in both elite and popular sources, was assimilated to that of the rogue. In *Irish Highwaymen*, a chapbook collection of criminal biography, two robbers travelled through the country dressed as pedlars. One of them, 'observing that some of the pedlars [at a fair] took money pretty fast', decided to become one, buying 6/8 worth of goods from Belfast, 'tapes, garters, laces, needles etc., which he carried in a bag that he had made from his mother'; another pedlar 'taught him the canting speech . . . and made him a mould for the imitation of Clement's buttons, a famous maker of silver buttons in London'. ('Canting' was the name given to thieves' and beggars' slang in the rogue literature.) Similarly, in a folk tale collected in Co. Cork in the 1930s, a 'Peidléar Bán' (white or fair-haired pedlar) outwits a highwayman who has attempted to rob him and eventually joins the highwayman himself.[49] This mixture of admiration and distrust, characteristic of the popular view of rogues, continued until at least the nineteenth century, when, in France, glossaries of the 'pedlars' language', to help a customer avoid being tricked, were still being printed.[50]

Pedlars did have their defenders, however, among those who recognised their importance in opening up the countryside to retail trade,
and particularly among those wholesalers who supplied them with goods.
Dublin printers, to judge from the way their advertising wooed the
pedlars, clearly approved, but the most influential support came when
a bill was introduced into the British Parliament in 1785 to tax shops.
As a concession to shopkeepers, the measure also proposed making
peddling illegal. This was strongly opposed by a variety of interests,
who petitioned parliament in support of pedlars. These included the
major textile manufacturers in Britain, who appreciated the pedlars'
role in 'introducing [their goods] into parts of the country where they
would not otherwise have been sold'. All the petitions stressed the
large sums of money and the long lines of credit involved in the trade.
One supplier of textiles in Shrewsbury was owed £16 000 by pedlars.
The final form of the bill did not suppress pedlars, but increased their
licence fee and restricted the areas in which they could operate. These
restrictions in turn were opposed by petition, and in 1789 most of the
restrictions were removed and the old licence fees restored. According
to the Muis, the controversy 'illustrates the power wielded by extra-
parliamentary forces to influence the course of legislation' and that
'the connection between supplier and hawker had long since been firmly
established'.[51]

Consumers in small towns and rural areas must also have appreciated the pedlar, to judge from an exchange of letters in a Co. Tipperary
newspaper in 1827. A Thurles shopkeeper wrote to the paper complaining of 'the practice of encouraging strolling hawkers of goods to
sell in their respective towns to the injury of the fair trader, a sort of
article ingeniously made up for sale to catch the eye'; moreover, 'the
very best room in town (the public court house) is given up to every
stroller that comes', and there are 'armed policemen to protect [their]
temporary counters from the idle and curious'.

The next issue contained a reply by 'an inhabitant' who clearly looked
forward to pedlars' visits: 'the last person of the description alluded to
had an assortment of articles not generally sold in any shop here, namely,
jewellery, plate, plated ware, and books . . . his ware room was at night
full of the beauty and fashion of our little town . . . These hawkers are
always licensed, and cannot be legally prevented from hawking their
goods . . . when books are exhibited for sale, and that sale discour-
aged, it is in fact a blow at the liberty of the press, and augurs little
for the civilisation of a town.' Similar defences of pedlars by readers
and consumers are found in eighteenth-century France, one even coming

from Malesherbes, the state supervisor of booksellers.[52]

To judge from the folklore collected in Ireland in the 1930s, referring to the second half of the nineteenth century, the popular view of pedlars seems on the whole to have been positive. They were known to people and liked, and were frequently referred to by name. In Kilworth, in north Co. Cork, for example, 'Old Mr. Morris's father was a pedlar. He used to be travelling selling combs and thread and all kinds of things . . . he made a lot of money and set up a shop and educated a family. He had three sons priests and two daughters nuns, another son a doctor and another a poet.'[53]

There were therefore both negative and positive images of pedlars, probably confirming and reinforcing the view of the books being sold. To moral reformers and to shopkeepers, pedlars were unsavoury characters hawking subversive literature; to many consumers, they were welcome visitors bringing otherwise unavailable goods and sometimes buying the people's own domestic manufactures.

4 Chivalric Romances

Contemporary commentators were unanimous about the prominence of one type of text within the cheap printed literature of the eighteenth and nineteenth centuries, and surviving printers' lists and advertisements bear them out. This genre was the romance of chivalry, which had been a fundamental element of popular literature since its beginnings, not only in Ireland, but in Britain and Europe as well. None of the printed romances popular in Ireland was in fact indigenous, unlike the texts in the other genres to be considered. This is probably because of the way the 'country market' evolved in Ireland, being supplied initially from London, and later with Dublin reprints of English texts. Romances, being among the earliest titles produced for that market, were also among the most likely to be imported. Native romantic tales did exist, of a type very similar to the printed romances, but they were in manuscript and in the Irish language. A printing trade that functioned in English would not necessarily have been aware of them, or interested in having them translated.

The cheap printed romances which circulated in Ireland, therefore, formed part of an international corpus, and were all as frequently printed elsewhere as in Ireland. The genre originated in the courtly literature of medieval Europe, and reflected the values of a medieval aristocracy. The characters are all noble, and the principal virtues of the heroes are those of a society based on military service. They are good fighters, honourable and loyal to a king, who is represented as good and wise. The world view is that of medieval Christendom, the enemies usually representing Islam, being Turks or Persians, and much of the action takes place in Asia Minor and the eastern Mediterranean.

Valentine and Orson is a prototypical romance of this kind. The story, of medieval French origin, concerns two brothers, the sons of the emperor of Greece, who were separated at birth. Valentine was brought up in the court of his uncle, the king of France, while Orson was brought up by bears in a forest. They later meet and fight, and when neither manages to defeat the other this leads to their recognising each other. The rest of the text is taken up with a series of military adventures against Saracens and giants, frequently conquered by magical means.

The romance as a genre underwent a revival in the sixteenth century, beginning in Spain. Many of the medieval texts made a success-ful transition to print, and an enormous amount of new texts was pro-duced. Precisely why this happened remains unclear. It may have been a reaction on the part of the aristocracies to social change, or may possibly also have satisfied a demand on the part of a new urban read-ership which was looking for models of socialisation. The new ro-mances were frequently even more extravagant than the old. The Spanish neo-chivalric romances had a great impact throughout Europe, includ-ing England, where they inspired a plethora of new texts in the late sixteenth and early seventeenth centuries, the best known of which is probably Richard Johnston's *History of the Seven Champions of Chris-tendom* of 1596.

The seven champions of the title are the patron saints of Ireland, Britain, France, Spain and Italy. The story centres on St George, who was kidnapped by an enchantress at birth. At the age of 14 he outwits her and sets himself and the other six champions free. Each of them has a series of adventures and combats in which the adversaries are Islamic, and the story switches regularly from one to another. Nearly all of the material was taken from the Middle English romance *Bevis of Hamden.*[1]

Don Belianis Of Greece is another neo-chivalric romance, written in Spanish in the sixteenth century. Belianis, like Valentine and Orson, is one of three sons of the emperor of Greece. A picture of a woman he has never met appears on his shield, and he searches for her, fighting on the way against Persians and Turks. He is watched over by an enchantress who cures him magically of his wounds and sends magic chariots to move him from place to place. An English translation of *Don Belianis* was published in 1591, and a second and third part were added in 1671 by a London bookseller and writer, Francis Kirkman, some of which is set in medieval Ireland.[2]

Valentine and Orson, *The Seven Champions* and *Don Belianis* were the most frequently reprinted chapbook romances in eighteenth- and nineteenth-century Ireland. A fourth popular text, *The Seven Wise Masters of Rome*, is not strictly speaking a romance, but can profitably be con-sidered alongside the others since its setting is an emperor's court, its structure, like that of the romances, is episodic, and a good proportion of it concerns knights and chivalry. It is in the form of a storytelling contest: the second wife of the emperor falsely accuses her stepson of attempting to seduce her, and the emperor therefore condemns him to death. The stepson's seven teachers in turn tell the emperor fables which show the folly of judging by appearances, while the empress responds to each of the fables with tales whose theme is ingratitude and treachery.

These romances were already common in Ireland by the late seventeenth century, and are included in the earliest advertisements directed towards pedlars. The Preface to a copy of *The Seven Wise Masters* in the Pepys collection (from the 1680s) claims that the story 'is held in such esteem in Ireland that it is of the chiefest use in all the English schools for introducing children to the understanding of good letters.'[3]

In the wider long-term printing history a pattern is discernible. The early editions were expensive quartos, and contained very long texts (*Don Belianis*, for example, was originally in three volumes). By about 1650 in England, these were beginning to be replaced by shorter, smaller and cheaper editions, printed by ballad and chapbook publishers. Kirkman's preface to his 1671 translation of *Don Belianis*, for example, after recommending a course of reading in romances of chivalry 'to give thee some order and method that thou mayest proceed in', beginning with *The Seven Wise Masters* and continuing through *Don Belianis*, *Valentine and Orson* and *The Seven Champions* among others, lamented that:

> although they are excellent pieces, and were not long since in great esteem with the French and English nobility and gentry, yet they are also thrust out of use, by the present slighting and neglecting of all books in general, and by the particular esteem of our English stage plays.

They seem to have continued as elite luxury literature slightly longer in Ireland, and quarto editions of *Valentine and Orson* and *The Seven Champions* were printed in Dublin in 1749 and 1770 respectively. By the late eighteenth century in Ireland, however, they were purely small books and were strongly condemned by elite commentators on popular culture.[4]

It could be argued that these romances were unlikely candidates for making the transition into popular literature, in Ireland or elsewhere. Their ambience, attitudes and values must have meant little to the peasantry since they were so far removed from everyday experience. It might even be claimed that this literature glorified the very class the peasantry might have seen as oppressors. This problem has indeed presented the principal historiographical issue concerning the significance of chivalric romance in popular literature. There are two ways in which this proposition needs to be severely qualified, however. In the first place, the romances were magical and fantastic tales entering and supplementing a corpus of folktale and legend, and it is misleading to treat them purely as realistic. In the second place, the ideology of the texts could be used to problematise social relations as much as reinforcing them.

ROMANCE AND ORAL LITERATURE

An approach to the romances which treated them as folklore would direct attention towards questions of structure and form as well as social ambience. The aristocratic setting of the stories is an external feature of the tales, whereas their structures are more like magical folk tales than real events in the lives of the medieval nobility. Indeed many episodes within the romances are also international tales, possibly adapted by scribes and bards for their aristocratic audiences. If these had an 'ordinary' hero, he or she could be replaced with a knight or a princess.[5]

One of the international tales in *The Seven Wise Masters*, for example, concerns a dog which its master left to mind the master's child. A snake tried to kill the child, but the dog fought it off. When the master returned he found the cradle upset and the dog covered in blood; he concluded that the dog had tried to kill the child, and therefore put the dog to death. This is a version of Aarne-Thompson tale type B524 and was the basis of the unusual Alpine cult of St Guinefort in the thirteenth century.[6] Later in *The Seven Wise Masters*, a story about marital infidelity and jealousy, is a version of Aarne-Thompson type 1377, a story which is also found in the *Decameron*.

Such motifs from the international repertoire also occur in some of the chapbook literature of Irish origin, particularly in the Irish criminal biography. The motif of two equal champions not recognising each other, fighting with neither winning, and becoming friends, which is one of the crucial features of the plot of *Valentine and Orson*, recurs in the life of Redmond O'Hanlon, in *Irish Highwaymen*. O'Hanlon, the great outlaw of Ulster, fights Captain Power, 'the greatest robber in Munster', and when they discover each other's identity after an equal fight, they become sworn friends.

Romances were popular with non-elite audiences, therefore, because they were continuous with traditional narrative forms. They could easily enter the same oral channels of transmission, and indeed the medieval originals were probably intended to be read aloud, and have many of the characteristics of oral literature. In particular, their structure is episodic, and they can therefore conveniently be divided up, for reciting on successive nights, for example. Precisely this practice is implicit in the plot of *The Seven Wise Masters*, which, like the *Arabian Nights*, features stories being told in this way.

In the long-term movement of romance from elite to popular surroundings, therefore, we can see the effects of a shift in reading practices in the early modern period. Among the elite, as literacy gradually became universal, there was a shift from group reading towards individual, usually silent, reading. At the popular level restricted literacy meant that reading aloud in groups still had a social role. Romances, being suited to being read aloud, gravitated to the milieux where this was still the commonest practice.[7]

In Ireland, moreover, the printed romance in English entered a tradition of reading aloud of manuscript romance in Irish. As in Europe, this derived ultimately from texts composed for medieval aristocratic audiences and recited by professional bards. These originally featured native saga cycles such as the stories of the Red Branch knights, but after the Norman conquest of the twelfth century, more European elements appeared as the new Anglo-Norman aristocracy introduced romances of French and English origin. These were slow to be adopted, however, and until the end of the fourteenth century the repertoire of bards, even in the households of Anglo-Norman lords, was still largely of Irish origin. By the end of the fifteenth century the Irish-language manuscript corpus began to include translations of English and continental texts such as *Guy, Earl of Warwick*, *Bevis of Hamden*, collections of tales such as *The Seven Wise Masters*, and sources of exotic description like the travels of Marco Polo and Sir John Mandeville. These influenced successive versions of Irish romance, which began for example to include adventures in the Middle East, in Persia, Syria and Greece.[8]

Newer romances are common in the manuscripts of the seventeenth and eighteenth centuries, by which time, following the destruction of the Gaelic aristocracy in the seventeenth century, most of the scribes were schoolmasters or farmers rather than the professional learned classes of medieval Ireland. The reading aloud of romances in Irish from manuscripts is well attested for the eighteenth and nineteenth centuries. One manuscript collection of romances, for example, was called *Gadaidhe Géar na Geamhoíche* [The cunning thief of winter nights], since, according to the preface, 'it steals away the night not only from the reader, but also from the audience'. The Gaelic scholar Standish O'Grady in 1857 described manuscripts being 'read aloud in farmers' houses on occasions when numbers were collected at some employment, such as wool-carding in the evenings, but especially at [funeral] wakes'. These tales then entered the oral tradition and were collected by folklorists in the late nineteenth and early twentieth centuries.[9]

The Irish-language romances were located in non-elite circles throughout the eighteenth and nineteenth centuries, and formed a corpus of texts, as well as a set of reading and reciting practices, into which the printed chapbook romances in English could easily penetrate. This penetration is illustrated by the fact that some poet-scribes of the early eighteenth century composed romances which derive from Spanish sixteenth century models, particularly *Don Belianis,* and that the printed chapbook romances also entered the oral tradition in Irish. A tale about St. George deriving from *The Seven Champions* was recorded in 1937 in Co. Kerry, and a version of *Don Belianis* in Co. Mayo in the 1920s.[10]

The gradual change in the social location of romance had similar effects on both printed and manuscript texts. These include a simplification of narrative structure and stripping away of ornament. Early manuscript versions contain long and stylised descriptions of people and actions, for example, with alliterative runs of adjectives, which are omitted in versions from the eighteenth and nineteenth centuries. In print, the long and elaborate texts of the sixteenth and seventeenth centuries were severely compressed in later, smaller books, with detailed description of places and attitudes being similarly suppressed, simplifying the story while retaining the action.[11]

There are varying views about the effect of this process among historians of popular print. Whether these reflect differing manners of compression by printers or differing styles of reading by historians is not clear. Chartier considers abridgements in the *Bibliothèque Bleue* to be careless, leading sometimes to incoherence; this is attributed to the commercial necessities of a business with low profits. Simon, on the other hand, finds a certain integrity in the process:

> The compiler of the chapbook [of *Guy of Warwick*] went carefully about his or her work ... Far from being a brutal and unreflective assault on a complex narrative, there has been a real effort to identify and preserve a central core of experience in the romance.[12]

The Irish-printed corpus contains examples which could be viewed in both ways. Most versions of *The Seven Champions of Christendom* are coherent and have a tight uncluttered narrative. In some editions of *Valentine and Orson,* however, material constraints are very evident. Chapters become progressively shorter through the text, and where at the beginning they may last two or three pages, by the end they are reduced to ten or twelve lines.

The implications of such compression for styles of popular reading are of two kinds. The first relates to the possibility of the content of a text being reproduced without that text itself being physically present. A written or printed text in a mainly oral culture frequently functions as a base from which a storyteller or a singer can operate. As Murphy writes about manuscript texts, some incidents are 'summarised briefly but doubtless narrated at length in real tellings of the tale.' The second possibility is that shorter, compressed stories formed a corpus on their own, and that particular storytellers specialised in them. According to Bruford, the telling of stories derived from books in English 'was left to specialists who used a more matter-of-fact style with much dialogue and no runs [of words].'[13]

An example of such a specialist was the Co. Mayo narrator Pat Caine, from whom a version of *Don Belianis* was collected in the 1920s. According to the transcriber, a Catholic priest, 'these tales of knightly chivalry . . . have been handed down and remained to the last an exclusive family inheritance', but it is clear that the printed book is a close source. Unfortunately, we do not know whether Caine himself learnt the story directly from the book, or what edition he or his source might have used. The printed text is followed closely, with all names being preserved accurately, while, as might be expected, some details are omitted. However, it is only the first of the three parts of the printed text which is retold. The second part is given an extremely rapid summary, while the third part is omitted altogether. Such a style of compression suggests that the printed text was too long for the style of oral narration, which ideally consisted of four or five basic episodes. When that limit was reached, the rest of the text could be summarised rapidly. What is striking about this procedure is how it parallels the transformation of *Valentine and Orson* in some printed versions. Printer and oral narrator both had a pragmatic approach to the text. The storyline was followed in a linear way from the beginning, and when the limits of format or genre were reached, the remaining text was foreshortened or omitted to fit. Such compression, in other words, whether it appears sensitive or not to a twentieth-century reader, did not prevent a printed book becoming a satisfying narrative in a popular milieu.[14]

THE IDEOLOGY OF ROMANCE

As regards ideology, however, the apparent disjunction between the values of the romances and those of a peasant readership remains something of a problem. Most writers agree in stressing the unreal nature of these romances, their distance from the life of the ordinary reader. According to Spufford, for example, 'above all, [they] had no relevance to the urban classes or to the countrymen who read [them].' Mandrou notes that non-nobles are hardly ever mentioned, and indeed that characters are sometimes insulted by being accused of having non-noble origins. As far as the common reader is concerned, Mandrou quotes Michelet: 'Chivalric romance is exactly the opposite of the truth.'[15]

Among the writers who discuss this question, there are two views. The first, that of Spufford and Adams, sees the romances as being escapist wish-fulfilment: 'A stupid ineducable fellow might kill a giant . . .' So, 'the whole point of this literature is that it is useless . . . [it is] truly a pass-time . . . and it does not serve any other ends polemical or political.'[16] There is undoubtedly much to be said for regarding the romances as being essentially escapist. The picture of the ruling class they give is far removed from eighteenth- or nineteenth-century realities. It would be difficult, for example, to make any straightforward connection between the aristocratic heroes of the romances and contemporary ruling classes. The aristocracy in the romances is shown in a purely military, adventurous, travelling role, never as settled landlords.

One would have to regard as escapist, for example, the peasant reader described by John O'Donovan, the antiquary, in Co. Londonderry in 1834:

I met yesterday one of the name Maguiggan who is one of the most extraordinary men Ireland ever produced. He is capable of reasoning well and perfectly moral, sober and correct in his conduct, but from reading Don Quixote, the Seven Champions of Christendom and other books treating of knight errantry, he has undertaken to perform surprising feats, and thinks he has exceeded any knight or hero that ever appeared in this world.[17]

To regard the stories purely as escapism, however, is not entirely satisfactory. In the first place, the idea of a totally escapist literature, as Spufford has it, without 'any ends political or polemical', seems at least of limited use, and possibly untenable. Fiction must connect in some way with the life of the reader, or else it will be incomprehensible. Sympathy with its heroes must imply an understanding of their motivation, and probably a sharing of their values.[18]

The second view, held by Mandrou and in a more extreme version by Muchembled, supplies a political dimension. They see the romances as instilling a ruling-class ideology in the people. The romances, in this view, construct a mythic historical past from which social conflict is missing, and in which the most laudable virtue is loyalty to the established order. Consequently, the relative quiescence of rural France in the eighteenth century, as opposed to the seventeenth, is partly explained by the increasing lower-class readership of the *Bibliothèque Bleue*, and the absorption of the 'false consciousness' contained there. Muchembled describes 'optimistic stories that corresponded poorly to the sufferings of the French peasantry at the end of the seventeenth century, but that perhaps helped the reader to forget his troubles for a moment.' Therefore, 'like drugs, they tranquilised a popular world that was alienated, crushed by taxes and tempted by revolt'.[19]

Romance certainly had a role in what Muchembled calls 'the acculturation of the rural world'; a non-elite readership may well have used the texts as models for socialisation. A newly literate, and possibly newly prosperous, farmer, might use them to discover or explain the values of the upper classes to whose manners he might aspire. There are suggestive connections, for example, at the production end between the romance and the manuals of behaviour. John Shirley, a writer of the 1680s, who produced a chapbook version of *Don Belianis*, as well as writing versions of the romances *Guy of Warwick* and *Palmerin of England*, also wrote manuals of behaviour such as *The Triumph of Wit or Ingenuity Display'd in its Perfection; being the newest and most useful academy . . . with instructions for dancing*. Of course, given the economic position of a 'hack' writer, this may have been strict necessity; nevertheless, the concentration by one author on the two genres is suggestive. Moreover, romance survived within the elite as children's literature. *Valentine and Orson*, for example, was printed in New York in 1810 with the subtitle, 'A tale for youth', and was followed by similar editions in Boston in 1811, 1813 and 1814. Of course, this survival partly reflects the fact that oral literature such as romance or fairy tales became children's literature within modern literate societies, since it was among children that oral recitation survived. By the same token, however, their use as children's literature suggests that they formed part of the socialisation process there also.[20]

Nevertheless, to view the romance literature as acculturating to a coercive degree also seems somewhat simplistic. There is, in the first place, no evidence that printing of romance was sponsored or supported in any way by authority, elites or aristocracy; nor is there any reason to think that printers thought of them in this way. When popular literature was produced with socio-political aims in mind, as in the case of the tract societies, that intention is stated very clearly. Moreover, if chivalric romance acted as a pacifying, socially cohesive force, then the strong elite disapproval of it which had emerged by the late eighteenth century becomes problematic. Of course, since the texts had become principally located in a popular milieu, we might expect a certain aesthetic distaste, since they were no longer a cultural 'luxury', and did not conform to the canons of contemporary elite literature. We find, though, that the disapproval is ideological as well. Robert Bell, describing reading in schools in Ireland in 1804, maintained that romance 'describes the manners of barbarous and superstitious ages . . . it is not calculated to inspire youth with correct notions of government.'[21]

In the second place, if the values contained in the romances were so radically different to the real interests of the peasantry, then an acceptance of these values through the influence of popular literature imputes an enormous power to this literature. The readers or listeners are easily indoctrinated in this presentation, moving rapidly from acceptance of the authority of the printed word to acceptance of social hierarchy. The argument contains even a suspicion of circularity, since the audience is passive in its acceptance of a literature which is held to have produced that passivity in the first place. It seems more likely that at least some of the values were present among the populace before their adoption of the romances, and that this can partly account for their extraordinary popularity.

In any case, although the romance literature is underpinned by a particular set of values and a particular cosmology, it should not be assumed that these necessarily produce passivity. What emerges from a more sustained consideration of the texts is that the values and hierarchies they express were capable of being creatively reworked. The printed romances, that is to say, might set out the moral ground rules and the vocabulary for describing heroism, real or ideal. These are then available for use in other circumstances.

This becomes clear from a consideration of the romance literature in the context of the ritual and vocabulary of popular politics. Within these, an ideology which emphasises the importance of rank and deference, and which glorifies those at the top of the social scale, while frequently or even usually directed towards stability and continuity, is also capable of being used as a vehicle for criticism. This ideology constructs an idealised version of social relations, ideal types of kings and lords, against which reality can be measured and often found wanting. Popular political ideas, therefore, were mythic and folkloristic and these 'guiding myths' were the underlying world-view of early modern popular political action.

In the case of the seventeenth-century rebellions against taxation in southern France studied by Bercé, the first step in protest was to formulate a petition for relief which is sent to a king who, as in the romances, was distant, wise and just. If the petition was unsuccessful, it was inferred that the king was being deceived by evil advisers who kept the truth from him, precisely the situation dealt with in *The Seven Wise Masters*, whose subtitle refers to 'the treachery of evil counsellors [being] discovered and innocence cleared'. It was consequently justifiable to attack those counsellors, often local agents of the royal or state power. Ultimately, though rarely in popular rebellion, if it became clear that the king was less than wise and just, his legitimacy would be called into question.[22] The legend of the just king, therefore, could be used to legitimate power and also to subvert it, but it did not in itself do either. The same can be said of the rest of the ideology of the romance. It is not simply that nobility is thought to bring with it virtue and bravery, but that the absence of these qualities can also cast doubt on the nobility of a person or group.

Within the wider corpus of printed popular literature, the vocabulary of the romance also had the possibility of other subversive applications. The most immediate use was as a model for the construction of the forms of criminal biography, which partly derive from the romance by the intermediary of the picaresque and rogue literature. We have already seen a case of the borrowing of motifs from *Valentine and Orson* in one of the lives in *Irish Highwaymen*. The connection is made explicit in another of the lives in the same collection, that of William Peters. His early life and education are described as follows:

> In his youth he was put to school . . . he had read the Seven Wise Masters, Don Belianis of Greece, Valentine and Orson and Reynard the Fox, and was accounted on the mountains a complete scholar. The reading of Reynard gave him a taste for politics, but it was very much to his disadvantage that he was not continued at school, at least till he had passed through the history of the Seven Champions, and the Destruction of Troy; he might have understood feats of knight-errantry, and have advanced himself to the dignity of a highwayman; but by studying such mean authors as before mentioned, [never] attempted any thing more than petty thefts . . .

This was not necessarily a realistic description, although it could well have been, as is clear from the examination of the use of chapbooks in schools. What is important is that the connection between the genres was clear to the author, and presumably also to his readers.

This study will follow the author of *Irish Highwaymen* in treating romance and criminal biography as essentially complementary, as mirror images of each other. In the Irish context, the most potent idea they share is the traditional aristocratic emphasis on the importance of blood and descent in producing the bravery, fighting qualities and sense of justice of a true hero, an idea discussed in Chapter 10.

5 Criminal Biography: *Irish Highwaymen* and *James Freney*

Criminal biography, the lives and actions of robbers and highwaymen, was, like the romances of chivalry, a frequent, if not universal, feature of popular literature in western Europe. While some romances, such as *Valentine and Orson*, were printed in many countries, the literature of crime tended to be more national. At the same time, however, there were striking similarities between texts from different countries, in chronology, structure and content, suggesting common or mutual influence. The typical criminal figure was active in the seventeenth or early eighteenth century, and the printed lives followed shortly after, many remaining in print until the nineteenth century. Both England and France had a corpus of texts based on an urban gangleader active about 1720 in the capital city, Cartouche in Paris and Jonathan Wild in London. Ireland and France both witnessed the success of texts featuring comparatively late figures, James Freney whose life was published in 1754, and Mandrin, the first of whose lives dates from 1755. Collections of criminal lives were issued in early eighteenth-century England, inspiring a collection of Irish lives, *The Lives and Adventures of the Most Notorious Irish Highwaymen*, a decade or so later. There are also similarities in content, such as the representation of criminals as constituting an 'underworld', an alternative society mirroring conventional society, and similar moral attitudes, such as that of the successful criminal as a gifted individual who has gone wrong due to circumstance or innate character flaws, but whose cleverness is to be admired.

Behind these texts, in all three countries, is the folkloric figure of the noble robber, the bandit-hero as Hobsbawm has described him, who is just, generous and virtuous. In some cases, a real historical figure is mythologised in successive printed lives, each moving closer to the noble robber. Examples of this are Guilleri in seventeenth-century France and Redmond O'Hanlon in seventeenth- and eighteenth-century Ireland. Other texts which were not themselves examples of the bandit hero were read by audiences who transformed their subjects into noble robbers. Such was the case with the life of James Freney.[1]

Of course, the strictures that have been made in the European historiography about romanticising the actual historical criminals as 'primitive rebels', engaged in social protest, also apply to Ireland. As Blok
and others have pointed out, the description of such figures by Hobsbawm
involves the conflation of a popular myth of the bandit with the historical reality.[2] In the case of the chapbook literature, we are looking
primarily at mythical figures or constructs, and, in the case of *Irish
Highwaymen* particularly, emphatically not at real historical events. We
need then to look at the literary conventions which underlie these
constructs.

ORIGINS OF CRIMINAL BIOGRAPHY

One strand of the genealogy of criminal biography comes from the
representation within 'official' culture of those who were outside it or
marginal to it. This literary genre originated in discussions of the poor
and beggars in the sixteenth century and was extended to other elements in the seventeenth. It represented these groups in structural terms
as 'counter-cultures' which paralleled or were inversions of conventional society. Thus beggars or robbers were shown as forming organised
hierarchies, with a leader such as the 'king of the beggars', with their
own rules, rituals and laws, and frequently featuring an alternative
language such as beggars' cant or thieves' slang. This literature was
found throughout western Europe; sixteenth-century English examples
include the *Fraternity of Vagabonds* (1561) by John Awdeley, which
divides beggars into 19 'orders', giving a slang term for each one, and
*A Caveat or Warning for Common Cursetors, vulgarly called vaga-
bonds* (1566) by Thomas Harman, which explains the tricks and cheats
used by thieves, beggars, card tricksters and the like. These books were
read partly as explanations and taxonomies of groups which were on
the margins of society, partly as practical guides to dealing with them.[3]
    This strand of the genealogy continues in the picaresque narratives
of the sixteenth and seventeenth centuries, which share the concern
with the marginal and criminal. Indeed the rapidity of the spread of
picaresque from its sixteenth-century origins in Spain throughout Europe in the early seventeenth century is partly accounted for by the
way in which it fused with the earlier vagabond literature, incorporating elements such as the glossary of slang. It differed from the vagabond literature by being a narrative and concerned with one rogue
rather than the society of rogues. In this way, picaresque shifted the

literature of criminality away from the purely taxonomic and towards the biographical, or even the autobiographical, since the hero is usually the narrator in the picaresque novel.

English translations of Spanish picaresque novels began to appear in the late sixteenth century, beginning with *Lazarillo de Tormes,* one of the earliest Spanish examples, which was published in London in 1576. By the mid-seventeenth century original English works were being published, such as *The English Gusman* (1652) by George Fidge, whose title echoes *Guzman De Alfarache,* the other earliest Spanish text. The best known example of English picaresque was *The English Rogue described in the Life of Meriton Latroon* (1665) by Richard Head. It is a straightforward description of a life of crime and debauchery ('vulgar, coarse and pornographic', according to one commentator) which also has many features derived from the vagabond literature. Chapter V contains a taxonomy of gypsies (22 sorts) and a lengthy glossary of their slang; later the author 'gives some general instructions to his countrymen, first how to know padders [robbers] on the road, by infallible signs ... directions, if robbed, how to follow the thieves ... and infallible instructions for the innkeeper, how to know thieves from his honest guests.'[4]

The source from which criminal biography most immediately derived was the scaffold literature which proliferated in the late seventeenth and early eighteenth centuries. This sprang from similar concerns to those of vagabond literature and the picaresque, and shared some of their characteristics. It was concerned mainly with condemned criminals, often being produced to accompany the execution of those criminals. Amid a vast mass of printed material, it is convenient to isolate three textual forms. These are the 'trial', the 'last speech' and the 'confession' or 'life'.

The 'trial' was a straightforward account of the court proceedings leading to condemnation. The 'last speeches' were highly stylised productions, in which the repentant criminal denounced his (or her) past life as immoral and told the crowd (or the reader) to benefit by his example. In this way, the last speech sold at executions formed part of the ritual of the public execution, or, sold elsewhere, served to bring that ritual to a wider print audience.[5] The 'confession' or 'life' was an account of the crimes of the condemned, often in his own voice. These accounts, according to Linebaugh, 'minimise the repenting tone' of the last speeches and provide instead a detailed description of the crimes themselves. Although these are not entirely fictionalised accounts, they have certain similarities to fictional criminal biography, and provided a source for the latter which needed little adaptation. The different forms were frequently combined, giving pamphlets with titles like 'The last speech and confession of . . .' or 'The trial and last speech of . . .' One publication which combined all three was the *Account* of the Ordinary (chaplain) of Newgate prison in London, a serial publication of the last speeches and lives of condemned prisoners in that institution, which was printed from the seventeenth century right through the eighteenth century.[6]

These texts combine the fascination of the picaresque with the ingenious rogue and his tricks on the one hand with the practical and taxonomic features of the vagabond literature on the other. Titles such as *The Life of Martin Bellamy . . . necessary to be perused by all persons, in order to prevent their being robbed for the future* and *A Genuine narrative of all the Street Robberies Committed . . . by James Dalton . . . To which is added A Key to the Canting Language, taken from the mouth of James Dalton*, both printed in London in 1728, are representative. Robbers' lives such as these formed the basis of large collections of criminal biography in the early eighteenth century, of which the best known were Alexander Smith's *Complete History of the Lives and Robberies of the Most Notorious Highwaymen . . .* (1713–14), and Charles Johnson's *A General History of the Lives and Adventures of the Most Famous Highwaymen* (1734).

IRISH HIGHWAYMEN

Printed production in Dublin of criminal literature was very active in the same period, and a substantial corpus of trials and last speeches of Irish criminals survives from the seventeenth and eighteenth centuries. There were also Dublin reprints of the last speeches and lives of many of the better-known London criminals of the early eighteenth century, such as Jonathan Wild and Jack Sheppard, along with a translation of a life of Mandrin which had a Dublin edition in 1755.[7] The demand for these may be illustrated by the fact that differing versions of the same criminal's supposed speech were produced by different printers. A 'last speech' of 1725 claimed that 'I had no thought of making a speech had I not heard a false and scandalous paper cry'd about, called my speech, printed by one Brangan . . .'[8] The genre became so common in Dublin that it was parodied, as for example in *The Last Speech and dying Words of J-n A-b-kle, author of the Weekly Journal* (c.1725), which is an accusation of plagiarism, i.e. robbery of verse.

*The Lives and Actions of the Most Notorious Irish Highwaymen,
Tories and Rapparees* was to Irish crime literature what the collections
of Smith and Johnston were to that of London. Although it is smaller
and shorter than either, being a single volume containing nine lives
(13 in later editions) rather than a multi-volume compilation, it was
clearly intended as their Irish equivalent. Its title echoed theirs and it
borrowed the few criminals of Irish origin which appeared in those
books: Patrick Fleming, William Maguire and Richard Balf. Indeed,
half of the figures in the first surviving edition are highwaymen who,
while born in Ireland, had most of their careers in London and were
executed there.[9] *Irish Highwaymen* first appeared some time in the 1730s
or 1740s, and covers a period from the 1650s to 1735. About its author, J. Cosgrave, nothing is known.

In terms of its conception and representation of crime, what is immediately striking about *Irish Highwaymen* is the absence of explicit
condemnation. The preface makes the conventional claim that the book
has 'no other design than to discourage young men from falling into
such company as may lead them into a shameful way of living', but
there is little evidence of such an intention in the lives themselves.
This can be demonstrated by setting the lives within the typology constructed by Faller in his recent study of English criminal biography, a
typology based on the lives contained in Smith's *Complete History*.[10]

Faller distinguishes three types of criminal: the brute, the buffoon
and the hero. The brute is the most negative, being extremely violent
and inflicting the maximum suffering on his victims. He does not observe some basic social norms, and sometimes lives outside society
altogether. The classic example in Smith's collection is Sawney Beane,
who lived in a cave in sixteenth-century Scotland, robbing passers-by
and then eating them. The second type, the buffoon, is morally neutral
and is used for humourous effect, usually playing tricks on his victims. The hero, finally, is the most positive – he is 'gallant, witty,
judicious in his selection of victims, he uses the minimum force necessary... though an outlaw, he maintains a sense of social justice'.

In *Irish Highwaymen* the brute is completely absent. There is no
inhuman figure, or even any episode in which a particularly nasty pun-
ishment is inflicted on a victim. Moreover, although Smith's *Complete
History* in fact contains a 'brutish' Irish highwayman, Patrick O'Bryan,
who rapes and murders a young woman while robbing a house, he
does not appear in *Irish Highwaymen*.

On the other hand, Cosgrave does include two buffoons taken from
Smith. These are Patrick Fleming, whom Faller uses to exemplify the

prototypical buffoon, and William Maguire, alias Irish Teague, whose comic value lies in his Irish speech. The flavour of these characters may be gauged from an episode in the life of Maguire: he robbed a lady on the highway by asking her to lend him money. She replied that Maguire was not borrowing but robbing, to which Maguire answered: 'By my shoul and shalvation, Madam, I am stranger upon the country, and I want your monies, and what's lying good for; af you lend it to me I won't give it to you again, and af I rob you, I will keep it, and that's all the difference I make between robbing and borrowing.' Maguire therefore fits neatly into the comic genre of English representations of Irish (or Hiberno-English) speech. His alias, Teague, was one of the stock names for the comic Irishman – the classic text which established the genre, a joke book published in the late seventeenth century, was known as *Teague-Land Jests.*[11]

The absence of brutes is particularly striking when we bear in mind the extent to which *Irish Highwaymen* derives from English models, during a period in which the brute and the buffoon were precisely the two most powerful representations of the Irish. The representation was in transition 'from barbarian to burlesque', from brute to buffoon in Faller's terminology, in the late seventeenth and early eighteenth centuries, but both images were present throughout the eighteenth century.[12] The image of the Irish as brutish or barbarian was not only general in England, particularly after the rebellion of 1641, but was sometimes used explicitly in English criminal biography. One of the lives of Jonathan Wild published in London just after his execution traced his genealogy to 'his great-grandfather's father, whose name was Patrick MacJudas Wild, and lived in a cave on the mountains of Newry in Ireland ... [Patrick and his family were] in nature savage beasts, not only void of religion, government etc., but also of Christianity universally ... they lived by robbing the travellers as they passed on foot over the mountains of Newry.'[13]

Cosgrave, therefore, in constructing an Irish counterpart to English collections of criminal biography, accepted the Irish buffoon figures while rejecting those of the Irish brute. By far the dominant figure, however, is the hero, presented in a favourable light. Paul Liddy was 'a very handsome well-set young man, about six feet high and every way proportionable, and in strength outvied most of his age in the kingdom.' John MacPherson 'was always a leading man at hurlings, patrons and matches of football, and acquired such fame by his wondrous activity that no single person dared oppose him at any exercise. He was accounted in his time the strongest man in the kingdom.' Other accomplishments are listed. James Butler 'spoke Latin pretty fluently', MacPherson '[while being] carried to the gallows . . . played a fine tune of his own composing on the bagpipe, which retains the name of MacPherson's tune to this day', and William Peters 'composed several songs and put tunes to them, and by his skill in music had gained the favour of some of the leading men's sons in the country, who endeavoured to get him reprieved'.

Most importantly of all, these criminals were 'gentlemen', either of good birth or capable of correct behaviour. Redmond O'Hanlon was 'the son of a reputable Irish gentleman.' Captain Power, 'a genteel robber . . . was the younger son of a worthy gentleman.' Paul Liddy 'was the son of very reputable parents who had him educated after a genteel manner by the best masters in the country.' They therefore have an exalted code of behaviour. Liddy, when engaged in highway robbery, 'always behaved agreeably to his education, more like a gentleman than any of his comrades', MacPherson 'was very cautious of striking unless in his own defence', and Peters was 'very diverting in company, and could behave before gentlemen very agreeably'.

If, as Lusebrink argues, the popular literature of crime can represent 'a fundamental questioning of justice by a significant proportion of the population', then the good breeding of the criminals, in a society in which deference was still very strong, was certainly a major factor in legitimising a challenge to authority and property. Moreover, they were not simply gentlemen but also leaders, and they frequently controlled entire alternative power structures. In the French eighteenth-century popular literature, Mandrin commanded a 'captain', 'lieutenants' and 'soldiers', issuing laws and levying taxes. Similarly, in *Irish Highwaymen*, O'Hanlon is described as 'Protector of the Rights and Properties of the Benefactors, and Captain-General of the Irish Robbers'; he issued his own laws, levied tolls on pedlars 'who acknowledged his jurisdiction', and even sent one individual, who had been robbing in his name, to the gaoler of Armagh, with instructions to try him at the next assizes.[14]

This theme is found throughout *Irish Highwaymen*. Fleming greeted his highway victims with 'I am the chief lord of the county and collector of the road, and you shall pay tribute to Patrick Fleming.' Paul Liddy was the 'captain' of three bands, with 'subalterns' and a 'brigade of twelve of the most resolute fellows among them, whom he was to command in person'. Charles Dempsey, as well as having a network of cattle stealers throughout the country under his command, set up his own training system:

He had likewise never less than four apprentices at a time, who were always bound for the term of seven years, and paid a pretty round sum for learning his art and mystery, in which he had such a great skill, that boys were sent to him all the way from the county of Kerry to be bound.

Here, the taxonomic aspect of the vagabond and picaresque tradition is being used, not to explain marginal people to conventional society, but implicitly to question that society and the forms of power within it. The hierarchies among highwaymen are similar to, even mirror images of, conventional power structures and particularly those of the state, but they are clearly in opposition to those structures and to the extension of their control – soldiers and tax collectors are favourite targets. The legitimacy of this opposition is derived ultimately from the social position of the bandit himself and his command of an alternative structure. It is a reaction of traditional hierarchies to new ones, and typical of a pre-modern political outlook.

In Ireland, where the personnel of the landed classes had changed enormously during the seventeenth century, the break between the old and the new was very marked. The landed class of 1600 had been mostly dispossessed by 1700, and either emigrated, became tenants on or near their old estates or became outlaws. These outlaws, called tories and later rapparees, flourished particularly in the disturbed aftermath of the Cromwellian and Williamite settlements. The post-dispossession context of Cosgrave's text is evident from its title, with its reference to 'tories and rapparees', and is underlined by the fact that the first and longest life in the book is that of Redmond O'Hanlon, a dispossessed aristocrat and in many ways the prototypical tory. An examination of the way in which O'Hanlon's life was adapted for the chapbook text reveals much about the political outlook of the collection as a whole.

It is fairly clear that the historical O'Hanlon was far from being a bandit-hero leading a loyal band for the protection of the poor. He made peasants pay him tribute money, for instance, and offered to turn his colleagues over to the law in return for a few years protection. By the mid-eighteenth century, however, the myth had already been firmly established. In Cosgrave's text, O'Hanlon fulfils many of the criteria set out by Hobsbawm for the bandit-hero, robbing the rich to give to the poor, being a master of disguise, and, being invulnerable, dying through treason.[15]

The gradual mythification of O'Hanlon can be seen in the way in which Cosgrave's account is adapted from previous ones. The earliest surviving text about O'Hanlon is a pamphlet from 1681, the year of his death, and is a factual piece of news reporting, describing, in seven pages, his betrayal by his foster-brother, his capture and death.[16] The following year, a longer, 23-page, text appeared, *The Life and Death of the Incomparable and Indefatigable TORY Redmond O'Hanlyn, commonly called Count Hanlyn*.[17] This began the fictionalising process by treating O'Hanlon as a conventional picaresque hero, giving him for example a remarkable birth, predicted to his mother by a fortune teller: he was born with a 'T' on his chest, which was interpreted by neighbours as a cross without a head, signifying that O'Hanlon would be a martyr. In fact, the author tells us, it stood for thief or tory. Moreover, O'Hanlon was born 'in the year 1640, the year preceding the last Irish rebellion as if fate had sent him a harbinger to the confusion and mischief following, or as if the birth of so great a man ought to be attended by no less than a universal conflagration.'

The picaresque intention is made explicit early in the narrative, when the author declares that 'the Spanish Guzmond, the French Duval and the English Rogue were but puisnes in the profession' compared to O'Hanlon. In this text, O'Hanlon begins his career early, by robbing his schoolfriends, his teacher, and then his parents. The second half of the narrative consists of a series of classic rogue stories in which O'Hanlon outwits soldiers, goes about in disguise and has narrow escapes. He is summed up as 'naturally bold but not cruel, shedding no blood out of wantonness . . . had his inclinations been virtuous, as his parts were quick, he might have proved a good subject to his king and serviceable to his country.' O'Hanlon was therefore already free from condemnation in a text which appeared one year after his death. Half a century later, using the 1682 text as its principal source, *Irish Highwaymen* completed the process of constructing a bandit-hero by altering the story in two ways.[18]

Firstly, the narrative was dehistoricised to a large extent. No birthdate is given, and there is consequently no mention of the 1641 rebellion; and an episode was altered in which, after the Restoration in 1660, O'Hanlon lived respectably for a few years, becoming a collector of poll money and hearth tax, not an occupation to make a man popular. In Cosgrave's version, 'Redmond was presented with the King's protection for three years', without mentioning a date or the king's name. Secondly, the features of the picaresque unsuitable to the bandit-hero were dropped. There is no birthmark, and a note in some editions explicitly denies that there was one: this is 'a story and a fiction'. In particular, O'Hanlon's youthful wickedness was omitted, and he became an outlaw in adult life by 'happening to be at the killing of a gentleman in a quarrel.'[19] Before this, there is an important new beginning:

> Redmond O'Hanlon was the son of a reputable Irish gentleman, who had a considerable estate . . . . The nation being reduced by the English forces, several Irish families who had a hand in the wars of Ireland were dispossessed, and their lands forfeited; by which means a very great alteration was made in this family, and several of the O'Hanlons were obliged to travel, in hopes of retrieving their fortunes . . . poor Redmond [was] in this unhappy condition . . .

Here we move away from the notion that the individual personality is the source of crime, and towards an explanation which locates it in social conditions, and specifically in dispossession. None of the other figures in *Irish Highwaymen* is explicitly described as a tory or as dispossessed aristocracy. The emphasis on gentle birth in most of the lives, however, implies this background, and some of the figures have typically tory names. One of the lives is of Captain Power and the principal tory of Munster was Colonel Power, and Charles Dempsey's father is described by Cosgrave as 'a man of note among the rapparees of King James' time'.[20]

The ideological context of these texts, therefore, and the principle which legitimises a challenge to authority, is nobility of blood and the rightful ownership of land. This is a specifically Irish phenomenon, related to the unusual position of the native aristocracy. It is missing, for example, from a London edition of O'Hanlon's life in 1819, where, although favourably presented in a text largely derived from *Irish Highwaymen*, he is described as 'of rather mean extraction'.[21]

THE LIFE OF JAMES FRENEY

The motif of dispossessed aristocracy also underlies the other principal criminal biography in the Irish chapbook literature. This was *The Life and Adventures of James Freney, told by himself* which first appeared in 1754, a description of the career of a highwayman and housebreaker and his gang in Co. Kilkenny from about 1744 to 1749. It gives fairly full details of house robberies, the hijacking and holding to ransom of merchandise in transit, a series of highway robberies, the various chases and captures in which the gang were involved, as well as some accounts of the court procedures after their captures.

The Freneys, or De la Freynes, had been a leading Anglo-Norman family in Kilkenny until the mid-seventeenth century, when they forfeited their land after the war of the 1640s. It is not clear whether James Freney himself was one of this family, but the name certainly had 'tory' associations. The same may well have been true of Freney's accomplices also. His principal ally in the gang was James Bolger, and a James Bolger was one of the forfeiting Jacobite landowners in Kilkenny whose estates were sold at the beginning of the eighteenth century.[22]

It appears from the text of *Freney* that this gang, headed by landless gentry, operated with a certain amount of protection from local elites. When two gang members were captured and tried, for example, they were discharged by a jury after the intervention of 'a man of power and interest' to whom Freney himself had supplied stolen silver. The magistrate 'left the court in a rage', because people were 'protecting and saving the rogues they had under their eyes'. This protection was due to the fact that Kilkenny was one of the areas in Ireland in which social structure had changed least in the sixteenth and seventeenth centuries, and in which many features of late-medieval society survived. It was consequently a region in which the historical phenomenon of banditry (as opposed to the literary genre) was likely to be persistent, and in which state law was opposed effectively by local interests.[23]

This ambivalent relationship between criminal, society and authority accounts for one of the more unusual features of *Freney* as criminal biography. At first sight, its genre appears to be that of the 'last confession', in which the criminal before his death enumerates his crimes baldly, and without overt repentance or moralising. However, *Freney* is not the confession of a man about to die. Although condemned to death at Wexford assizes in 1749, he was pardoned in return for testifying against others and for having previously turned most of his gang over to the law. A large part of the narrative is made up of his evidence against them, consisting of detailed description of house robberies and other crimes. The full names of the accomplices are specified, and their share of the booty is minutely explained, with items such as silver spoons and tankards being enumerated and valued.

As Linebaugh points out, one of the functions of the 'last confessions' was to make discoveries, that is, to indict other criminals.

At a time when the administration of justice depended for its effectiveness on either private prosecutions or the betrayals of those caught in its nets . . . whenever possible the Ordinary sought to transform those confessions into judicial discoveries. It was a nasty possibility, but one that seems hardly ever to have been successful, a dying person having nothing to gain from it.

If the discoverer was turning King's evidence, however, as Freney did, there was everything to gain. The publication of discoveries was not as widespread as that of last confessions, but other examples did exist, such as an English chapbook published the year before Freney's, *The Discoveries of Poulter, alias John Baxter . . . admitted King's evidence and discovered a most numerous gang of villains . . .* Freney himself appears to have benefited enormously from discovery and publication, receiving a royal pardon, the local protection of Lord Carrick, to whom he had given himself up, and ultimately, apparently, a position as a customs officer.[24]

As a result, *The Life and Adventures of James Freney* appears an unlikely candidate for popularity in cheap format. Most notably, it does not conform to the ideal of the bandit-hero and his followers. If the bandit-hero dies, it should be through a single act of betrayal. Instead, Freney testifies against most of his accomplices who are then hanged. Before that, rather than being 'admired, helped and supported' by his followers, Freney is repeatedly betrayed by them to the authorities. If the bandit-hero survives, he should return to being a respected member of the community; in the text, Freney is represented as having to leave the country because of his unpopularity after the trials. Despite this, it became one of the standard chapbooks of the late eighteenth- and early nineteenth centuries, and Freney himself entered folk tradition as a bandit-hero.

This transition was facilitated by some features of the text. In the first place, it is episodic, and it is possible to extract (or emphasise) those sections or stories which best fit the folk image of the bandit hero. There are in fact two types of crime described in the book, burglary and highway robbery. The burglary is done in groups, and is discussed in minute detail. This is because it was for burglary that the gang was tried, and the descriptions were part of the evidence. On the other hand, interspersed between the burglaries is a series of possibly fictional highway robberies. These often feature Freney on his own, without his gang, behaving with chivalrous decorum and indulging in good-humoured badinage with his victims. Thus, he stops an officer's wife who was travelling on her own, but:

finding no money, ... I was about taking my leave of the lady, but she begged me to give her as much money as would defray her expenses to Duncannon. I told her I would, and at the same time drew out [her] purse, in which I found only two guineas and a half with some silver ... I returned her the money, saying I had a particular liking to a carbine which her servant had, but as her husband was not with her, I would not deprive her of it, for I was always very civil to the ladies.

The second feature of the text which may explain its popularity is a total absence of repentance, and indeed of any 'moral' reflections whatsoever. In this respect it is instructive to contrast the success of *Freney* with the lack of success of another highwayman's life published in Dublin and London two years before *Freney* and also a first person narrative. This was *The Life of Nicholas Mooney, alias Jackson, born at Regar, near Rathfarnham in the County of Dublin.* Mooney has some ingredients at least of a prospective popular hero, including daring robberies, travels and even fighting as a Jacobite soldier in Scotland in 1745. Mooney later became a Methodist, however, and wrote his life at least partly as a religious exercise. The text consequently has an extremely moralising tone, and almost every action calls for a comment such as 'How easily does a rash head, an ambitious desire and a corrupt conscience, spurred on by ill counsel, make a rebel!' The judicial context of Freney, on the other hand, avoids the need for any such moralising, and makes the transition to bandit-hero much easier. Mooney's text was reprinted once in England in 1776 by Methodists, but does not seem ever to have been reprinted in Ireland.

RECEPTION

Unlike the romances of chivalry, which moved from large expensive formats to smaller cheaper ones, and consequently from an elite to a more popular audience, both *Irish Highwaymen* and *Freney* were initially published in a small format. At the same time, a similar change in readership can be inferred from both contemporary commentary and some changes in the presentation of the texts themselves.

The first edition of *Freney* was published by subscription, the list of purchasers including the provost of Trinity College Dublin and a number of the newer landlords in Kilkenny. The publication of the book, therefore, like the trial of Freney's gang, was very likely an episode in conflict over law and order between local gentry groups in Co. Kilkenny. By the early nineteenth century, however, it was being condemned unanimously by elite commentators, and seems to have had an exclusively popular audience. A similar transition can be seen in the case of the *Irish Highwaymen*, by the fact that later editions omit the buffoon figures, such as William Maguire, who featured in the first editions. The comic value of Maguire derives from the fact that his speech and logic are those of an oral culture, appealing to a reader who values literate thought and expression as a form of social and intellectual distinction. A popular readership located in a culture which was still intensely oral, and which may even have listened to *Irish Highwaymen* being read aloud, might not have appreciated such an external and deprecating view of verbal dexterity.[25]

By the late eighteenth century, these texts were located well down the social scale. Immediately after the rebellion of 1798, Whitley Stokes pointed to the reading of 'histories of robbers and pirates' by 'the lower class' as part of the background of the uprising. The use of these books in schools is confirmed by some surviving documentation as well as the recollections of some of those who were educated in hedge schools. Both books are recorded as having been in use in a small school in West Kerry in the 1790s, *Irish Highwaymen* being read by a 14-year-old pupil, and *Freney* being read by a 16 year old. Henry Cooke, the nineteenth-century moderator of the Presbyterian church, who had been educated in hedge schools in Tyrone in the late eighteenth century, remembered the use of *Freney* in school: 'another extravagant tale I recollect having read, the history of a Captain Freney, a robber'. There is also the well known description of a more general readership by the folklorist Crofton Croker in the 1820s:

> A history of rogues and rapparees is at present one of the most popular books among the Irish peasantry, and has circulated to an extent that seems almost incredible; nor is it unusual to hear the adventures and escapes of highwaymen recited by the lower orders with the greatest minuteness and dwelt on with the greatest fondness.[26]

One consequence of the omission of buffoons in later editions of *Irish Highwaymen* is that the collection then became one exclusively of bandit-heroes. This tendency towards a heroic or at least sympathetic presentation of the criminal is a feature of the publication and the reception of both of these texts. In the case of *Irish Highwaymen*, it is visible in the selection of characters and in the way the principal life, that of O'Hanlon, was adapted from previous works. In the case of

Freney, it is more evident in the later folklore and balladry which accumulated around the text. These selected the episodes of highway robbery, with their wit and gallantry, rather than the more businesslike descriptions of housebreaking. A nineteenth-century broadside ballad took as its subject *Freney*'s description of robbing a tailor:

> He drew out of his pocket some gold and silver, amongst which was a thimble. I asked him what he was; he said a tailor. I then asked him what the deuce sent him my way, charging him not to discover that ever I attempted robbing him; at the same time gave him his money and thimble, saying I would rob nobody but a man.

Tailors were often figures of fun in folklore, and the ballad underlines this:

> 'Your dirty trifle I disdain'
> With that I returned him his gold again.
> 'I'll rob no tailor if I can –
> I'd rather ten times rob a man'
> And it's oh, bold Captain Freney . . .[27]

The success of *Freney* can be gauged from the speed with which Freney himself became a mythical figure, independent of the text, to whom stories of robberies and other escapades were attached. A mid- or late-eighteenth-century verse exists, attributed to the east Co. Cork poet Piaras Mac Gearailt (1702–95), in which he pokes fun at another poet for having been robbed of his shoes by Freney, 'an t-am do bhain Fréinigh a bhróga de ar bhóthar Bhaile Atha Cliath' [when Freney robbed him of his shoes on the road to Dublin]. The verse uses the name 'Fréinigh' as a rhyme and does not explain precisely who he was; 'Freney' was therefore well enough known to be used as a synonym for highwayman. In Co. Tyrone in 1790, a group of burglars entered a doctor's house; two of them were disguised, but the third was not, and he said he was called 'bold Captain Freney'. In the 1830s, a traveller in Co. Limerick was told that Cratloe woods 'were sometime the haunt of the celebrated Freney, the robber, where he successfully eluded all attempts at arrest'. The *Dublin Penny Journal* in 1834, as part of a series about robbers, had a story in which Freney was given hospitality in a house in south Co. Dublin 'in 1772 or 3', and that, while robbing many houses in the area later that year, he left that house alone. A number of tales heard by a priest in an Irish-speaking area in north Co. Cork in the 1870s places Freney in the mountains of that area 'some time ago', and includes the verse by Mac Gearailt. In these stories (only one of which is even vaguely connected with the original text) we have a classic bandit-hero:

> The people supported him. He would share with the poor most of the money he took from the rich.

Freney had therefore become the archetypal highwayman and bandit-hero by the nineteenth century in many parts of the country, almost certainly through the circulation of the chapbook.[28]

In both *Irish Highwaymen* and *Captain Freney*, we can observe the gradual assimilation of the figure of an actual robber or criminal to that of the bandit-hero. In the case of the former, this process is already visible in the printed text itself and in the way in which it re-interprets its sources, to such an extent that the preface makes a point of disavowing the favourable image of the criminal. The preface was not included in later editions, and it is no surprise that the book came to be regarded as potentially subversive. Freney, on the other hand, is an example of a figure from print becoming established within folk-lore, independently of the printed text. Narratives from within the wider oral culture subsequently attach themselves to all of these figures, particularly those of O'Hanlon and Freney, who ultimately attain a mythic status.

6 Time, Ritual and History: *The Battle of Aughrim*

Many of the texts of printed popular literature contain a strong historical dimension and present a variety of different conceptions of time. Mandrou emphasises the historical aspect of chivalric romance, which he calls 'historical legend', describing a mythical past, an origin legend of the early modern French state and of its ruling classes. Bollème and Capp have discussed the presentation of time in the annual almanacs which were among the most widely circulated printed items. These structured short-term time around the agricultural and commercial year, listing the dates of fairs and suggesting times for various farming activities such as sowing. In the longer term, they also embodied a version of history by giving anniversaries of historical events, usually events in the formation of the national states of France or England.[1]

Calendars and almanacs in early modern Europe therefore gradually defined the year less in terms of saints' days and more in terms of days on which historical events occurred. This process happened soonest in Protestant, particularly Calvinist, countries which no longer accepted many of the saints of the medieval church. It was a general phenomenon, however, and by the early seventeenth century, French calendars typically gave the dates of events, from the early middle ages onwards, which were important in the formation of the French state.[2]

The case of England has been documented in two recent studies of church festivals by Cressy and Hutton. Both show the adaptations of calendar ritual moving towards a specifically English sense of time. Two events in particular stand out, the defeat of the Armada in 1588 and the discovery of a conspiracy to blow up the Houses of Parliament in 1605. The latter was commemorated on 5 November, usually by a sermon, followed by the ringing of bells and the lighting of bonfires. Both events stress the deliverance of a Protestant people by supernatural means: favourable weather conditions in 1588 and fortuitous discovery in 1605. These contributed to a Protestant sense of time and of identity, the identity being that of a community under threat from Catholic enemies both external and internal. This calendar was reflected in printed almanacs throughout the eighteenth century.[3]

The English (or British) sense of history emphasised the role of

Catholics as an external threat, particularly in the shape of French or Spanish invasion. In Ireland, by contrast, Catholics were the majority, and conceptions of the historic calendar were more contested as a result. There were throughout the eighteenth and nineteenth centuries two diametrically opposed views of Irish history and of what were seen as the defining events of recent history and the foundation of state and society, the wars of the 1640s and 1690s. These wars resulted in large-scale change in land ownership, as a predominantly Catholic landed elite was to a great extent replaced by a newer Anglican one, and the creation of a state which was overwhelmingly Anglican, in which access to power was forbidden to Catholics or non-Anglican Protestants.

The state calendar in eighteenth- and nineteenth-century Ireland was similar to that of Britain in that it stressed deliverance from Catholic enemies. Its high points came during two well-defined periods. The first was at the end of October and beginning of November, between 23 October, which commemorated the massacre of Protestants which took place at the beginning of the rebellion of 1641, and 4 November, the birthday of William III. The former, 23 October, was the more important, and the massacres were a centrepiece of Protestant historiography, representing a general Catholic conspiracy for the extirpation of Protestants, similar in many ways to the Gunpowder Plot and the Armada in England. The commemoration was established by statute in 1662, and followed a pattern similar to that in England, with sermons, bell-ringing and bonfires. The ceremonies varied from place to place and from year to year, being particularly marked at times of threat of French invasion.[4]

There was a lesser peak in early July, with the anniversaries of the two principal battles of the war of 1689–91, both Protestant victories. The battle of the Boyne had taken place on 1 July 1690, and the battle of Aughrim on 12 July 1691. Both dates were marked by parades and processions during the eighteenth century, and Boyne societies were formed in larger towns. On a smaller scale, the anniversary of the siege of Londonderry during the same war was the occasion of marches and celebrations in the town itself.[5] It is this latter period of the year which is fundamental to the Protestant calendar in the north of Ireland today. Its most striking manifestation within the popular printed literature of the eighteenth and nineteenth centuries is in the form of a folk play *The Battle of Aughrim*, first printed in 1728, and which had well over twenty editions between 1750 and 1850. The performance of this play constituted a re-enactment, and consequently a commemoration, of the battle.

To set *The Battle of Aughrim* in context, we can examine another historical play, *The Siege of Londonderry*, which was often printed with *Aughrim*, as well as two of the most frequently printed popular historical texts dealing with the seventeenth century. These are *The Impartial History of Ireland* by Hugh Reily (or O'Reily), which gives a Catholic view, and the *History of Ireland* by R.B. (Robert Burton, the pseudonym of Nathaniel Crouch), which gives a Protestant version of events.

REILY'S *IMPARTIAL HISTORY*

Reily's *Impartial History* was originally published in 1695 as *Ireland's case briefly stated*. Hugh Reily came from Co. Cavan, where the Reilys had been the principal landholders until the seventeenth century. He was a lawyer, and had been Clerk of the Council in Dublin under James II and accompanied James to France after the war of 1689–91. The text therefore presents a Catholic elite view of the sixteenth and seventeenth centuries, beginning with the accession of Elizabeth I and ending in the 1680s.

Reily's book is important in that, as Kelly points out, it was the 'sole major statement of the Catholic view to appear in print between 1691 and the middle of the eighteenth century', and as such it had regular editions throughout the eighteenth century.[6] Other documents illustrating Catholic grievances were added in these later editions, including the text of the Treaty of Limerick which ended the Williamite war, the last speech of Oliver Plunkett, an Archbishop of Armagh who was executed in 1681, and *The Case of the Roman Catholics of Ireland* (1724) by Cornelius Nary, Catholic parish priest of St Michan's in Dublin.[7]

Reily therefore remained a basic political document for Catholics of all classes, adding material as circumstances changed. It was still being added to in the nineteenth century, and an edition of 1837 includes a biography of Daniel O'Connell. All of these editions, even the first, were small and cheap, and the text needed no adaptation for the chapbook market. By the early nineteenth century it was an exclusively popular text, classified with the mass of chapbook material.

The tone and outlook of Reily's history have been accurately characterised by Hill as 'long-suffering Catholic'.[8] The Catholics of Ireland, particularly the landowners, are shown as fundamentally loyal, attempting to defend themselves against an aggressive campaign of conquest. The text presents itself as an answer to the propaganda campaign in support of that conquest, a campaign which vilified Catholics in order to seize their land. As the preface puts it, 'In all cases, [the conquerors'] chief text was, Throw dirt enough, and some of it will stick.'

The classic justifications of loyal rebellion are used by Reily; the revolts of the 1590s and 1640s are presented as defensive, reacting to religious persecution. Reily is careful not to criticise the monarchy in any way. Charles II, for example, 'was so far from intending to deprive the Catholics of Ireland of their birthright, that he was fully resolved to do them all the justice imaginable; and would have certainly done it, but that he was perfidiously circumvented by those he confided in.'

This argument is purely legal and political, and religious affiliation as an independent cause of conflict is avoided. Protestants are accused of bad faith in stressing religious divisions: 'Religion was made a stalking horse to violence and rapine, and gospel liberty turned into all manner of licentiousness.' Similarly, aggressive Counter-Reformation Catholicism is ignored, and the assertive papal nuncio of the 1640s, Rinuccini, is only mentioned once, and in a negative light, when he excommunicates those who were in favour of peace with Charles I in 1646.

Reily's position, therefore, is Jacobite, loyal and legalistic, stressing the injustices done to the Catholic elite and the need to redress them. The inclusion in later editions of the Remonstrance of 1660, the text of the treaty of Limerick and Nary's *Case* is fully in keeping with the intention of Reily's text, and the whole is representative of Catholic upper- and middle-class attitudes to the state during the eighteenth century and continuous with the views of Catholic campaigns up to and including O'Connell's Catholic Association of the 1820s. (The inclusion of the O'Connell biography in the 1837 edition follows logically in the sequence of accretion of texts.)

Within popular or cheap print, Reily's work was the principal statement of history from a Catholic point of view. In its diffusion into the countryside, it was penetrating a world which already had its own different version of history, written in Irish and deriving from the historical works of the professional learned class employed by the Gaelic aristocracy until the seventeenth century. Compared to this other version, what is initially striking about Reily's work is its smaller time frame. It begins with the accession of Elizabeth and ends with the restoration of Charles II. Irish historiography during the eighteenth century, according to Hill, concentrated on three main themes and periods: firstly, the character of pre-Christian and pre-Norman civilisation in Ireland;

second, the nature of the early Irish church; and finally, the seventeenth century wars and land confiscations.[9] The first two are ethnic and religious issues, the third political. Reily addresses the third issue, and does not discuss the first two at all.

Reily therefore contrasts very much with Gaelic histories. The most prominent of these was *Foras Feasa ar Éirinn* [A Basis of Knowledge about Ireland], a synthesis of medieval Gaelic manuscript histories written in the 1620s by Geoffrey Keating, which stops before the Norman conquest of the twelfth century. Keating's concern was to provide a cultural critique of conquest by emphasising the antiquity of Gaelic civilisation and its equality with, or even superiority to, the culture of the Anglo-Normans and English. This was the basic historical text in Gaelic culture between the seventeenth and nineteenth centuries; it circulated widely in manuscript, an English translation was printed in 1722, and it would certainly have been known to many of the readers of Reily's work.

Both the time frame and the elite point of view of Reily also contrast with what we know of Gaelic popular culture. As representative of the latter, we may take *Seanchas na Sceiche* [The Tale of the Bush] by Antoine Raiftearaí (Raftery), a blind itinerant poet who was active in Connaught in the early nineteenth century. In this poem of some 400 lines, the history of Ireland is presented as being narrated by an old bush under which the poet had unsuccessfully sought shelter. Most of the bush's narrative (over 200 lines from the 300 which constitute the historical section) concerns pre-Norman Ireland, with Keating's *Foras Feasa* explicitly acknowledged as the source. When it comes to the sixteenth and seventeenth centuries, Raiftearaí's concerns are more with religion and ethnicity than with landed property. Only two lines discuss land, describing the Cromwellian confiscations, whereas 14 are devoted to explicit condemnation of the Lutheran Reformation. Reily's Jacobite loyalism also contrasts with Raiftearaí's anti-Stuart position: James II is described by the latter as 'Séamas an chaca, milleán géar air' [James of the shit, bitter blame to him].[10]

In looking exclusively at the sixteenth and seventeenth centuries, Reily is therefore concerned with the (relatively) short-term injustice of confiscation of land, and stresses the fundamental loyalty of the dispossessed Catholic landowners to the crown, as well as the legality of their claims. His text does not share the cultural, ethnic and religious views found in Keating or Raiftearaí. Reily's voice is that of the old Catholic anglophone landed elite, one which is echoed in the documents which are appended to later editions. Nary's *Case*, for example, criticising the law which forbade Catholics to carry arms, emphasises the injury to the Catholic upper classes consequent on their loss of status:

> Many gentlemen who formerly made a considerable figure in the kingdom are nowadays, when they walk with canes or sticks only in their hands, insulted by men armed with swords and pistols, who of late rose from the very dregs of the people. Servi dominati sunt nobis!

There is therefore a clear contrast between Reily on the one hand, and Keating and Raiftearaí on the other, between a view of Irish history in politico-religious terms and one in ethnic-religious terms, between a view which circulated in print and in English, and one which circulated orally or in manuscript and in Irish. Language shift and the spread of popular literacy therefore implied a certain change in historical views.

This is a clear example of the influence of a print trade centred in Dublin on a rural readership, since Dublin Catholic printers would be more in sympathy with the loyalist, civil rights views of Reily than with Gaelic ideas of ethnicity; moreover, their position within the Dublin print trade precluded an aggressive Catholicism, in the early eighteenth century at any rate. The inclusion of Nary's *Case* in the cheap editions illustrates this. Nary was a Dublin priest, and his text mentions the issue of quarterage, the legal bar on Catholics becoming full members of guilds, a grievance far more relevant to urban printers than to a rural reader. Moreover, Protestant printers saw the successive printings of Reily's book as a statement within Dublin politics and therefore expressive of Catholic complaints within the city. Finally, it is striking that no cheap abridgement of the 1722 translation of Keating's history seems to have been produced, despite the fact that it would have appealed to a rural Catholic or Gaelic audience. The Co. Cork scribe, Mícheál Ó Longáin senior, for example, in a compilation of genealogical material transcribed in 1774 quotes the large printed edition of Keating as an authoritative source.[11]

Reily's history in fact made the transition into the Gaelic manuscript tradition, but in a way which underlines the gap between their differing versions of history . A translation was made from the chapbook version in Co. Cork in 1772 by Uilliam Ó Murchú, a scribe and poet. The twentieth-century editor of the text found the translation literal and unidiomatic, however, and it does not appear to have been copied into other surviving manuscripts, despite the flourishing Gaelic scribal activity in Co. Cork in the late eighteenth and early nineteenth centuries.

Whether this lack of enthusiasm was due to the difference between Gaelic and anglicised Catholic versions of history, or whether Reily's history was felt to be redundant within a culture which was already well stocked with politico-historical literature, is not clear; either way, the lack of impact of the translation indicates that the gap between the two views remained.

CROUCH'S *HISTORY OF IRELAND*

Reily's *History* and Crouch's are almost mirror images of each other. Nathaniel Crouch (*c.*1632–*c.*1725) was one of the most prolific chapbook writers in seventeenth-century England, and was best known for his epitomes of longer histories. He published under the pseudonyms Robert and Richard Burton; the phrase 'Burton book' came to signify a chapbook, in England as well as in Ireland. His abridgement, like Reily's *History*, was originally issued in a small format and needed no further adaptation for chapbook publication. The parallel between the two texts was certainly clear to the printers of the 1746 edition whose preface declares that they are publishing Crouch because:

> there has been lately printed in Dublin, by some anonymous popish printer, a small book, intitled, The Impartial History of Ireland, under the name of Hugh Riley, esq., containing a heap of the most insolent and false reflections upon the Protestant authors of the history of Ireland.

The subtitle of Crouch's *History* is 'an abridgement of Dean Story's late wars in Ireland'. Story had been a chaplain in the Williamite army and published his *Impartial History of the Affairs of Ireland* in 1691. He was therefore a Williamite counterpart of Reily's during the wars, and the use of the term 'impartial' for later editions of Reily's book echoes Story's title.

There is a difference between the time frame of Story's work and Crouch's abridgement, however. Although Story is exclusively concerned with the years 1688–91, which he narrates in great detail, Crouch abridges this radically. Indeed there is little similarity between the two texts overall. Story's is a day-by-day account of the military campaigns of 1688–91, whereas Crouch begins with pre-history, devotes much space to the 1640s, and only reaches 1688 over two-thirds of the way through. Indeed, even for the period 1688–91, Story is not Crouch's only source.

There is far more direct quotation from Crouch's (unacknowledged) source for the 1640s, Sir John Temple, whose *History of the Late Rebellion* (1646) was the fundamental Protestant account of the period. Crouch quotes Temple as early as his introduction, and later presents long citations from Temple describing the massacres of Protestants by Catholics at the outbreak of the rebellion of 1641. The nature of the massacres was one of the principal bones of contention between Protestant and Catholic historians of the seventeenth and eighteenth centuries.[12]

For the period before the seventeenth century, about a fifth of the text, Crouch's source is not identifiable with precision, but the account fits into a fairly conventional English historiography of Ireland, stemming from Giraldus Cambrensis, the twelfth-century chronicler of the Norman conquest of Ireland. Cambrensis is the ultimate source for the series of descriptions of natural wonders with which Crouch begins his text.

In terms of attitude, Crouch presents a Protestant view, opposed to Reily's on most points but based on the same fundamental principles. Where Reily sees Protestantism as merely a means of conquest, Crouch presents the Catholic clergy as the principal fomentors of rebellion:

> [The Irish] have left no treacheries, murders or villainies unattempted, being encouraged thereto by their ignorant and superstitious priests, to whose dictates the stupid people entirely submit.

Politically, the two writers inhabit the same seventeenth-century world. Where, for example, Reily blames 'evil counsellors' for the failure of Charles II to do more for Catholics, to Crouch James II's favouring of Catholics had the same source, since '[James] gave himself wholly up to the conduct and counsels of the furious Jesuits.'

LONDONDERRY AND *AUGHRIM*

There was, as we have seen, a range of official ritual which commemorated the events of the seventeenth century from a Protestant point of view. Performance of the two folk plays would constitute an unofficial re-enactment of two of the military victories of that history. Of the two plays, *The Siege of Londonderry* would in theory have been the more faithful re-embodiment of the past. It is a very straightforward historical account, quoting troop numbers, defences and other matters in great detail, with authentic letters and proclamations reproduced verbatim in the text. *The Battle of Aughrim* on the other hand is much less factual, and one edition, printed in Dublin in 1777, felt it necessary to accompany it with 'a historical account of the battle'.

The atmosphere of *Londonderry* owes much to the circumstances of its author. An English-born professional soldier, John Michelburne was the Governor of Londonderry during the later stages of the siege, and had some difficulty with the traditional civic authorities, whom he felt to be less than fully committed to the defence of the city. Later in the war, when he was governor of Ballyshannon, he was accused of improper conduct during the siege of Sligo. He published a pamphlet in 1692 to answer his accusers, *An Account of the Transactions in the North of Ireland Anno Domini 1691 . . . with a particular relation to the taking of the town of Sligo by storm, by the Hon. Colonel John Michelburne, Governor of Londonderry*. He settled in Londonderry after the war, where he felt that his contribution to the successful defence had been insufficiently recognised and rewarded by the city authorities.

In the play, the difficulties of the Governor's position are outlined and shown to be successfully resolved. The last speech of the play, spoken by a Jacobite Lieutenant-General, maintains that the Jacobite army would eventually have conquered England had it not been for the defence of Londonderry:

> Eternal honour to you, Governor of Derry, your great conduct ought to be recorded forever.

Early commemoration of the siege of Londonderry, in the years around 1720, was organised principally by Michelburne and did not involve the city authorities. The play probably formed part of these celebrations, contributing to what McGovern calls 'the essentially plebeian nature of the siege myth'. It was therefore a folk play from the beginning, representing popular rather than official attitudes to the siege.[13]

The Battle of Aughrim contrasts in many ways with *The Siege of Londonderry*. Where *Londonderry* represents a localised commemoration, *Aughrim* was far more widely read and performed. Little is known about its author, Robert Ashton, although he may be the same as 'R. Ashton, one of the Brethren' who published a poem 'in honour of the Loyal Society of Journeyman Shoe-makers' in Dublin in 1725, which was written in the same poetic metre as *Aughrim*. A prologue to the first edition of the play mentions that the author was 'scarce tender twenty' at the time, and consequently, unlike Michelburne, was probably not a participant in the war. The text of *Aughrim* is quite different to that of *Londonderry*. Whereas Michelburne writes in prose, going into technical details, *Aughrim* is in rhyming couplets throughout; and while Michelburne concentrates on political and military aspects, Ashton's play presents a more conventionally heroic view of both sides, emphasising bravery and fighting qualities. A Williamite colonel rallies his troops with these words:

> Oh stand and bravely perish e'er you fly,
> For at the worst, brave souls, we can but die.
> Then bravely stand your ground, and scorn to flinch,
> But if they conquer, sell them every inch.

The play also includes a love interest. Captain Charles Godfrey, a Williamite soldier, is in love with Jemima, the daughter of a Jacobite colonel. As a result, he changes sides and fights with the Jacobites. During the battle, his father's ghost appears to him and accuses him of desertion. Godfrey changes sides again and is killed, being found by Jemima just as he is dying.

There are a number of indications that *Aughrim* was from the start a play performed exclusively by amateurs, and soon became a folk play. The rhyming couplets in which it is written had gone out of fashion in stage drama some decades before, there is no record of it having been performed professionally in Dublin before 1745, it does not occur in a recently compiled database of theatrical performances in Dublin up to 1796, and no professional performances are recorded outside of Dublin before 1800. This absence may have been part of a wider trend: the main historian of eighteenth-century Irish theatre has remarked that 'The companies in the country towns only sporadically tried to appeal to their audiences with works of Irish content.'[14]

The accounts of performances of *Aughrim* that did take place stress their informal or at least non-professional nature. According to a periodical of 1804:

> Perhaps a more popular production never appeared in Ireland; it is in the hands of every peasant who can read English; and like the songs and poems of the bards in Scotland, is committed to memory, and occasionally recited.

William Carleton in his autobiography recalled frequent performances in barns in Co. Tyrone in the early nineteenth century.[15]

The popularity of *Aughrim* as a folk play can partly be attributed to its oral nature. It was spoken from memory, or read aloud, rather than read silently. The printed text, like a ballad sheet, was therefore, in Shields' phrase, an 'aid to performance' rather than a self-contained text.[16] Its participants included both the literate and the illiterate, and Carleton recalled training people who could not read to take part:

It is astonishing what force and impetus such an enthusiastic desire
to learn and recollect bestows upon the memory.

The constant rhyming couplets would have facilitated such memorisation.
The play also includes references to classical mythology in a manner
which would have blended with eighteenth- and nineteenth-century folk
poetry in both English and Irish. The ghost describes the wandering of
his soul as follows:

> Sometimes I hover o'er the Euxine Sea,
> From pole to sphere, until the Judgement Day,
> Over the Thracian Bosphorus do I float
> And pass the Stygian lake in Charon's boat,
> O'er Vulcan's fiery court and sulph'rous cave
> And ride like Neptune on a briny wave.

Listing classical references in this way is characteristic of both the
poetry of the lower class 'rhyming weavers' in early nineteenth-century
Ulster and of eighteenth-century Munster *Aisling* (vision) poetry in the
Irish language. Overall, therefore, Ashton's play had many of the characteristics of the oral culture of eighteenth-century Ireland, particularly anglophone Ireland, and was able to make the transition into that
culture easily.[17]

Of course, orality is not the only reason for *Aughrim*'s success. It
had a specific political and ideological role in eighteenth-century Ireland, conveyed by Carleton, who noted that it was initially performed
by a Protestant peasantry. Later, when Catholics wished to take part,
they took the roles of the Jacobite soldiers. In one sense, this type of
performance would have been an unusually faithful re-enactment of
some of the foundation myths of eighteenth-century Ireland: Protestant
victory and, to a lesser extent, Catholic glorious failure.[18] Although
there is no explicit record, it seems very likely that *The Battle of Aughrim*
would have been performed on the battle's anniversary. There are certainly some pointers in that direction. On 12 July 1780, a mock battle
between two Volunteer brigades was held near Birr, Co. Offaly, and
the event was described as 'the anniversary of Aughrim'. That Ashton's
text may have been used is suggested by the fact that it was considered appropriate for performance by another Volunteer corps in
Newtownards, Co. Down in April 1782.[19] A mock battle eventually
became one of the features of popular Orange ritual in the north of
Ireland, and one has been performed since 1835 in Scarva, Co. Down,
every 12 July. It seems likely that this derives in some way from *The*

Battle of Aughrim. According to Adams, 'the existence in the eight-eenth century of a popular and much acted unsophisticated play be-tween Williamite and Jacobite forces would almost certainly be the genesis of the sham fights of the Orangemen.'

There is one crucial difference, however. The sham battle enacted at Scarva is the battle of the Boyne rather than of Aughrim. Popular Prot-estant celebrations since the early nineteenth century have in fact con-centrated overwhelmingly on the Boyne, although Aughrim was militarily the more decisive of the two battles, at least in the context of the war in Ireland. There was a sudden shift of emphasis at the end of the eighteenth century, and of an unusual kind. What happened was not a change from one date of commemoration to another date, but from one event to another on the same date. Throughout the eighteenth cen-tury, 12 July referred to Aughrim, whereas since the nineteenth cen-tury it has referred exclusively to the Boyne. This shift coincided with a period of realignment both in Protestant–Catholic relations and in relations within Irish Protestantism.

All of the major anniversaries, those in October and November as well as those in July, were the site of contesting politics in the late eighteenth and early nineteenth centuries. The precise issues and events are not clear, as the study of popular Protestant culture before the twentieth century, particularly in areas outside Ulster, has been rela-tively neglected. Even writing on Ulster Protestantism tends, under-standably, to concentrate on seeking the origins of the present situation and of current Orange ritual rather than exploring a wider cultural context. What emerges from Hill's study of state celebrations, however, is that in the course of the eighteenth century 'respectable' Protestants, along with church and state, withdrew from the July military commemora-tions and identified more with the October and November events. Simi-larly, McGovern shows that, in the early eighteenth century at least, participation in the August commemoration of the siege in the town of Derry itself was plebeian, and was critical of the civic elite.[20]

In the early 1790s, after the repeal of most of the remaining penal laws against Catholics, as well as the growth of sectarian tensions in Armagh and elsewhere, the subject of Protestant identity re-emerged sharply. As Hill points out, a resurgence of 23 October celebrations might have been expected, but this did not occur. Both it and 4 November went into decline; 23 October sermons were no longer printed, and the principal text describing the massacres, William Temple's *History of the Late Rebellion*, was not reprinted in the first half of the nineteenth century. The July commemorations, and particularly the Boyne, were now the centre of attention. There are therefore two shifts to be explained, one from November to July and the second within July, from Aughrim to the Boyne.

Hill offers two reasons for the first shift. First, the 1641 massacres had been the subject of extended controversy after the mid-eighteenth century, and Catholic historiography had succeeded in tempering the worst aspects of the image of 23 October, making it therefore less of a providential deliverance. Secondly, the specific conjuncture of high politics in the early 1790s was that of conflicts of authority between the Protestant Irish parliament and the British government and crown which had been the main force behind the repeal of the penal laws. A renewed emphasis on the revolution of 1688–91 was a way of underlining the primacy of parliament and people over monarchy.

These reasons would apply principally to readers of elite historiography and those involved in representative government. At a popular level, Hill suggests that neither 23 October nor 4 November offered a 'direct opportunity for vicarious triumph over popish king and rebels' as the July anniversaries did. To this we can certainly add the popularity of *The Battle of Aughrim* both as a printed text and as a ritual play. In the play, popular Protestantism had evolved a more attractive and more participatory ritual than the sermons of 23 October, some of which could last up to four hours.

The shift from October to July corresponds mainly to changes within elite culture. Reasons for an increased emphasis on the Boyne rather than Aughrim, on the other hand, are probably located within the culture of popular commemoration, and particularly related to the rise of the Orange order as a conservative popular Protestant organisation after 1795. There are a number of possible reasons for this latter change. Firstly, there was a coincidence of dates due to the change from the Julian to the Gregorian calendar, which happened in 1752. This brought Britain and Ireland into line with the rest of western Europe, which until then had been 11 days ahead. According to the old style, the battle of the Boyne took place on 1 July, according to the new style it was on the 12th; the battle of Aughrim took place on 12 July old style, 23 July new style. By the law of 1752, the dates for commercial transactions, fairs and other events, were to be moved forward 11 days; the ecclesiastical and political calendars were to remain the same. After 1752, therefore, the Boyne continued to be celebrated on 1 July, Aughrim on the 12th.

The change in the meaning of the 12th, from old style to new style, from Aughrim to Boyne, can be dated with precision in Ulster. In the

Belfast Newsletter in 1796, the 12th referred to the anniversary of Aughrim; the following year, it referred to the Boyne, 'conformable to the old stile'. Usage elsewhere followed later: in the *Dublin Journal*, for example, the change occurred between 1799 and 1800.[21]

The timing of this change corresponds to the emergence of the Orange Order, which was founded in Armagh in 1795 during the intensification of organised sectarian violence, and spread through the rest of Ulster and Ireland in subsequent years. It became the principal institutional expression of popular Protestant conservatism, and the main promoter of the 12 July commemoration of the Boyne. It may be that resistance to the Gregorian calendar, which was papal in origin, might have appealed to an determinedly Protestant organisation. It appears, however, that it was a regional rather than a religious phenomenon. The Rev. John Graham, an Anglican minister who was familiar with both Ulster and Munster, noted the dates of celebrations among the 'native Irish', almost certainly Catholic:

> It is worth observing, that so tenacious are the native Irish in Ulster of their ancient customs that it is on the 1st of May 'Old style', namely the 11th day of that month, they put up their May bushes and strew flowers around them.[22]

The explanation is more likely to lie in the logic of calendar ritual, whereby the efficacy of commemoration of specific events is linked to a conception of time which is cyclical, to a belief that a certain date in the calendar offers a privileged access to the events of the past which happened on that day. This is particularly the case with 'incorporative' commemoration, the re-enactment of past events in the present, such as mock battles and military parades. Altering the calendar would diminish that access and break the link with the past.[23]

At the time of the calendar change of 1752, there was unease about the unchanged dates of religious festivals. In the following year, for example, some areas of England began to celebrate Christmas on 5 January, a practice that continued until the early nineteenth century.[24] Celebrating Christmas on 25 December after 1752 could be justified, however, on the grounds that the calendar change restored the feast to that point in the year at which it would have taken place in the first century. Keeping the same dates for the Boyne and Aughrim could not be justified in the same way, since the half century which had elapsed between them and 1752 would not have caused major distortion.

Changing the dates in the 1790s therefore re-established the power of an incorporative ritual at a time of heightened political and religious conflict. That the re-enactment of these battles retained an occult force can be seen in the reactions to the rebellion of 1798, such as that of the *Dublin Journal*:

> Marquis Cornwallis came to this country at a very awful period, when British subjects were as much menaced as at the day when the illustrious William on the banks of the Boyne smote the superstitious legions of James . . . The battles of Aughrim and Ballinamuck [in 1798, against an invading French force] had similar striking features . . .

Such a pattern of repeated Catholic attack was also fundamental to British Protestant identity in the same period.[25]

Simple calendar adjustment, however, would imply a continuation of Aughrim commemoration on 23 July. That did not happen, and 12 July remained the most important date for Orangemen from 1800 on. This second shift, from Aughrim to the Boyne, was probably due to the relative symbolic weight of the two battles. For the Orange Order, the presence of William of Orange at the Boyne and his absence from Aughrim may have been decisive. This is not an entirely satisfactory explanation, however, since it would make the Order's relative neglect of 4 November, William's birthday, problematic.

The changeover may also have been influenced by the character of Ashton's play as a principal vehicle of Aughrim commemoration, and the political differences between the attitudes of the play and those of popular Protestantism after the 1790s. The latter included a definition and defence of hierarchy and political power in religious terms rather than in terms of orders or classes. This ideology, discussed in Chapter 10, included a view of the seventeenth-century conflict in providential rather than aristocratic military terms. The wars of the 1640s and 1690s in this view had been an appeal to divine judgement and a victory over 'Popish tyranny and superstition', a religious event more than a political one. This perception extended to the ritual calendar as a whole, as Dublin Corporation maintained in 1839:

> Protestants will continue fondly to cherish the Glorious Pious and Immortal memory of the great and good King William – the triumphs of Aughrim and the Boyne – the defeat of Popish treachery and gunpowder treason – and all those memorable interpositions of a gracious Providence.[26]

The religious dimension is not absent from Ashton's text. In the very first scene, the French general St Ruth envisages Jacobite victory and refoundation of Catholicism:

> James shall return and with great pomp restore
> Our Romish worship to the land once more
> And drown these heretics in crimson gore.

This is echoed by the Irish commander, Sarsfield:

> Then shall our monks and Jesuits all return
> And holy incense on our altars burn.

Overwhelmingly, though, the issue is presented as being resolved through military skill and bravery rather than divine intervention. Both sides compliment each others' fighting qualities. Sarsfield tells St Ruth:

> You know not yet what Britons dare attempt
> I know the English fortitude is such
> To boast of nothing, though they hazard much.

The Williamite general Talmash goes so far as to compliment Sarsfield on his previous attack on an ammunition convoy:

> If you are Sarsfield, as you bravely show
> You're that brave hero whom I long to know
> And wished to thank you on the reeking plain
> For that great feat of blowing up our train.

Emphasising the martial qualities of the Jacobites suits Ashton's purpose, since it consequently magnifies the military achievement and bravery of the Williamite forces, and he exaggerates the size of the Jacobite army for the same purpose. The issue is summed up by the Williamite commander, Ginkel:

> This day Hibernia's fortune shall be tried,
> Whilst war and blood-shed shall the cause decide.
> Then shall my English handful surely free
> This famous Isle from Romish tyranny.

Such an aristocratic-martial presentation leads to a portrait of the Jacobites which is favourable in many respects, and which may have been less suitable to Protestant ritual in the atmosphere of heightened sectarian tension of the early nineteenth century. Even structurally, the action of the first two acts is entirely within the Jacobite camp, and the Williamites do not appear as a group until Act III. What Thackeray was later to call the 'even-handedness' of the play must have increasingly appeared to Orangemen as sympathy for Catholics. One writer in 1804 even attributed a Catholic background to Ashton:

> Ashton's father, like Hamilcar, has sworn his young Hannibal at the altar, *not* to be a *mortal foe* to Rome, but a *devoted fanatic* to its interests, through, and in, every mode of blood, bigotry and superstition.[27]

The love story in the play may well also have been deemed unsuitable for what became a male-dominated ritual vocabulary.

The battle of Aughrim, therefore, did not become a central event in popular Orangeism in the same way that the Boyne did, and is a very muted presence in its ritual and literature. A *Standard Orange Song Book* of 1848, for example, contains songs on 12 July (meaning the Boyne), 4 and 5 November, but nothing on Aughrim. There are other shifts within the printing of Protestant historical works over the same period. Crouch's *History* was not reprinted in the nineteenth century, and neither was its elite counterpart, Temple's *History*.

Changes in ritual and in attitude were not as sudden or as sweeping as this account might suggest. Even among Ulster Protestants, the change of date was not uniformly accepted. The Anglican rector of Maghera, Co. Derry, in about 1812 described an Orange march 'on the 12th of July, the anniversary of the Battle of Aughrim'.[28] Newspapers and almanacs adjust at different points in the early nineteenth century. Equally, the market for reprints of Ashton's *Battle of Aughrim* was buoyant in the early nineteenth century, and it remained a staple text in the cheap book market.

As regards attitudes, the absence of reprints of Temple and Crouch did not mean that the massacres of 1641 were no longer a potent symbol, or that their repetition was no longer a Protestant preoccupation. The episode of the 'Blessed Turf' in June 1832 demonstrates this vividly. The Catholic peasantry in Ireland reacted to the cholera epidemic of that year by distributing lighted sods of turf said to have been lit originally by the Virgin Mary in Co. Cork, and which were believed to have the power to ward off the disease. The sods were carried rapidly throughout the country on foot over the next five days. Protestants were deeply frightened by the event, suspecting that 'it was the signal for a general rising of the Catholics to murder them'. The proof, according to Mortimer O'Sullivan, an Anglican minister in Co. Tyrone, was that 'the massacre of 1641 is said to have been preceded by fiery signals'.[29]

By the 1840s, both Reily's *Impartial History* and *The Battle of Aughrim* had been in print, more or less continuously, for over a century, and were fundamental works in religio-political perceptions of Irish history since the sixteenth century. However, while some aspects of their world-view had become generalised, in other respects they had been superseded.

In the case of Reily, the elite sense of grievance about expropriation of land which it expresses had become characteristic of a broader section of rural Catholics by the early nineteenth century, a process outlined in Chapter 10. At the same time, however, the social and political outlook of those same Catholics was much more sectarian than that of Reily. Whether this was the result of rising inter-denominational tensions, or whether popular attitudes had always been more aggressively religious is uncertain. The history of *The Battle of Aughrim* describes an almost symmetrical pattern. Having contributed to the institutionalising of the memory of the military campaigns of the 1690s at the levels of both ideology and ritual, its outlook in turn was left behind by the increasingly sectarian sentiment embodied in Orangeism.

This process can also be traced at the level of overall printed production. In the eighteenth century, these texts dominated the Irish historical material within popular print. The early nineteenth century, however, saw the production of enormous amounts of other material which both reflected the greater denominational strife and helped create it. The activities and printed production of Protestant missionary societies from about 1810 onwards, coupled with the Catholic response, focused attention on more religious issues; while the publicity machine of Daniel O'Connell's Catholic Association consolidated the sectarianisation of political ideas. In these circumstances, even though the *Impartial History* and *The Battle of Aughrim* remained in print, they were less dominant and less representative.

7 The Catholic Reformation, Irish-Language Printing and Song: the *Pious Miscellany*

Nowhere is the potential disjunction between popular printed literature and popular or local cultures greater than in the area of religion. Most of the printed devotional or pious literature intended for mass consumption was produced by institutional churches, and reflected the ideals and attitudes of those churches rather than the everyday belief and practice on the part of adherents of those churches. It was frequently produced in forms which facilitated comprehension and use by as wide a public as possible. A case in point is the catechism, probably the most widely possessed religious text in both Protestant and Catholic countries, whose content summarised the minimum of doctrine necessary for an individual believer, whose form, question and answer, was appropriate to a culture which was still largely oral, and whose distribution aimed at standardising belief over as wide an area as possible. Catechisms printed in Ireland, even those of Irish origin, consequently differed little from those printed elsewhere.

Some of the other principal genres of devotional literature, such as printed sermons and hymns, have Irish examples which can be compared with similar productions from other areas. This chapter will consider a collection of Catholic hymns, or spiritual canticles, in the Irish language, which was the most frequently printed book in that language before the twentieth century, and which offers a case study of a regional religious culture and of printing in local languages. This is the *Pious Miscellany* of Tadhg Gaelach Ó Súilleabháin (Timothy O'Sullivan, c.1715–95) which had 18 or more editions between 1800 and 1850 in south and south-eastern Ireland. Written by a layperson, it was originally printed with the support of the institutional church, but it remained in print due to a popular demand of striking intensity. It offered a version of belief and practice that was orthodox in most ways, but which was not entirely representative of the direction of the official Catholic church. To see why this was so, we need to look at the somewhat unusual position of the Catholic church in eighteenth- and nineteenth-century Ireland.

The period between 1750 and 1850 saw a long campaign by the Catholic church in Ireland to ensure that post-Tridentine standards of religious practice were adhered to among the laity. As in the rest of Catholic Europe, these standards included universal attendance at a minimum of religious services (particularly at Christmas and Easter), basic knowledge of church doctrine as contained in catechisms, and the discouragement of popular, 'unofficial' religious practices which were felt to be 'superstitious' or 'disorderly'. This process has been written about extensively in recent years, initially by Larkin and Miller, and most fully by Connolly.[1]

Ireland differed from most of Catholic Europe, however, by the lateness with which these reforms were undertaken on a large scale. There were a number of reasons for this. First, there was Ireland's peripheral location, which made clerical discipline and general reorganisation difficult, as these were directed from Rome. Secondly, there were the wars of the 1640s and 1689–91, in both of which Catholic forces were on the losing side, together with the penal legislation which followed these, under which the Catholic church had a quasi-clandestine existence (at least in the early eighteenth century). There were also financial problems. Not being part of a state church, Irish clergy were supported by their parishioners, whose means were frequently insufficient to sponsor extensive church building, missionary drives and other prerequisites of full orthodoxy of practice. Finally, there was the problem of language, since the official church recruited principally from English-speaking groups and functioned almost entirely in English, while attempting to reach a largely Irish-speaking lower class. Contemporaries remarked on the extent to which English-speaking priests ministered to Irish-speaking congregations.[2]

The first and third of these reasons explain why the new forms of religious practice made their initial impact, from the mid-eighteenth-century onwards, in the south-east and along the east coast. These were the areas which had the closest contact with Catholic Europe, as well as being the regions containing the wealthiest and most confident Catholic population, in the form of large farmers and urban merchants. From the early nineteenth century, the reforms began to be implemented in the rest of the country, and were finally consolidated in the aftermath of the Great Famine of the late 1840s.[3] One of the principal aims of the church in this process was the encouragement of a knowledge (or a better knowledge) of church doctrine, and this doctrine was frequently conveyed in the form of cheap print. It is no surprise to find that the middle of the eighteenth century marks the beginning of large-scale production of catechisms within Ireland, and consequently the gradual conformity of Catholic belief in Ireland to European models.[4]

The other frequently printed Catholic texts of the period also tended to 'europeanise' Irish Catholicism. Among them were *Sixteen Irish Sermons in an easy and familiar stile*, written in Irish by James Gallagher, bishop of Raphoe, first printed in Dublin in 1736, and the works of Richard Challoner, particularly *Think Well On't* and *The Garden of the Soul*, first printed in London in 1728 and 1740 respectively. (Gallagher's book cannot be described as popular in format, being large and intended for the use of priests. However, the introduction to an English translation published in 1835 suggests that it was bought by 'the poor', and in the 1830s individual sermons from that translation could be bought for threepence. In any case, it can be taken to be representative of contemporary preaching).[5]

These books are adaptations of principal elements of French Catholic Reformation thought, Gallagher's being principally derived from seventeenth-century French sermon collections, and Challoner's adapted from François de Sales. Both are suited to a 'popular' style of reading, being capable, for example, of being read episodically. Gallagher in his preface suggests 'giv[ing] them each Sunday a part of the loaf, by preaching a point, or even a paragraph, for there are some [sermons] which by their length can afford to be divided'. Challoner's devotional works, according to one commentator, are intended to be read in small sections: 'If [they] resist extended reading, it is precisely because they are written on a method which has a particular object – daily devotion – in view.'[6]

CANTICLES

The sermon, the meditative work and the catechism were three of the principal forms in which religious doctrine was conveyed to large audiences in both Protestant and Catholic regions. Other forms, such as images or songs, are less well documented in Ireland. It is to the second of these, and specifically to the genre of the canticle, or devotional song, that Ó Súilleabháin's *Pious Miscellany* belongs. Canticles had been a form of devotion and instruction since the early church, but their use increased enormously from the early sixteenth century in Protestant and Catholic churches alike. Reformed churches, both Lutheran and Calvinist, produced large amounts of religious music, emphasising in particular the principal biblical lyric, the psalm.[7] The Catholic church consequently tended to avoid psalms, concentrating instead on newly written texts.

Historians of the canticle in France have tended to see two principal periods of production, corresponding to the periods of most intense reform activity. The first, in the mid-sixteenth century, was controversial and polemical in tone, with the competing churches attempting to supplant each other's productions as part of a wider conversionist strategy. The second period, the mid-seventeenth century, when confessional boundaries had stabilised, saw the production of mainly Catholic canticles as part of the 'Catholic Reformation', the missions to establish more orthodox belief and practice within Catholic France. Here the intention was to supplant profane songs of which the church disapproved, often by writing devotional words to the melodies of those songs, 'drive out those songs which could lead to impurity' as the introduction to a 1738 collection put it. (Like the canticle itself, this was an older tradition, and the practice of writing 'parodies', religious words to secular songs, was well established in the later middle ages.) The canticles were originally introduced in liturgical settings, during a mission for example, but were later used in domestic religious practice, sung from cheap printed editions.[8]

The *Pious Miscellany* conforms to most of the characteristics of the second period. The poems are devotional but non-liturgical and were usually sung, with four of the songs specifying the secular melodies used. The intention to provide an Irish equivalent to European models is explicit in the preface to post-1820 editions:

As Hymns and Spiritual Canticles are recommended by St. Paul, as a mode of devotion highly acceptable to God – to introduce thus this pious Miscellany into the hands of the rising generation cannot (with the blessing of God) fail of contributing much to the reformation of the wicked and corrupt morals of the present time . . . During the long nights of winter, a hymn or song out of this little book may be sung in every Roman Catholic family. – It would be better to do so, than suffer the vile compositions that have been daily sung through the public streets, to be introduced therein.

There were in fact precedents for such a production in Ireland. In 1684 Luke Wadding, Catholic bishop of Ferns in Co. Wexford, had printed a collection of religious songs in English set to folk melodies, under the title *A Pious Garland*, and as far back as the early fourteenth-century, Bishop Ledrede of Ossory had been writing sacred texts (in Latin) to secular melodies.[9]

What distinguishes the *Pious Miscellany*, however, is that it was not written in Latin or English, the principal languages of the official church, but in Irish, the local vernacular. Printed canticles of this type were produced in all of the Celtic languages in the early modern period. At least 36 editions of the Psalms were printed in Welsh before 1800, for example. A Scottish Gaelic translation was produced in 1659, and their texts and metre came to form the basis of a unique tradition of congregational singing.[10] Closer in character to the *Pious Miscellany* are two of the most frequently printed texts in Breton and Scottish Gaelic. *Cantiquou Spirtuel*, written by the Jesuit Julien Maunoir for the missions which he conducted in Brittany in the mid-seventeenth century, was first printed in 1642 and continuously reprinted until 1821. In Scotland, *Laoidhe Spioradail* [Spiritual Lays], by Dughall Buchanan, was first printed in 1767, and had 21 editions by 1850.[11]

These three texts represent varying degrees of accommodation between vernacular cultures and centralising churches. At one end is Maunoir, who was not originally a Breton speaker but learnt the language for evangelical purposes. He distrusted the previous Breton literary tradition and in his missionary texts virtually created a new form of the language. The printing of the *Cantiquou* was overseen by Maunoir himself, who distributed it at missions. Buchanan, by contrast, came from a bilingual area in the southern Highlands, speaking and writing both Gaelic and English with apparently equal facility. He wrote a spiritual diary in English, supervised the printing of the Gaelic New Testament and worked as a schoolmaster for the anglicising Scottish Society for the Promotion of Christian Knowledge. Some of the *Laoidhe Spioradail* are in fact renderings of English hymns of the seventeenth and eighteenth centuries. They were probably written with evangelical intent, Buchanan himself, like Maunoir, being responsible for their publication.[12]

Laoidhe Spioradail offers some striking parallels to the *Pious Miscellany*. They were the most frequently reprinted texts in their respective languages (leaving aside catechisms) before the twentieth century. They were written by contemporaries, Buchanan having been born at the same time as Ó Súilleabháin, though dying some 25 years earlier. They both presented their lives in somewhat evangelical terms, with a mis-spent youth followed by a conversion, Ó Súilleabháin in his poetry, Buchanan in his diary. Consequently, comparing the eight songs in Buchanan's collection with the first six in Ó Súilleabháin's, which, on the evidence of surviving manuscript versions, were written earlier, their content is very similar, allowing for denominational differences.

The emphasis is almost exclusively on repentance for sin in the face of death and the last judgement.[13]

Where the *Pious Miscellany* differs from *Laoidhe Spioradail*, and also from the *Cantiquou Spirtuel*, is that the poems or songs in it were not written specifically for printing. They were transmitted separately and in manuscript form initially, and their collection and printing did not take place until after Ó Súilleabháin's death. In this respect, it was the editors and printers of the *Pious Miscellany* who offer parallels with Maunoir and Buchanan. The writer of the preface to the *Pious Miscellany* who quoted St Paul was in fact invoking one of the classic biblical texts used to justify devotional singing, one which is also used by Buchanan in his subtitle, in which he urges the singing of 'Salmaibh, laoidhibh agus cantaicibh spioradail a' deanamh ciuil don Tighearn' [Psalms, songs and spiritual canticles to make music for the Lord]. Ó Súilleabháin was therefore composing within a vernacular literary tradition to an extent slightly greater than Buchanan, and far greater than Maunoir, while at the same time, as we shall see, incorporating newer forms of religious devotion and practice into that tradition.

THE *PIOUS MISCELLANY*

The *Pious Miscellany* consists of 25 poems or songs. Eighteen concern sin and repentance: they are litanies of sins, descriptions of the Last Judgement and pleas for forgiveness and intercession. Of the others, two advocate the recitation of the rosary, one is in praise of St Declan, patron saint of Ardmore, Co. Waterford, and one is an exhortation to chastity and virtue. As literature, they are firmly in the tradition of stressed verse (*amhrán*) typical of eighteenth-century Munster, and many of the poems are well-established in Gaelic manuscript culture from the 1760s onward.[14] The word and sound patterns are complex and resonant, using much alliteration and long decorative sequences of adjectives. Formally, therefore, the work is a product of a native and largely lay culture rather than of centralised Roman clerical culture, and was in fact the only case of successful transition into print of texts of any kind from that native culture. Moreover, the printed text remained close to the continuing manuscript tradition, and later manuscript copies of the poems probably derive from the printed text.

That the *Pious Miscellany* made that transition was probably due to some form of institutional church support. The first edition in 1802 was published by subscription, and although clergy do not by any means dominate the list of subscribers, they are a substantial presence, 38 out of over 200 names. Some features of the list of clergy, moreover, suggest institutional backing. Some priests took multiple copies, the parish priest of Dungarvan, Co. Waterford, for example, taking 12. The bishop of Ossory was also a subscriber, as were the Presentation Convent, Cork and the Ursuline Convent, Thurles. There are surprisingly few in east Co. Cork, although this would have been an area of high Irish-language literacy, as later Cork printings of the *Pious Miscellany* would suggest. This may well be connected with the fact that the area lies within the diocese of Cloyne, from which hardly any clergy subscribed, and that the initiative of printing was centred on the dioceses of Ossory and Lismore (south Tipperary, south Kilkenny and Waterford).

A clerical origin for the first edition is also suggested by the manuscript which is most likely to have been the source of the printed version. This manuscript was written in 1792, and the scribe was the Rev. Laurence Morrissey, a curate in Owning, Co. Kilkenny. Morrissey was later a subscriber to the first edition, and his manuscript bears a great deal more resemblance to the eventual printed text than do the other pre-1802 manuscripts of Ó Súilleabháin's poetry. In particular, the manuscript seems, like the printed text, to be directed at a readership whose principal literacy was in English. It contains a grammar of Irish written in English and melodic indications in English for some of the poems. The melodic suggestions, which are not in earlier manuscripts, are also reproduced in the printed text.[15]

If institutional backing explains the *Pious Miscellany*'s initial transition into print, its frequent reprinting was due to sustained popular demand. This demand was clear to the book trade, and a Cork edition of 1821 contains an advertisement soliciting further religious material in Irish:

> [The printer] wishes it to be known to all who may have rare or scarce books of devotion in the Irish or English language, that he is most desirous of printing new and correct editions ... R.C. clergymen are most earnestly solicited for translations into Irish of such approved works as *Think Well On't, Imitation of Christ, Spiritual Combat* etc.

The printer in this case was approaching the clergy, rather than vice versa. In fact, two separate translations into Irish of Challoner's *Think Well On't* had just been produced at the time of the advertisement, but they had nothing like the commercial success of the *Pious Miscellany*.

Ó SÚILLEABHÁIN

Little is known about Ó Súilleabháin himself.[16] He was born about 1715 in central Munster, and lived most of his life in east Co. Cork and Co. Waterford. He was a member of a confraternity in Dungarvan, and died in Waterford city in 1795. He was in contact with, and a participant in, newer forms of lay religious sociability, therefore, in the area in which those forms had made most impact, and it was his endorsement of those forms and their accompanying models of behaviour which made his poetry attractive to the church.[17]

In the first place, some of the poems describe relatively novel forms of devotion, such as the cult of the Sacred Heart, which was an eighteenth-century innovation.[18] In addition, there are two poems which recommend the rosary, and which were probably written for the poet's confraternity in Dungarvan. The confraternity was one of the most frequent ways in which the reform movement encouraged lay observance: in seventeenth- and eighteenth-century Brittany, Rosary confraternities were frequently established during or immediately after a parish mission, to prolong the effects of the mission.[19] They were being founded in Ireland, particularly in the south, from the 1770s onwards. Confraternities were therefore very close to the official church, and according to one writer 'it is probable that becoming a member of a confraternity was often a first step on the way to becoming a nun.' The Rosary was the principal Tridentine Marian devotion. It seems to have been introduced on a large scale to Ireland towards the end of the seventeenth century, and to have been well established in Ó Súilleabháin's area by the mid-eighteenth: the visitations of Cashel in the 1750s mention that 'the beads is duly observed by most of the people'.[20]

Secondly, Ó Súilleabháin's concerns, his ideas of sin in particular, are as much social as personal, compared for example to the Irish religious poets of the seventeenth century, whose poetry was principally meditative.[21] Ten of the 25 poems are concerned with the behaviour of the community and of Ireland as a whole. The depravity of Ireland in particular is deplored, for example in *Duan an Spioraid Naoimh* [The hymn of the Holy Spirit]:

> Is Éachtach an t-éirleach so in Éirinn le spás
> Dar gcaochadh, dar dtraochadh 's dar dtréin chur chun báis
> Ar n-éitheach, ar ngéarghoin, ar gcraos nimh ag fás
> Do léas linn, do léirigh mar mhéirlachaibh ráis.

[There has been terrible destruction in Ireland for some time, blinding us, tiring and killing us; our lies, our deep wounds and our poisonous gluttony are increasing, showing us to be abandoned wretches.]

In *Duan Chríost* [The hymn of Christ], a topographical description of Ireland serves to list the locations of sin; *Duan an Spioraid Naoimh* contrasts the virtue of the rest of the world with the vice of Ireland; and *Slán le hÉirinn* [Farewell to Ireland] envisages all of Ireland being excommunicated because of its vice, probably referring to one of the many sanctions imposed during the reforming campaign. Although the descriptions of sin are frequently generalised and vague, specific sins mentioned are adultery, swearing, drunkenness, gossiping and fighting.

An emphasis on the sins and moral failings of the Irish in general had been a feature of historico-political (as opposed to devotional) poetry in the Irish language during the seventeenth century, and similar lists to Ó Súilleabháin's occur in that poetry. Their meaning is different, however: in the earlier poetry, the sins are explanatory of political catastrophe, and the solution is prophecy of divine intervention; for Ó Súilleabháin, the sins are simply observed, and the solution is a reformation of manners.[22]

Ó Súilleabháin is therefore concerned with questions of public behaviour. Religious observance and discipline are recommended, in particular attendance at mass and obedience to clergy. In *Slán le hÉirinn*:

Fáth mo chumha le tréimhse na scéalta seo againn na rás
I n-áitreamh Mumhan gan géilleadh don chléir chirt nó cin le spáis

[I have been saddened for some time by these stories that come pouring in, that Munster has not been obeying or respecting its rightful clergy.]

Overall, the concern with disorderly behaviour and lack of strict religious observance accurately reflects the priorities of the reforming church in this period. Gallagher's sermons, noted above as the principal guide to Irish language preaching during the eighteenth century, have a similar message: disorderly behaviour is condemned, with one entire sermon devoted to the subject of swearing; eight of the 16 sermons discuss requirements of observance; and Ireland's sins are national – 'seo na peacaí a thug léirscrios ar mhuintir na hÉireann, agus a thug a ndúichi agus a dtalamh do náisiúin eile' [These are the sins which have destroyed the people of Ireland and which have given their native land to other nations].[23]

Although his strictures are sometimes vague, Ó Súilleabháin is clearly in sympathy with many of the more detailed initiatives of the reforming church. There is, for example, in *Duan an Domhain* [The hymn of the world], written in 1791, a specific condemnation of organised fighting at fairs, which reflects accurately one of the church's preoccupations at this precise time: the bishops of the province of Cashel (which includes most of Munster) had condemned fighting at fairs in 1777 and imposed ecclesiastical sanctions on those involved.[24] Similarly, the unfavourable comparisons with Europe and the world suggest an aspiration towards uniformity of practice and social order with other Catholic countries.

Ó Súilleabháin reflects not simply the negative side of the reforming church, what it condemned, but also the positive conduct and practices it recommended. This is very clear in the two poems on the Rosary where new devotions are an antithesis to old sins:

> Bladaireacht, blaodhmann, baoth-bhroid, braduigheacht
> Préimh na bpeacaí chráidh sinn
> 'S banaltra an Aon-mhic glaodhaigh mar charaid
> Péarla an Pháidrin Pháirtigh.

[[Avoid] flattery, boasting, foolishness, thieving, the roots of sin which plague us, and ask the protection of the nurse of the only Son, the Pearl of the Rosary.]

As for everyday life, *Duan an Domhain* gives a good picture of the new civility:

> Bíom rialta súgach múinte béasach
> Ciallmhar clumhail ciúin deiscréideach . . .
> Bíom fonnmhar fiúntach ag cumhdach na cléire
> 'S go galánta cineálta craobhach.

[Let us be disciplined, cheerful, polite, well-behaved, sensible, well-reputed, quiet, discreet . . . let us protect the clergy gladly and well, and be courteous, kind and successful.]

Although these poems were principally a means of advocating new forms of Catholicism, the new elements are mixed with some older motifs. The first two poems in the collection in particular (which are the two longest) are very traditional meditations on the Last Judgement and the transitory nature of life.

Some of the older elements come from the poetic tradition within which Ó Súilleabháin was working, such as the occasional interpretation

of theology in terms of pre-seventeenth-century Gaelic social organisation. Thus damnation or purgation for sin is thought of as an 'éiric',
in Gaelic law the honour price paid as reparation for having wounded
or done ill to someone, in this case Christ:

> An corp 's an t-anam dá ngreadadh 'sna stéidhgibh
> I ndoimhnidh ifrinn uile mar éiric.

[Body and soul being scorched like steaks in the depths of hell as
an éiric.][25]

This is, however, a minor survival, and more fundamental conceits of
medieval Gaelic religious poetry, such as addressing praise poems to
Christ or Mary as if they were secular patrons, are not found in the
Pious Miscellany.

Nevertheless, Ó Súilleabháin's attachment to 'respectable' forms of
religion is not so overwhelming as to stop him indulging in a relatively risqué pun in *Slán le hÉirinn*, which is a pious farewell to life.
The last verse addresses an unspecified (but from the context probably
clerical) patron, and incongruously wishes him:

> Mo sheascadh ghlan-bhab gheal ghradhmhar ghnúis-lonnrach
> Ó bhathas go sáil gan snáithe clúda iompa
> Acht carn-fhuilt bhláith go fáinneach fionn-bhúclach
> Tabhairt le báidh go bráth dam chlumhail-phrionnsa.

[Sixty clean bright-faced loving girls without a thread on them from
head to heel but with thick blond curly hair, to give for ever to my
famous prince.]

This is a standard pun in eighteenth-century Irish poetry whereby the
poet, instead of giving his patron 'seascadh beannacht' [sixty greet-
ings], gives him 'seascadh bean nocht' [sixty naked women].[26]

MANUSCRIPT AND PRINT

These differences between the discourse of Gaelic poetry and that of
the Catholic church point to the ways in which Ó Súilleabháin's poems
had different connotations in different physical forms. In the earlier
manuscripts, they occur individually, mixed in with other material,
sometimes religious but more frequently secular, from the corpus of
Gaelic literature. The publishers and subscribers of the printed version, on the other hand, thought of it as forming a single collection,

separate from secular poetry. It was to be used in a specifically devotional context and formed part of a wider genre of reforming Christian literature which was aimed at improving the religious beliefs and practices of the laity. However, because of its roots in a tradition outside the institutional church, the *Pious Miscellany* is representative of an attitude which tried to incorporate and purify popular practice within newer forms of religion, rather than condemning or suppressing it. This is visible both in the content and in the use of the printed book.

One poem or song, for example, celebrates a type of local religious practice of which the church had come to disapprove. This was the pattern, a pilgrimage to a well associated with a saint, which took place on that saint's day. In the mid-eighteenth century, condemnations of these rituals, mainly on the grounds of the accompanying disorder, began to be issued by the church. In 1777, for example, the bishops of the province of Cashel, which included Ó Súilleabháin's region, forbade attendance at patterns.[27]

'Duan Naoimh Dhiaglain' [The hymn of St Declan], however, describes the pattern of St Declan with approval:

A Dhéaglain ordha onoraigh, a easpaig,
Is ort thriallas go diadha 'n-a ndreamaid
Pobal gcal Dé le cléir na salm,
Is a nguí dúthrachtach urnaitheach dod agall ...

Is ciallmhar clumhail a dtiúin 's a dteagasc
Is rialta a ngreann os cionn na mara
Is deachroidheach a n-aithridhe 's a machnamh
A Dhéaglain ghléghil ar naofa do bheatha.

[O Declan of gold and honour, O bishop, to you the multitudes travel piously, the bright people of God, together with the clergy of psalms and address their devout prayers to you ... Their melodies and teaching are renowned and sensible, their gaiety is restrained there by the sea, their repentance and meditation are good-hearted, O bright Declan, whose life was holy.]

What is envisaged here is a pattern purified of its disorder, taken under clerical supervision rather than suppressed altogether. (The pattern of St Declan at Ardmore, Co. Waterford, was in fact one of the patterns which suffered little as a result of clerical condemnation. In the 1840s it was still attracting between 12 000 and 15 000 people, and over 60 entertainment tents.)[28]

Apart from clerical supervision, another way to purify rituals or festivals which the church felt to be supersitious or disorderly was by providing approved devotional material. This appears to be the principal use made of the songs in the printed *Pious Miscellany*. They were recited or sung, for example, at funeral wakes in Munster. The traditional wake, 'tórramh', was, like the pattern, one of the principal targets of the reforming movement, and was condemned repeatedly by pastoral letters and diocesan statutes after the middle of the eighteenth century. The wake took place in a private house, with the corpse present, and featured various games, often with sexual overtones, drinking, reading aloud of manuscripts, narration of long stories, singing and a type of ritual lamentation known as keening. From the church's point of view, promoting the recital of sacred poetry or the singing of sacred songs within the wake was preferable, and perhaps more effective, than banning the wake altogether. Such a process had taken place already in early nineteenth-century Co. Londonderry, according to an Anglican clergyman:

> The ancient cry has fallen into disuse here, and its place is supplied by solemn hymns in the Latin language . . . such as *Dies Irae*. The change has been effected but very lately, and we state it as a record of the great influence the Roman Catholic clergy possess over the peasantry of Ireland.

In southern parts of Ireland, the *Pious Miscellany*, and particularly the poems on death, offered a way in which domestic religious practice might be permeated with newer values. The 1821 Cork edition even added a translation into Irish of the *Dies Irae*.[29]

It is unlikely that the *Pious Miscellany* had the effect of altogether replacing or suppressing 'vile compositions' as its publishers intended. Such replacement could and did happen, particularly in Calvinist areas where the singing of psalms became common. Folklorists in the Cevennes in the nineteenth century found few folk songs but many psalms. The way in which evangelical conversion had a musical aspect is evident in the experience of one of the participants in the popular religious revival in Cambuslang, near Glasgow, in 1742. John Parker, aged 23, frequented fairs and weddings, but:

> was made to see . . . the evil of carnal delights, of getting songs and ballads by heart and whistling and singing them . . . the matter of these songs not being very chaste ofttimes . . . therefore I broke off these practices . . . and got some psalms by heart . . . and often sang them when I was following my work.[30]

In a far less acculturating way, the *Pious Miscellany* embodied and partially created a regional religious culture, a type of reformed Catholicism in the Irish language, using indigenous literary and musical forms to infuse new ideas into traditional rituals. It was fundamental to popular religious practice in Irish in Munster for most of the nineteenth century. John O'Daly, who was from Waterford and whose father had known Ó Súilleabháin, published editions in Dublin in 1858 and 1868 which were intended, according to O'Daly's preface, for 'the peasantry, to whom, in Munster particularly, its contents are as familiar as household words'. Some survived in oral tradition into the twentieth century: one of the poems on the Rosary was sung to a folklorist in Co. Clare in 1932 by a woman aged 74 years. Moreover, they were known not only in Munster, but in other areas. There is a manuscript copy of one poem made in about 1818 in the Meath/Cavan area; the printed version was one of a small number of devotional books in use in Donegal at the end of the nineteenth century, and also read, perhaps as a schoolbook, in west Co. Galway in the late nineteenth century:

> While my father was going to school, Irish was being taught. He was able to read Irish, and his father before him also. My father had a book in Irish by Tadhg Gaelach Ó Súilleabháin.[31]

As the geography of its editions indicates, however, the heartland of the religious culture of the *Miscellany* was in east and south Munster. That regional publishing history came to an end in the 1840s, and the last popular editions, in 1858 and 1868, were published in Dublin. This pattern was due partly to the recentralisation of the print trade in Dublin after the middle of the nineteenth century; partly to the decline in the number of Irish speakers in east Munster during the Famine of the 1840s; and partly to changing attitudes to religious music within the Catholic church in Ireland in the later nineteenth century. There was a strong emphasis on purity and authenticity in musical practice, and all seminarians were instructed in chant. The principal target was the use of secular, often operatic, music in church, but it is likely to have had an inhibiting effect on more indigenous music also.[32] As a consequence, Ó Súilleabháin's canticles, originally printed with the intention of infusing local and domestic religious practice with newer forms of orthodoxy, became themselves marginalised and archaic, along with the regional vernacular religious culture of which they were one of the most effective expressions.

8 'Improving and Practical Literature'

The historiography of popular culture in Europe traces, and is the product of, a growing divide between the culture of the elite and popular culture from the sixteenth century onwards. Within elite groups, economic change, literacy and the growth of the private sphere led to new forms of cultural practice, and the gradual but definite withdrawal from a common culture in which they had previously participated, and the development of views of popular culture as different. These views then led to efforts to reform popular culture, to suppress those aspects which were held to be dangerous or disorderly. One of the earliest such efforts was the Reformation, both in its Protestant and Catholic forms, which attempted to remove or modify a magical world-view and promote orthodoxy of belief and religious practice.

By the eighteenth century, elite withdrawal from participation in popular culture was fairly complete, and efforts at reform had become secular as well as religious. There were campaigns and legislation against certain forms of popular festivities and sports, accompanied by the distribution of printed tracts encouraging more orderly and 'moral' forms of behaviour. In England, societies for the 'reformation of manners' were established in the 1690s, and continued their activities throughout the eighteenth and nineteenth centuries. Similar societies were also active in Ireland since the early eighteenth century.[1]

Later in the eighteenth century, and particularly in the revolutionary climate of the 1790s, there was unprecedented activity in the distribution of the printed literature intended to reform popular culture. In Ireland in the 1790s and after, different sections of the elite were competing in these campaigns, seeking popular allegiance to their ideologies. Political radicals, in the form of the United Irishmen, and conservatives, in the form of new tract societies, both circulated vast quantities of printed material which attempted to infiltrate and replace pre-existing printed popular literature.

Both groups shared with elites elsewhere a certain distrust or dislike of popular culture, as well as an instrumental attitude towards it, attempting to control and direct it through social action. The political reforms of the United Irishmen had as one of their aims a moral reform of the people, according to a letter from the Dublin section printed in the newspaper of the Belfast section, the *Northern Star*:

> Then will every right obtained, every franchise exercised, prove a seed of sobriety, industry and regard to character, and the manners of the people will be based on the model of their free constitution.

In subsequent months, the paper published a poem on temperance and a criticism of 'the barbarous practice of boxing', two favoured subjects of reformers of popular culture. Conservatives, on the other hand, did not envisage sweeping political change, but aimed to promote similar models of behaviour through education and exhortation.[2]

As regards popular literature, the similarity in attitude can be illustrated by the juxtaposition of two descriptions, one from a radical viewpoint, the other from a conservative. The first is in a letter written in 1788 by Matthew Carey, a printer who had been involved in radical political activity in the 1780s and had left Ireland in 1784 after allegations of libelling the government. He was writing from Philadelphia to Patrick Byrne, a Dublin printer and bookseller who was later a member of the United Irishmen. He referred to:

> the vile tales and burton books, whereof thousands are annually disseminated throughout Ireland, and which corrupt the taste (and may I not add, the morals) of the youth of both sexes.[3]

Precisely the same attitude was expressed eight years later by the Anglican Bishop Magee in a sermon to a conservative tract society, the Association for Discountenancing Vice. He disapproved of:

> the pernicious tendency of most of the cheap publications, commonly entitled story books and ballads, which formerly constituted almost the whole of the literary entertainment of the lower classes.[4]

Both groups adopted the strategy of infiltrating this popular literature with texts which were similar in appearance and style to the older literature, using forms which were small, cheap, and suited to oral transmission, such as ballads, catechisms and dialogues. Both operated almost entirely in English, and used similar means of distribution, through pedlars or even giving the texts away free.

The efforts of the United Irishmen have been written about extensively in recent years. Their printed propaganda has been seen as effective in communicating their programme, in democratising political culture and encouraging a broader base of participation in political activity. On the other hand, most writers also allow for the potential of a popular readership to modify or alter the message of this propaganda, notably introducing elements of the sectarianism which was such a strong feature of certain parts of rural Ireland into what was originally a universalist political discourse.[5]

Less has been written about the efforts of conservatives, although they were active at precisely the same time and in the same way. The first large tract society, the Association for Discountenancing Vice (ADV), was founded in 1792, a year after the United Irishmen, and was active on as large a scale during the 1790s and after. This chapter will therefore focus on the conservative societies for the reform of popular literature and culture, tracing their activities up until the middle of the nineteenth century, and attempting to evaluate their impact on popular culture.

The ADV was followed in the 1790s and after by many other societies, the most important of which was the Society for Promoting the Education of the Poor of Ireland, known as the Kildare Place Society, founded in 1811. The motives and operations of these societies were closely linked with and influenced by similar groups in Britain, and their texts were initially reprints of those published by British societies. To begin, therefore, the background of tract societies in Britain needs to be considered.

TRACT SOCIETIES IN BRITAIN

Late seventeenth- and early eighteenth-century Britain saw the appearance of a number of tract societies which printed and distributed quantities of small moralistic books intended to change the behaviour of the lower classes and to turn their minds away from 'disorderly' popular culture. In the long term, this was part of the preoccupation of elites with the question, not only of popular culture, but also of poverty and the growth of the poorer classes since the sixteenth century, and the consequent questions of social order. The problem became acute in the eighteenth century, when growing urbanisation increased the difficulty of maintaining social order. Many aspects of traditional popular culture began to be perceived as problematic in the new urban environment. Popular festivities and leisure, for example, were felt to be disruptive and to pose a threat to public order. Traditional mechanisms of control did not adapt quickly enough to new circumstances, and the social hierarchy of the countryside was not reproduced in towns and cities. Instead of a well-established gentry, the dominant class was the middle class of trade and industry, and it was from this class that much of the impetus towards moral reform came.[6]

Since the mechanisms of suppression and control were weak, however, there was an increasing tendency towards using techniques of persuasion such as elementary education and free distribution of religious or moral pamphlets. Tract societies, which often combined the printing of pamphlets with the foundation of schools, were increasingly in evidence in the eighteenth century, They were reinforced in many cases by evangelical impulses, which recommended the reading of the Bible and its use in schools, since it was felt that a Bible-reading lower class would be an orderly one.

The use of education and tracts for the reform of popular culture did not meet with universal approval, however, and there was a debate throughout the eighteenth century on the desirability and utility of educating the people. Those in favour of popular education, deriving their arguments principally from Locke, viewed it as a solution to the problems of disorder and poverty. Education would inculcate thrift, hard work and religion among lower-class children in particular, counter the malign influence of their environment, and make them useful members of society. Popular education would therefore be primarily an influence for social stability. On the other hand, critics of this position such as Bernard Mandeville maintained that, on the contrary, popular education would destabilise society, since it would make the lower classes dissatisfied with their situation: an educated lower class would feel that it was above hard labour.[7]

The pro-education position was further developed from the mid-eighteenth century onward, under the influence of the French Physiocrats, and was incorporated in classical economic theory. The lower classes needed to be made aware of the 'natural order' of society, on which their own prosperity, as well as that of society as a whole, was dependent. Popular education was therefore crucial to economic development and political order.[8]

In Ireland, this view was widely shared by the 1780s, and a plan for the provision of primary education by the state was presented by the government to the Irish House of Commons in 1787. Introducing it, the Chief Secretary, Thomas Orde, gave a classic expression of the argument:

You have been obliged to correct the unfortunate consequences of a want of education with a rude and severe hand ... [It would be preferable] to introduce the balm of information into the wounds of ignorance . . . [by] introducing into their minds some little notion of the compact and the duties of society.[9]

This argument, both in Britain and Ireland, assumed that the people did not receive any education worth speaking of, and that they were both ignorant and illiterate.

During the 1790s, however, the debate ceased suddenly to be theoretical, because the assumption of lack of education, or at least of literacy, was seen to be false. In both Britain and Ireland, printed material played a large part in radical political movements such as the United Irishmen. Pamphlets and ballads, often on the subject of France, were widely circulated, and Paine's *Rights of Man* had numerous cheap editions. There was clearly a public ready to buy and read such texts, or at least willing to listen to them read aloud.

For those who believed that education led to social stability, this was an alarming development. It was not, however, taken to mean that education *per se* was dangerous, but that the people were clearly receiving the wrong sort of education and reading the wrong sort of books. From then on, traditional chapbook literature, characterised as 'pernicious', was increasingly blamed for popular agitation. Of course, this older chapbook literature had been around a long time without having had such evil effects, and it was recognised that the French Revolution was the catalyst. As Hannah More, probably the best known conservative tract writer of the 1790s in England, put it:

Vulgar and indecent penny books were always common, but speculative infidelity, brought down to the pockets and capacities of the poor, forms a new era in our history.[10]

If the content of popular literature was regarded as bad, while education itself was held to be good, the obvious response was to attempt to control that content. The initial approach was to renew the activities of the tract societies, and this happened in both Britain and Ireland in the early 1790s. It soon became clear, however, that this was not having the desired effect, and that a new strategy was needed. The new strategy, infiltration of popular literature rather than straightforward distribution of tracts, was developed in England by Hannah More.

More initially answered Paine's *Age of Reason* with a short dialogue called *Village Politics*, published in 1792. It soon became clear to her, however, that the work was not being read by those for whom it was intended, but by the middle and upper classes. Her bookseller, for instance, told her that most of the purchasers were 'people of rank'.[11]

The problem was therefore not one of simply answering republican arguments but also of infiltrating the channels of communication through which they passed. This meant producing literature which might be sold by pedlars alongside, or better still instead of, existing popular literature. More therefore collected chapbooks to study their format and content, and soon possessed 'the best sans-culotte library in Europe'; moreover, along with the Bishop of London, Porteous, and the Bishop of Dromore in Ireland (a member of the ADV), she evolved a strategy of selling to pedlars at competitive prices.

The result was the Cheap Repository Tracts, printed from 1795 onward, a set of over a hundred texts, half of which were written by More herself. They were short and cheap, being generally 24 pages long and costing a penny. The Cheap Repository Tracts organisation operated on a very large scale, and it claimed to have circulated two million copies of its texts in its first year of operation.

As Susan Pedersen has argued, More's tracts represented an innovation not simply in the manner and scale of their distribution, but also in their content and presentation.[12] To attract pedlars and shopkeepers, More adopted the outward forms of the chapbook literature of the time. The tracts tried to be entertaining, presenting a story with a moral rather than a sermon; they included woodcuts, and their covers were made to look as like chapbooks as possible; and they were given catchy titles such *as The true story of sinful Sally, shewing how from being Sally of the Green she was first led to become Sinful Sally, and afterwards Drunken Sal.*

This desire to adopt the forms of popular literature was reflected in the third new departure, the fact that these tracts were written in simple and direct language, and addressed an audience which was presumed to be capable of being persuaded by rational argument rather than by pure exhortation. They marked, therefore, the introduction of a new type of relationship between elite and popular culture, by which the elite would infiltrate popular literature, and, working from within, attempt to reform it and accommodate it to the social order. A good example is the tract entitled *The Wonderful Advantages of Adventuring in the Lottery!*, which was of course anti-gambling.

There is little that is innovative about the ideology of the tracts. There is an emphasis on the value of hard work, sobriety, strict sexual behaviour and a subordination of secular concerns to religious. Above all, the acceptance of the established order is stressed, along with the importance of deference. Deference, however, must be rewarded, and here More departs a little from previous tract writers. The duty of

the rich to care for the poor is emphasised, using stories in which the
virtuous poor are ultimately saved and taken care of by the rich. The
tracts therefore envisage a moral reform of society as a whole, and not
simply of the poor. More's activities before the 1790s had in fact been
directed at precisely such reform of the elite. Her *Thoughts on the
Importance of the Manners of the Great to General Society*, published
in 1788, maintained that the rich must reform their behaviour to set an
example to the poor. It had a Dublin edition, also in 1788.

EARLY TRACT SOCIETIES IN IRELAND

More's tracts were reprinted and distributed in Ireland by the Association for Discountenancing Vice, which had as one of its objects the
publication of 'such tracts and essays as may tend to impress a due
sense of religion on the minds of the people'. One of the three founding members was William Watson, a Dublin printer under whose im-
print the Association's tracts appeared, and whose firm was still its
printer in the late 1820s. By 1794 it had 240 members, largely Anglican clergymen, who subscribed £300 per year.[13] The Association's pre-
More tracts were heavily moralistic, including *Admonition to servants*
(10 000 copies printed) and *On the observance of Good Friday* (7500).[14]
    The Association seems to have worked fairly closely with More.
She was a member by the mid-1790s, and recorded suggestions about
'a good plan for hawkers' from the Bishop of Dromore in 1795.[15] It is
not surprising, therefore, that More's tracts were printed more or less
simultaneously in London and Dublin, and that Watson used the same
general title of Cheap Repository Tracts.
    The scale of the Dublin operation, while not nearly as large as More's
in Britain, was substantial. The Association claimed to have distributed 120 000 tracts in 1796 alone, although this was clearly an *annus
mirabilis*, since it also claimed a figure of 251 900 'religious books
and tracts sold at reduced prices or distributed gratis' for the decade
1792–1802.[16] This may well be accurate, since More's productions sold
most in Britain at the beginning of operations, in 1796.
    The Association was placed on a sounder financial footing after 1800,
when it began to receive a parliamentary grant – after 1803, this amounted
to £1000 per year. Later, however, its energies were mainly directed
towards its schools, although it continued to print and sell or distribute the Cheap Repository Tracts until at least the 1820s. Its 1829 report claimed to have distributed altogether 1.3 million books and tracts.[17]

It has been claimed that the Cheap Repository Tracts in England may have been instrumental in preventing revolution there.[18] The same is clearly not true of Ireland, and in the aftermath of the rebellion of 1798, it was felt that the tract idea needed to be pursued further. The government also commissioned a long series of reports on popular education, culminating in a large-scale inquiry in the early 1820s. These reports noted the existence of 'pernicious' literature, and the necessity for its replacement. According to the *Fourteenth Report of the Commissioners of Irish Education* (1813–14):

> [the lower classes] are actually obtaining [education] for themselves; and though we conceive it practicable to correct it, to check its progress appears impossible – it may be improved, but it cannot be impeded.[19]

These words were written by Richard Lovell Edgeworth, one of the commissioners and an advocate of Rousseau's ideas on education, who was in the forefront of the movement for educational reform. Following the publication of the *Fourteenth Report*, his son sponsored the publication of a pamphlet on agricultural improvement, and the introduction provides a classic statement of the tract idea after 1800:

> It has been justly observed by the Board of Education that 'the poor will read whether the higher classes of society attend to their instruction or not'; it therefore becomes a duty incumbent on the benevolent and well-informed to supply books suited to the industrious labourer, to whom the idle man of letters is so indebted.[20]

Before this, however, a similar project had emerged in a strictly religious context. The Association for Discountenancing Vice had been followed in the early nineteenth century by a number of societies with similar aims, but whose activities centred almost entirely on distributing Bibles and sections of scripture in Ireland, in some cases in the Irish language. These included the London Hibernian Society (1806), the Baptist Society for Promoting the Gospel in Ireland (1814), and the Irish Society for Promoting the Education of the Native Irish (1818). The Bible is not strictly speaking popular literature, and these societies are usually (and correctly) presented as proselytising agencies, early manifestations of the 'second reformation' or 'Protestant crusade', as Protestant evangelism in nineteenth-century Ireland came to be known. Nevertheless, they are included here since they form a part of the project of reform of popular literature. Their aim was not simply to spread scripture and convert, but to replace the previous popular literature and thereby achieve the same moral reform and reinforcement of social order as the tract societies. Moreover, by sharpening sectarian tension in Ireland, they influenced the climate in which the later tract and book societies worked.[21] In any case, the reception of the Bible in Irish popular culture provides an interesting case of appropriation, which will be discussed in Chapter 11.

A new stage in literature for the peasantry by elite reformers in Ireland appeared in the work of Mary Leadbeater (1758–1826), whose *Cottage Dialogues* was published in 1811. Leadbeater came from a Quaker family in Co. Kildare which had kept an 'improving' school there since the late eighteenth century. Kildare was one of the locations of the rebellion of 1798, and Leadbeater and her husband narrowly escaped death, their house being occupied first by soldiers and then by insurgents.

Cottage Dialogues followed More's literary example, consisting of conversations between peasant characters, during which the approved point of view emerges through discussion. As far as the content is concerned, however, there are two important differences. In the first place, religion as a subject was avoided, partly reflecting Leadbeater's own situation as a Quaker, and partly reflecting the increased sectarian tension in early nineteenth-century Ireland. As one of her correspondents put it:

> Religion should undoubtedly be the first object of any writer who aims at improving human nature, but her lessons are the more efficacious for not being formally announced as such; and perhaps in your peculiar situation, publishing tenets which do not wholly agree with those of the majority, on one hand, or with those of the established church on the other, to have given any direct lessons of religion would have diminished the general utility of your admirable works.

The book was nevertheless criticised by the evangelical *Christian Observer* for not containing enough religious material.[22]

The second new element was the extension of the emphasis on hard work and thrift to include a great deal of technical advice, both domestic and agricultural. There are dialogues on cookery, for example, and on washing, smallpox, pig-keeping and manure. This aspect was probably due to Leadbeater's friendship with William Lefanu, the editor of the *Irish Farmer's Journal*, who had suggested the original plan for the *Dialogues*.[23]

Unlike More, however, Leadbeater did not envisage distributing the *Dialogues* through the channels of popular literature. The book was fairly long and relatively expensive at one shilling and sixpence. It was printed by subscription, some subscribers taking as many as 100 copies, and then distributed free, '[promoting] their circulation among that class of readers for whom they were intended, in a more expeditious manner than it could have been effected by other means.'[24]

THE KILDARE PLACE SOCIETY

Leadbeater's project was taken up in the following years by the Society for Promoting the Education of the Poor of Ireland (better known as the Kildare Place Society).[25] This was founded in 1811, principally to organise schools. Finding books for use in its schools was soon seen to be a problem, and from 1816 the society began to write and publish its own texts. These were not only schoolbooks but also books of more general interest, whose distribution outside the schools was envisaged. The Society received a government grant from 1816 until 1831, and its book production reached a peak in the early 1820s, with figures of 185 000 in 1821 and 173 000 in 1824. By the time the grant was discontinued in 1831, with the establishment of the national school system, its production had already declined considerably and was down to 58 000 in 1831.

The society adopted More's strategy of penetrating the chapbook market by undercutting the existing productions. It told the Education Commissioners in 1825 that:

> by an offer of their books at a price somewhat below their prime cost [they] have induced the hawkers, pedlars and other dealers (who had been in the habit of supplying the country with the objectionable works) to become extensive purchasers . . . and they are now among its principal customers.

One member told the inquiry that 'to the southwards we found no instance of those pernicious works being reprinted.'[26]

A look at the society's own records, however, shows the difficulties that even a highly organised and well-financed body faced in doing this, and casts doubt on the success of the enterprise. The book project was initially set out in a memorandum in about 1814. It maintained that the principal reason for the popularity of 'vile trash' was its cheapness, rather than any attractions in the subject matter. Therefore, for purely commercial reasons, good cheap books, well distributed, would soon supplant it in the bookshops. A low price would be achieved by subsidy, and the society's capital would permit the use of stereotype, making the books even cheaper.[27]

The society appointed a book subcommittee and employed a literary assistant, and between them they selected or wrote the texts. By 1817, when sales began, four books were in print, three in press, three before the committee and three in preparation. Editions were in general of 10 000 copies and were sold either unbound in sheets or already bound. The sale in sheets was rapid and by 1818 some titles were being reprinted.[28]

It seemed that the market was accepting the product, but there were complications. It emerged that the booksellers who bought sheets were printing their own title pages, showing a higher price than the society's. The books were therefore being sold to a higher social class than was intended. Initially, this did not cause concern, since it was felt that middle-class reading 'prepares the way' for lower-class reading.[29]

By 1819, however, reports were reaching the committee that their books were being rebound and sold in Scotland, while at the same time 'in many parts of Ireland the cheap books have never been heard of' (perhaps since, as the committee noted, a quire of sheets was too large an investment for a country bookseller). Many of the books, then, seem not to have gone in the desired direction, either socially or geographically. This applies potentially to the vast bulk of the society's production, since sales in sheets were over ten times greater than sales in the cheap paperbound format.[30]

By the 1820s the society had nearly 80 titles on its list. Like Leadbeater's, these books strove to avoid confessional controversy and placed a heavy emphasis on 'useful knowledge'. Thirty-two of the books were voyages and travel accounts, ten were described as 'natural history', and ten as 'arts and economy', altogether over 60 per cent of the total.[31] Initially, the list impresses by its diversity of subject matter, but this is more apparent than real. 'Natural history' and 'travel accounts' are very similar, consisting of topographic and biological 'facts', into which moral lessons are (not very subtly) woven. If the books are classed by didactic purpose, a much more uniform picture emerges, since they are nearly all about the necessity for orderliness, thrift, hard work, subordination, sobriety, self-reliance and self-improvement generally. It is perhaps more convenient to classify them according to the way in which the lessons are imparted.

Explicit exhortation is found in a series of books on agricultural practice and domestic economy in the style of Leadbeater. In fact, one of them was commissioned by the Society from Leadbeater herself.

This was *The Pedlars*, in which two travelling pedlars are used as a peg on which to hang a series of observations about the different agricultural practices they see, such as crop rotation and growing mangel-wurzels. *The Cottage Fireside* is the domestic equivalent, a series of dialogues between a grandmother and granddaughter on bacon curing, potato cookery and butter, together with lectures on 'The economy of time' and 'Whiskey drinking at fairs'.

In most other books the lessons are inserted into the narrative, as in the travel accounts. The accounts themselves are dry collections of information, such as this passage, near the beginning of *Travels in Northern Italy*:

> Mr. Ivers and his family were, at the period when the narrative commences, setting out for Pisa from Leghorn. The latter is the seaport town of Tuscany, situated on the Mediterranean sea, in latitude 43° 33' North, and longtitude 10° 16' East . . . the distance between them is 14 miles; the road lying in a north-easterly direction through part of the forest of Arno, having the lofty chain of the Appennines on the right and the sea on the left.

Moral lessons are arbitrarily introduced. This is part of a description of boating on Lake Como:

> In a part of the mountain on our left, as the boatman informed our party, were some traces which are believed by the people to be the footsteps of Noah's family leaving the Ark.
>
> 'What is there', said Mr. Ivers to his sons, 'too absurd for ignorant people to believe! and therefore how anxious should our countrymen at home be, to profit by the schools established in almost every part of the country.'

The books which had the greatest commercial success were those in which the moral was implicit in the narrative, or which blended well with previous popular taste. An example of the first would be *The Shipwrecks of the Alceste and the Meduse*, which was intended to demonstrate the values of cooperation, subordination and obedience. Although this is stated explicitly in the preface, the main narrative is left fairly much to itself. The point of the stories is that the crew of the *Alceste* did not panic, remained obedient to its officers and survived, whereas on the *Meduse* it was *sauve qui peut*, with disastrous consequences.

An example of the second type is *Elizabeth, or The Exiles of Siberia*, an abridged translation of a novel in French by Sophie Cottin, originally published in London in 1807. In the chapbook form at least, this novel is very much a traditional fairy tale. Elizabeth and her parents are in exile in Siberia, her father having been involved in the Polish revolt; Elizabeth determines to make a plea to a higher authority, and after many adventures and setbacks, finally manages to reach the emperor, who pardons her father:

> Deeply rooted as his prejudices had been against [Elizabeth's father], they were instantly removed; the father of so virtuous a daughter, he conceived, must be innocent of the crimes laid to his charge; but had he even supposed him culpable, Alexander would, at such a moment, have forgiven him.

The journey to plead with a distant, wise and forgiving ruler would fit perfectly with folk narrative. It is noteworthy that *Elizabeth* was the society's best-seller, and shows that success depended not simply on approximating to the physical appearance of chapbooks, but also to the content of popular literature. This was the view of the folklorist Crofton Croker:

> As further proof of the natural good taste [of the Irish peasantry] it may be mentioned that of all the books printed and circulated by the Kildare Street Society, none is found to equal in sale *Elizabeth* ... Much may be said respecting educating the lower orders according to their taste and through the medium of their superstitions as the most attractive and effectual mode of instruction.[32]

One of the reasons for the decline of the Kildare Place Society after the mid-1820s was that it had become in Catholic eyes increasingly identified with Protestant evangelism. Thereafter, 'moral' (as opposed to 'practical') literature directed at a popular audience became more confessional in tone. To combat the activities of Protestant Bible societies, the Catholic church set up its own book society to print literature of a purely confessional sort, such as catechisms and titles like *Grounds of Catholic Doctrine* and *Defence of Catholic Principles*.

Established in 1827, the Catholic Book Society was run by a committee of clergymen and a Dublin printer, W.J. Battersby. Funds were raised from the clergy themselves, and the books were also to be distributed through them, thus using church structures to avoid conventional commercial channels altogether. Despite the fact that local church structures were being used successfully for fund-raising and politicisation in that decade by O'Connell (at the peak of whose campaign for Catholic Emancipation the Catholic Book Society was launched), this was not notably more successful as a strategy than market infiltration. The first two appeals for funds produced a disappointing response, and the society had continuous financial problems until it was wound up in 1845.[33]

The Catholic Book Society is a useful counter-example to some arguments which might be used to explain the apparent failure of other book and tract societies. It shows that alternatives to market penetration were not any more effective; and that the fact that most of the other book societies were Protestant, directing their products at a predominantly Catholic (and perhaps therefore hostile) peasantry, is not a satisfactory explanation of their lack of success.

'USEFUL KNOWLEDGE'

Other cheap 'improving' literature of the late 1820s and 1830s tended to follow the practical rather than the moral strand of the Leadbeater/ Kildare Place Society formula. It concentrated to a greater extent than that Society on the diffusion of 'useful knowledge' in the areas of economics and agriculture. This was partly a way of avoiding sectarian controversy and partly due to a belief in the moral benefits of scientific knowledge. It was also, however, attempting to address the economic problems of pre-Famine Ireland, particularly the rapid increase in population and the creation of an enormous rural poor. Literature aimed at economic and moral progress emphasised two main themes, knowledge of the theory of political economy, and knowledge of superior agricultural technique and practice.

Orthodoxy, following Malthus and Ricardo, attributed poverty, and particularly Irish poverty, to overpopulation.[34] In this view, population growth could best be limited by 'moral restraint', and this would be brought about through education in the principles of political economy. An early example of this reasoning being applied to Ireland is found in Daniel Dewar's *Observations . . . on the Irish* (1812), which maintained that education would have 'a tendency to impose those moral restraints which limit the extent of population to the means of subsistence'. Later, McCulloch '[urged] as a remedy for the poverty, wretchedness of the labouring classes and part of the peasantry of Ireland, the instruction of labourers in that branch of political economy which would induce a restraint upon the practice of marriage.'[35]

The clearest example of a popular work on these lines was produced in 1833 by Richard Whateley, the Anglican Archbishop of Dublin who was also a Commissioner for National Education and who chaired the government Poor Inquiry of the early 1830s. Whateley had been a professor of political economy in Oxford and had written a well-known textbook introduction to the subject. This was abridged for a popular and young audience under the title *Easy Lessons on Money Matters for young People*. It went through several editions, was published in an Irish translation, and was incorporated in part into primary school textbooks.[36]

As for the second theme, agricultural technique, probably the best known works were those published in the 1830s by another Anglican clergyman, William Hickey, under the pseudonym 'Martin Doyle'. The preface to *Irish Cottagers* (1830) conveys his intention:

> The author's object has been to convey sound practical advice to the rural population of his country through a familiar and entertaining medium.

Hickey worked in cooperation with agricultural societies (he had founded the first such society in Wexford), and adapted much of his work from their publications, such as reports on agriculture in Flanders. His books are very practical, and seem well adapted to Irish agricultural and social conditions. *Hints addressed to the smallholders and peasantry of Ireland* (1830), for example, includes a discussion of the importance of ventilation in houses, including one-bedroom dwellings in which the entire family sleeps in one room. Similarly, a section on cookery focuses on potatoes, and includes the observation that:

> the great perplexity relating to the process of digestion with half of you, especially during the summer season, is to get any food at all.

This practicality is at the service of a strong social conservatism. He warns, for example, against women dressing extravagantly on Sunday, since this leads to confusion of social rank:

> When people keep within their own class of society they are respectable in it – let them pass the bounds and those above them will laugh at them or despise them.

(Although this is a standard motif of moral literature, it was perhaps a more noticeable phenomenon in the 1830s with the arrival of cheap factory-produced cotton clothes.)

Education is viewed in terms reminiscent of Mandeville:

> [Classical education] is a nuisance among you . . . a smattering of that sort of knowledge is dangerous . . . such knowledge creates pride;

a certain degree of it makes a man think he is born to be a learned man and that the handles of the plough or the business of the counter would disgrace him.

A practical, rather than a classical, education is therefore conducive to social stability, since 'the honest, industrious, well conducted, religiously minded farmer is the happiest man'.[37]

THE IMPACT OF THE SOCIETIES

It is difficult, if not impossible, to estimate what influence these publishing enterprises had on a popular readership. The reports of the various societies are often very positive about their success, but this is certainly due in part to their desire to impress their members and supporters. The Cork Religious Tract Society, for example, founded in 1809, announced two years later that:

> The committee have the satisfaction of informing the public that their exertions have not been fruitless ... their tracts have found their way to the cottage of poverty, the bed of sickness, and to the cell of the criminal. These instructive treatises have occupied the room of idle stories, unprofitable tales, immoral and destructive ballads; a better taste is gradually spreading among the lower classes, as is already evident from the number of tracts already disposed of ... amounting in the short space of two years to 41 000.[38]

Adams suggests that Charles Bardin, the literary assistant of the Kildare Place Society, 'probably had a greater effect on Irish reading habits, and was more widely read, than many a famous mainstream literary author.' Consideration of the activities of the various societies, the difficulties they encountered and the nature of the literature they produced suggests otherwise.

At first sight, what is striking about the strategy of producing replacement popular literature is its fundamentally persuasive, rather than coercive, nature. The only society which mentioned outright suppression of the previous books was the Association for Discountenancing Vice, which attempted:

> to suppress the publication of immoral or obscene books ... by the interference of the magistrate in some cases, by the public prosecution of offenders in others, and in some instances by the destruction of the books in question.[39]

Otherwise, one shared feature of the whole series of enterprises was the assumption of the existence of a literate peasantry which was capable of responding to reasoned argument, and of appreciating and adopting practical knowledge and advice. The tone may frequently have been condescending, but the project as a whole was not, and may be said to show a new respect on the part of certain members of the elite for the lower classes and a willingness to address them as equals. Writing about temperance, to give one example, 'Martin Doyle' prefaced his remarks by the observation that "You and I like a drop of it and of course can find reasons enough for indulging ourselves."[40]

It is by no means clear, however, that the books were read by this intended audience. Those books which attempted to infiltrate and use market forces seem to have had a great deal of difficulty in doing so and in controlling the result, and in some cases, it is unclear whether the books reached the people at all. This had already been evident in the pioneering schemes of Hannah More, who had trouble persuading pedlars to take her tracts. 'They have been used to getting 300% for their old trash,' she wrote in 1796. 'Mrs. T- and others have condescended to spend hours with the hawkers, to learn the mysteries of their trade.'[41] In Ireland, de Brún has shown that the Irish Society for Promoting the Education of the Native Irish had difficulty in ensuring that its publications were distributed even by its own teachers during the 1820s.[42] For this society, moreover, there was the added difficulty of procuring Irish translations, culminating in a curious case of the intentions of a society being subverted by one of its own agents. It commissioned a translation into Irish of Whateley's *Easy Lessons on Money Matters* from Thaddeus Connellan, its principal Irish language adviser. When the translation was printed in Dublin in 1835, the Society discovered that Connellan had interpolated extensive quotations from medieval Irish saga literature into the text.[43]

The Kildare Place Society for their part had difficulties with booksellers, who bought their books in sheets and rebound them at higher prices, and frequently exported them to Scotland and England. Some pedlars even exported the cheap Bibles printed for the Bible societies. The Catholic Book Society was well aware of possible conflict of interest between itself and booksellers, and its initial prospectus declared that the society was 'Particularly anxious not to interfere with the trade of booksellers in the city or country'. Without government aid, it found market conditions more difficult to manipulate than most, and it had constant financial trouble.[44]

From a printer's point of view, of course, tract societies were a good source of business – a study of a Cork printer's workshop notes that 'the evangelical movement of the 1820s provided welcome trade for printers in an otherwise lean period.'[45] It is noteworthy that a printer, William Watson, was one of the three founders of the Association for Discountenancing Vice,[46] and was later prominent in the Kildare Place Society, and W.J. Battersby, a Catholic printer, was a moving spirit in the Catholic Book Society, which was run from his shop. No doubt both Watson and Battersby had the best of intentions. Nevertheless, the questioning of Watson by the Education Inquiry in 1825 focussed on the profit he made from being printer to the Association for Discountenancing Vice, and one may wonder with the commissioners whether, in some ways, the trade was using the societies rather than vice versa.[47]

The scattered references to the identity of purchasers in the documents of the various societies suggest that the books may not have been reaching those for whom they were ostensibly intended, or in the way the societies would have liked. The absence of direct evidence of lower-class purchasers is certainly not conclusive evidence, since the same could be said of much cheap printed literature. Nevertheless, the available accounts suggest that the buyers were middle or upper class, and if the texts reached a lower-class readership, it was most likely through free distribution.

In the 1790s, More had already noted that the Cheap Repository Tracts 'were bought by the gentry and middling classes full as much as by the common people'. Watson's Dublin editions of the same tracts announce 'great allowance to shopkeepers, chapmen and hawkers, and to those who buy to give away'.[48] The only specific purchasers mentioned in the reports of the ADV were army officers who gave them to the men under their command. The Kildare Place Society gave sets of their books free to schools which met the Society's approval, and the U.K. coastguard service bought 12 000 of them for distribution to their employees.[49] It is possible, therefore, that very few of the tracts actually entered the normal channels of distribution of popular literature and that the 'moral' publications never came close to supplanting the more traditional pedlar's books.

The middle and upper classes were therefore an important part of the market, and some aspects of the content of the tracts should be considered in this light. In the peasant dialogue, for example, the image of a lower class coming to responsible, conservative conclusions through rational debate is calculated to reassure elite purchasers and to convince them of the feasibility of reform of popular culture by persuasion.

As one of More's biographers wrote, the Cheap Repository Tracts 'discovered to the superior classes a new nation . . . the patient and laborious poor'. In this sense, the tracts are part of a wider project whose best known representative in Ireland was Maria Edgeworth: the appeal to the middle and upper classes to take their social responsibilities seriously, and thereby to avoid social unrest and revolution.[50]

The success of tract publishing from this perspective may be gauged by the extent to which it was imitated. A long series of similar societies was set up during the late nineteenth century and even into the twentieth in both Britain and Ireland. The Catholic Truth Society of Ireland, for example, founded in 1899, had as its aim: 'to combat the pernicious influence of infidel and immoral publications by the circulation of good, cheap and popular Catholic literature.'[51] The tract societies, therefore, had an added function within elite circles which did not depend on the ultimate effectiveness of the strategy among the population at large. As Neuberg has put it, 'contributing to the cost of tract production and buying them at wholesale rates to give away offered a satisfactory way of doing good at a reasonable cost'. Tract production, in other words, continued because it 'improved' the distributor as much as because it 'improved' the receiver.[52]

The appeal of the strategy within the elite was wider than this, however, and the vocabulary of the 'improvement' was taken up more generally by writers and publishers during the nineteenth century. When John O'Daly published in 1844 a small cheap booklet of translations of Irish political poems from the seventeenth and eighteenth centuries, *The Nation*, a nationalist newspaper, welcomed it in the following terms:

> Buy a ballad in any street in Ireland, from the metropolis to the village, and you will find in it, perhaps, some humour, some tenderness and some sweetness of sound; but you will certainly find bombast, or slander, or coarseness . . . a high class of ballads would do immense good – the present race demean and mislead the people as much as they stimulate them.

Both *The Nation* and the *Galway Vindicator* recommended the purchase of copies by temperance societies, the most conspicuous 'improvers' of the 1830s and 1840s. However, nationalist infiltration of the cheap print market in this case had no more success than the tract societies, and O'Daly's cheap editions were a commercial failure.[53]

In the case of some of the tracts, one could press the argument a little further and say that they are primarily about the 'discovery of a new nation', and were read exclusively by non-popular readers; that their principal function was ethnographic, to 'explain' the peasantry. There are certainly a few pointers in this direction.

Mary Leadbeater declared in 1809 that her intention in *Cottage Dialogues* was 'to write for the instruction of the lower classes' and the text would seem to bear this out. The first dialogue, for example, concerns the danger of leaving a baby unattended in a room with a pig, since the pig might bite the baby's hand off. However, when the Edgeworths read the book (probably in manuscript) they immediately suggested a London publication, and Maria Edgeworth wrote an 'Advertisement to the reader' for that edition, claiming that 'It contains an exact representation of the manner of being of the lower Irish, and an exact transcription of their language.'[54]

Similarly, the preface to the Kildare Place Society's *Cottage Fireside* hopes that the reader 'will not think that such characters as are here introduced are altogether imaginary; similar topics are often the subjects of discourse in the cottages of our industrious peasantry.' Martin Doyle's *Irish Cottagers*, whose avowed object was 'to carry practical advice to the rural population', notes in its preface some 'striking coincidences' between the stories contained in it and William Carleton's *Traits and Stories of the Irish Peasantry* (1830), one of the classic texts of the ethnographic genre. Later on, in the mid-1840s, Doyle's *Hints to the Small Farmers of Co. Wexford* was included in the first edition of Carleton's *Parra Sastha*.[55] Although the subject of these works is the peasantry, the point of view of the assumed or inscribed reader is outside that class.

Nevertheless, some of the tracts must have made their way into the hands of a lower-class readership. How were they read, or what influence did they have? It is possible, for example, that some at least of the practical advice was followed, although in general the role of print in the diffusion of technologies is a limited one.[56] The adoption of agricultural innovations depended in any case as much on material circumstances as on attitudes among farmers and tenants themselves. It has been pointed out, for example, that many of the traditional farming techniques criticised in the tracts were suited to a small-holding, highly subdivided land system, and that many of the innovations suggested would only make sense if the broader economic context changed.[57]

Taking this argument to a more general level, it can be argued that much of the improving and moral literature would appeal only to those whose circumstances predisposed them to such attitudes, and that a receptive audience was necessary for such literature to have any effect. The case of temperance is instructive in this regard. Alcohol, and whiskey in particular, was an intimate part of transactions and rites of passage among the pre-Famine rural lower classes, and adoption of temperance depended on broader changes in society and culture. Father Mathew's temperance crusade of the late 1830s and early 1840s was perceived in quite distinct ways in urban areas and in the countryside. In towns, temperance was accepted as part of a wider culture of improvement, as its sponsors intended. In the countryside, in contrast, Mathew was seen as a magical figure, and the certificates and medals of his movement were absorbed into folkloric religion as powerful magical objects.[58]

The evidence of some elite commentators also suggests that the impact of the tracts was limited. Martin Doyle, looking back from the 1860s, felt that he had failed: 'At the end of forty years I look back and look around and see but little of what I had hoped ... The improvement is, I am afraid, least ... in the class I endeavoured to instruct.' The social and political stability which was to be the result of better agriculture had of course not come about either, and the reason Doyle gives is consistent with his original linking of the two: '[Politicians] told you, you were oppressed slaves, and did not let you rest. Now the mind drawn off to such exciting themes has no room for other and better pursuits.'[59]

There are also some signs of resistance among lower-class readers to the content of the tracts. As early as 1810, the wife of the Anglican Bishop of Meath had told Mary Leadbeater that:

in all books intended for instruction to the lower class, care should be taken not to let the title or the preface imply that the book means to point out their faults and apply remedies to them. Their perceiving this intention, until they read the book, I have often known to prevent them from reading it at all; or at least, to make them so perfectly prejudicial against whatever might be the contents, as to put their being benefited by those contents quite out of the question.[60]

A similar argument is advanced, perhaps unwittingly, by a correspondent of the Hibernian Bible Society in Co. Sligo in the late 1820s:

I know that most of the common people do not accurately understand any thing read to them in any language, except a word here and there; and that even those who can read, do not in general understand what they read, being ill taught, and unused to exercise the mind. They can, however, *catch the spirit* of a rebellious harangue, or of a superstitious tale, and enjoy a filthy ballad, beyond any thing.[61]

It is probably more accurate to see this as a case of very selective reception on the part of the audience. That such selectiveness could be the result of the appropriation of printed texts by oral cultures is suggested by one of the few examples of 'ethnographic' literature, portraying the peasantry as viewed from outside, which has been recorded in oral narration. A number of stories by William Carleton were told by a well-known storyteller in west Cork in the middle of the twentieth century, and are instructive about the way such material might be viewed by a peasant audience. The conclusions of Earls's subtle analysis are worth quoting:

> The most immediately striking difference between Carleton's story and its derivative is one of length: [the printed version] is fourteen pages long, while [the oral] extends to a little less than a page and a half . . . In its oral form the story has been stripped down to its bare anecdotal outlines.

This is because of:

> the narrator's lack of sympathy with non-functional dialogue, or dialogue which is elaborated for its own sake, or for the purposes of achieving a deeper or more subtle characterisation . . . The storyteller has, as it were, abstracted the narrative elements out of the text in which they once formed a part.[62]

Bearing in mind the way in which moral lessons were interpolated into a narrative in the books of the Kildare Place Society, it is easy to imagine that if such texts entered popular culture, they did so without a lot of their 'moral and improving' elements.

9 Languages and Literacy

The discussion of the *Pious Miscellany* introduced the subject of popular printing and the linguistic situation in late eighteenth- and early nineteenth-century Ireland. The subject is worth examining in greater detail for the light it sheds not only on questions of literacy and of reading, but also of language shift, and more generally on the process of 'cultural modernisation' discussed in Chapter 11. This chapter will examine popular printing in the Irish language, focusing on three questions: first, what sort of literacy existed in Irish overall; second, what can be inferred from the printed corpus about print literacy in Irish; and finally, why so little was printed in Irish relative to English.

In 1750, Irish was the language of the majority of the population, and the absolute number of Irish speakers continued to increase until the 1840s. This was because of the rapid increase in population in the century before the Great Famine. The increase was greatest in the west and among the lower classes in the countryside, the regional and social strongholds of Irish. Overall, however, the linguistic balance was altering. Outside the elite, English began to spread rapidly from the late eighteenth century onwards, since English was the language of both the market and the state. The change operated particularly through the educational system, and literacy was usually acquired in English. This language shift was consolidated in the aftermath of the Famine, since Irish-speaking groups were disproportionately reduced by the population loss of some two million in that period. The extraordinarily rapid language shift of the mid-nineteenth century, however, should not obscure the existence of a large Irish-speaking community during the previous century, both monolingual and bilingual.

Because literacy was usually acquired in English, even for Irish speakers, the spread of literacy paralleled the spread of English. Maps of illiteracy and of Irish speaking as reported in censuses from 1841 onwards are almost identical. Both were heavily represented west of a line drawn from Derry through Limerick to Waterford, together with a weaker presence in north Leinster and south Ulster. Logan in fact found that in the later nineteenth century data literacy figures correlated better with language than they did with participation in schooling. Similar patterns are also found in eighteenth- and nineteenth-century France in areas where languages other than French were spoken.[1]

Irish speaking and illiteracy went together, therefore, but the precise relationship between them is not always clear. Tracing that relationship is difficult for two reasons: first, because linguistic scholarship has generally traced either the decline of Irish speaking or the spread of English speaking, devoting less attention to how the two coexisted; second, because literacy is broadly speaking a dichotomous variable, whereas language is not (one can speak two languages, but one cannot be both literate and illiterate). The link is made more problematic again by the fact that the chronologies of the decline in Irish and the rise in literacy do not coincide. Ó Murchú, on the basis of Fitzgerald's figures, sees the early to mid-eighteenth century and the mid to late nineteenth century as the periods of decline of Irish, whereas most accounts of literacy take the late eighteenth or early nineteenth centuries as the period of growth.[2]

Within Irish historiography, the standard view of the relationship is that of Cullen, who sees the decline of the Irish language as being 'essentially . . . related to the prestige of written above oral culture, and the explosive growth in the demand for literacy' from the late eighteenth century onwards. A similar view is expressed by Furet and Ozouf, who stress what they see as 'the oral character of culture in many under-literate non-French-speaking regions', and the absence in those languages of a literacy which would 'attenuate the strangeness of written culture'.[3]

The dividing line between languages is not precisely the same as that between orality and literacy, however. There can, for example, be language shift without the acquisition of literacy. The early twentieth-century censuses show that 'there were many in Donegal, especially men, who were illiterate but capable of speaking English'. This was because of the high level of seasonal migration, particularly harvest migration, from the area to Scotland and to English-speaking parts of Ulster. These migrants had increased contact with English and at the same time reduced participation in education, because many of them were young. Such migration had existed in different parts of Ireland, particularly the north-west and the south-west, since the early eighteenth century at least. Seasonal or return migration was equally a force for language shift in Scotland in the same period.[4]

If English could be acquired independently of literacy, literacy could also be acquired independently of English. There was a continuous and substantial production of Irish-language manuscripts throughout the eighteenth and early nineteenth centuries, as well as a minor explosion in Irish-language printing between 1800 and 1850. These indicate the existence of an Irish-language literacy, although its precise extent is unclear since quantitative sources measure literacy in English only. Similarly in Brittany, there was a substantial tradition of reading literacy in Breton, including a large amount of print which is discussed below. The non-French-speaking region discussed in most detail by Furet and Ozouf, therefore, would seem not to support their contention about the absence of literacy in regional languages. They do not seem to have been aware of literacy and print in Breton, and concentrate exclusively on signature data, assuming that to signify literacy in French only.

When literacy was achieved in a regional language, it often acted as a stepping stone to literacy in an official language. In late eighteenth- and early nineteenth-century Scotland, when evangelical societies established schools to teach the reading of scripture in Gaelic, pupils were disappointed if they did not proceed to reading and writing in English later on. It was not the desire for literacy *per se* which drove language shift. Literacy in regional languages was possible and desirable, but not as desirable as literacy in an official, high-prestige language. It is not entirely accurate therefore to see the demand for literacy as driving the demand for English in Ireland. English and literacy were acquired together, and for the same reasons: the prestige of literacy over orality paralleled the prestige of English over Irish as the language of the economic and political domains, rather than being logically prior.[5]

Some writers have viewed the relationship between language and literacy as being more openly ideological, and argue that language loyalty could produce resistance to literacy if that literacy was in a different language. François found that the regions of Prussia which had stagnating or declining levels of literacy between 1838 and 1871 were those with Polish-speaking populations, and he attributed this to opposition to Prussian state schooling based on 'a desire to preserve a cultural, linguistic and national identity'. Furet and Ozouf make a similar suggestion with regard to Brittany and south-west France. By the eighteenth century in Ireland, however, there is little evidence of a culturally inspired resistance to English, and in the early nineteenth century, the evidence all points in the other direction, with an extremely rapid and large-scale adoption of English. Moreover, the state-sponsored system of education established in the 1830s was rapidly accepted in most areas and by most institutions. The system was rejected for some decades in the Catholic Archdiocese of Tuam under Archbishop John McHale for reasons that were political and religious rather than linguistic. The Catholic church supplied an alternative system run by the Franciscan order, and the growth of English-language literacy in the region in this period was in fact more rapid than elsewhere, albeit from a lower base.[6]

As regards the dimensions of literacy in Irish between 1750 and 1850, no quantitative data whatsoever are available. The most frequently cited estimate is that of Whitley Stokes who in 1806 thought that about 20 000 people could read Irish, out of a total of one and a half million whose first language was Irish.[7] Qualitatively, we can distinguish two types within this literacy.

The first type was found throughout the Irish-speaking areas, but predominantly in Munster, where the Irish-speaking community was most socially diverse, and where most of the surviving manuscripts and the Catholic religious printing in Irish originated. Ó Conchúir has demonstrated the extent of scribal production in County Cork alone, counting over 200 scribes in the period 1700–1850, while more recently Cullen has looked at the mechanism of that production. Manuscripts were commissioned by patrons, ranging from farmers to clerics, and written by itinerant scribes, who were often poor, and usually combined transcription with teaching. This literacy probably encompassed both reading and writing, since the patrons were of relatively high social status, and was heavily influenced by manuscript practice.[8]

Evidence for a second type of literacy comes from the work of Protestant evangelical societies in the early nineteenth century. Some of these societies advocated the reading of scripture in Irish, and employed teachers to teach reading in Irish. De Brún has described the employment of between 250 and 300 individuals during the 1820s by the main society, the Irish Society for Promoting the Education of the Native Irish through the Medium of their own Language. The distribution of these teachers corresponded to the areas of activity of the Society and evangelical activity in general, with particular concentrations in south Ulster, north Connaught and on the west and south-west coasts. The literacy in the Society's schools differed from the Munster literacy in that it was more print-based, using reading primers and parts of scripture produced by the societies themselves (although many of the teachers were Irish-language scribes). Because of its religious inspiration, it probably contained a large proportion of reading-only literacy.[9]

PRINTING IN IRISH

Literacy in Irish therefore existed, with a potential readership for printed works in Irish, as well as a far larger audience for the recitation of such works. What printed texts were available to that audience?

In the historiography of popular printing in general, the possible existence of printing in minority languages is rarely treated at any length. For Ireland, the only monograph on popular print, Adams's *The Printed Word and the Common Man*, concentrates on Ulster-printed books in English and does not discuss what Irish speakers in the province in the eighteenth and nineteenth century may have been reading.[10] French studies focus on the *Bibliothèque Bleue*, whose texts were in French, and take two approaches to questions of other languages. Some writers, such as Mandrou, assume that the readership of the *Bibliothèque Bleue* was confined to French-speaking areas (in the eighteenth century, the region north of the Loire). Others, Muchembled in particular, suggest that they were read elsewhere, and discuss their role in the project of achieving linguistic uniformity within the French state as part of a broader process of acculturation of the people by the elite. The existence of popular printing in Breton or Occitan is sometimes acknowledged – Mandrou refers to translations of French texts printed in Quimper and Toulouse – but only in passing. Histories of education share this bias, inbuilt in the sources, towards the official languages. They sometimes show an awareness of the existence of literacy and of reading in other languages, but tend to view these languages as constituting greater or lesser 'obstacles' to the achievement of literacy in the official languages.

In Ireland, the high point in the production of popular print in Irish was the period 1800–50. This corresponds to the zenith of provincial printing, and many of these texts were printed in southern towns. Broadly, the corpus can be divided into three categories.

First, there was the Catholic religious literature. Ó Súilleabháin's *Pious Miscellany*, with some 20 editions, has already been discussed. There were of course catechisms, particularly that of O'Reilly, a mid-eighteenth-century Archbishop of Armagh. This was first printed in English about 1725. The Irish version survives in editions from every decade between the 1760s and the 1860s and was printed with particular frequency in the early nineteenth century. There were also other devotional works, principally translations of eighteenth-century English texts. Challoner's *Think Well On't*, for example, had two separate translations, which appeared almost simultaneously, *Machtnuig go maith air* in Clonmel in 1819 and *Smuain go maith air* in Dublin in 1820. The printing of this literature was concentrated in the south, particularly in Cork, Limerick and Waterford, but there were texts which came from other areas, such as *The Spiritual Rose*, a text of south Ulster origin which had three editions in Monaghan between 1800 and 1835.[11]

The second type of popular print in Irish was Protestant religious texts, consisting of catechisms, scripture and other devotional works, printed in Dublin and London by evangelical societies which formed part of the 'second reformation' of the early nineteenth century. Ideologically, these societies were similar to the tract societies of the same period, and in fact the Irish Society for Promoting the Education of the Native Irish was formed in 1818 as a secession from the earliest of the tract societies, the Association for Discountenancing Vice. The Irish Society differed from most of the other tract societies in two ways: in its emphasis on evangelisation in the vernacular and in its refusal to publish any secular 'improving' literature in Irish. When one of its principal Irish teachers recommended the publication of books in Irish on arithmetic, agriculture and geography, they were rejected as being 'manifestly unconnected' with the aims of the Society. Its productions consisted therefore exclusively of parts of scripture, prayer books, reading primers and dictionaries.[12]

The third type was the broadside ballad in Irish, a genre which survives in many examples from the early nineteenth century. (There were also a few, less directly 'popular' printed works in Irish during the period, such as Bishop Gallagher's *Sermons*, first printed in 1732, and which had gone through 14 editions by 1820. Despite its popular content, this was probably exclusively possessed by priests.)

What do these printed works reveal about the nature of print literacy in Irish? We can start with the question of typography, where a clear distinction can be drawn between the manuscripts and the Protestant printed texts on the one hand, and the Catholic and secular texts on the other. The former use Irish lettering, with fonts being commissioned by the bible societies themselves, while the latter used Roman type.[13] This is probably due to the fact that many of the non-Protestant texts were being produced commercially, within a printing trade that functioned almost entirely in English. Bishop Gallagher's *Sermons* explained its use of Roman letters in terms of practicability:

Why [should] Irish sermons come clothed in English dress . . . One reason is that our printers have no Irish types; and another, that our mother language ... is so far abandoned ... that scarce one in ten is acquainted with her characters.

This was still the case almost a century later, in the production of a devotional work in Waterford:

> It is a great dissatisfaction to me ... that I have been prevented from having this little book printed in the native Irish character, for the want of a native Irish type in Waterford, and because few only are acquainted with the language in its ancient characters.[14]

Such editorial remarks show that the intended readers were at least familiar with Roman letters, and probably more familiar with them than with Irish letters. As the introduction to a later (1858) edition of the *Pious Miscellany* puts it:

> Some may ask, why we have adopted Roman instead of Irish characters? Our answer is simply this, that if we did adopt the Irish, those for whom the work is intended would not be able to use it, being entirely unacquainted with that character, whereas every peasant who *speaks* Irish and *reads* English can master the work in its present form [my emphasis].[15]

Typographically, therefore, the Protestant texts were heirs to the manuscript tradition, while the literacy implicit in the Catholic and secular printed texts is closer to literacy in English; indeed, as the last quotation suggests, literacy for Irish speakers was often achieved first in English, and afterwards in Irish.

That many of these readers were literate in English is clear from other aspects of the commercially produced texts. The title pages were often in English, although the texts themselves were in Irish. The front page of the *Pious Miscellany* reads: 'Timothy O'Sullivan's, commonly called Tadhg Gaelach, Pious Miscellany' etc., the directions for singing were printed in English, such as 'Tune: The flowers of Edinburgh', and most editions contain a preliminary page, 'Instructions to the reader', in which the sounds of different combinations of letters in Irish traditional/manuscript orthography were explained.[16]

The texts which most clearly show the influence of English language literacy are those which are printed in a phonetic spelling based on English language orthography. Phonetic spelling had been used since the early eighteenth century, when it had been introduced in a Protestant catechism intended for Rathlin, Co. Antrim. By the early nineteenth century it had even infiltrated the manuscript tradition, particularly in Connaght. In print, phonetic spelling was used in many of the ballads and in the vast majority of the Catholic catechisms. A Waterford printed ballad from the 1820s begins with 'Is the ve ban oceal', which represents (in Irish orthography) 'Is do bhí bean uasal' [And there was a noble woman]; in the catechisms 'On teeryact rive nulle heel' represents 'On tsíorafocht roimh an uile shaoil' [Eternally prior to the whole world]. Thus, when these texts are read as if they were written in English, an approximation to the Irish sounds is produced.[17]

These printed texts therefore indicate a readership literate in both Irish and English, an audience which was clearly substantial in southern Ireland in the early nineteenth century. The evangelical texts, on the other hand, have a greater continuity with the manuscript tradition, and the Irish Society in particular, by employing many Irish scribes as teachers, contributed to the survival of that tradition by employing Irish scribes as teachers and by establishing contact between scribes in different areas. The Protestant texts therefore imply a style of reading and a readership different to that of the Catholic and secular, although there must have been a large overlap between the two audiences.

These differences demonstrate another facet of the difficulties of Irish language print culture in this period: the absence of established norms, whether of spelling or lettering. To this may be added the absence of literary norms for the language itself. According to Wall:

> There was the difficulty of electing for the rather antiquated literary language of the scribes and scholars . . . or for the simple colloquial Irish spoken by the people. This was an obstacle which, perhaps even more than the spread of English, lay in the way of the production of a popular religious literature in Irish.[18]

If the colloquial were chosen, as was probably the obvious choice for a popular literature, there was the further problem of dialectical variation – a text in the dialect of one region would not easily have been understood in another. This was a dilemma: the circulation of print in Irish was impeded by a lack of linguistic and orthographic uniformity; but such uniformity would have partly been created by the circulation of print in Irish in the first place.

This problem is referred to by a number of Anglican clergy in the north of Ireland, one of whom, the Rev. Robert King, while curate of Ballinascreen, Co. Londonderry, produced in 1849 his own translation of *The History of Our Blessed Saviour* in the local dialect of Irish. In the preface, he observed that:

The language of the Irish Bible is so unlike that which is in common use throughout Ireland, so unlike, for instance, to what is spoken here in Derry and Tyrone, &c., that any ordinary chapter of it,
read just as printed, would be quite unintelligible to the generality
of hearers around us . . . So that the many thousands who speak Irish
as their mother tongue in the district around here, have never had
printed for their use, in their own plain dialect . . . even such a short
life of our Lord . . . as is here for the first time supplied to them.[19]

PRINTING IN IRISH – LITTLE AND LATE

Taking all the printed literature in Irish into account, what is most
striking is its paucity, its domination by religious texts and its lateness. Why was there so little?

Cullen has approached the question from the perspective of the
manuscript tradition, and asks why:

a living language with such an immense written culture, one which
totally overshadowed that extant in any of the other secondary languages of Europe and one which enjoyed an upper-class backing,
however shifting its extent and motivation, did not spawn printing?

He offers two answers. The first, that manuscript production was essentially rural whereas printing was essentially urban, is somewhat
inconsistent with his description of Dublin as 'the Mecca for [manu-
script] transcribing activity from an early date'. The second answer is
that printing in Irish would need to have been actively sponsored in
the seventeenth century, before English had definitively become the
language of print.[20] Such sponsorship, when it appeared in other countries, invariably came from an institutional church, and points to the
importance of the religious context in Ireland.

The corpus of popular printing in Irish described above was predominantly religious, and points to the centrality of religious institutions in an explanation for the development, or non-development, of
print literacy in Irish. Discussions of motivations for popular literacy
in early modern Europe focus on three in particular: the economic, the
political and the religious. Since the languages of the market, the state
and politics usually coincided, the acquisition of literacy in a non-
official, regional language was dependent on an effective Reformation,
whether Protestant or Catholic, at a popular level. In Ireland, where
the religion of the majority was and remained Catholicism, the rela-

tive absence of print literacy in Irish was due initially to the lack of a comprehensive Protestant Reformation, and then to the lateness of Tridentine Catholic reform. Where that literacy was present, it was preceded and produced by Catholic reform. In most areas, however, by the time reform was undertaken, the Catholic church had begun to function in English, and as far as education was concerned, was becoming part of the state enterprise.

This argument can be supported by a comparison with the other Celtic regions, where the existence of a print culture in non-official languages was due to institutional church backing. In Wales, Scotland and Ireland, there were two main periods where such backing was crucial, the sixteenth-century reformations and the evangelical revivals of the eighteenth and early nineteenth centuries. In Brittany, Catholic church sponsorship of literacy in Breton was most influential in the 'Catholic reformation' of the seventeenth century. (There was some Protestant evangelisation in nineteenth-century Brittany, including a translation of the New Testament into Breton published in 1827, but the numbers of adherents remained small.[21])

In Wales, the early development of a print literacy based on Protestantism was crucial to the maintenance of the Welsh language in the long-term. The Protestant Reformation in Wales produced a printed prayer book in Welsh in 1546, and a complete translation of the Bible in 1588. According to Durkascz, 'these were the foundations on which mass Welsh literacy was later built – foundations which, by contrast with Ireland and Scotland, allowed a comparatively smooth transition from the medieval bardic heritage to the post-reformation tradition of printed literature.' A printing trade producing books in Welsh was well established by the mid-seventeenth century, and produced over 500 titles between 1660 and 1730. In the eighteenth century, print literacy in Welsh formed an important part of the Methodist evangelical movement, and 'sermons, tracts, epics, hymns and elegies multiplied in striking profusion, especially from 1760 onwards', according to Jenkins. Altogether, there were perhaps 3000 works printed in Welsh before 1820, compared to less than 200 in Irish, a statistic all the more striking when it is borne in mind that the population of Wales in 1800 was perhaps a tenth of the population of Ireland.[22]

It could be argued that Protestantism, with its emphasis on religious reading and practice in the vernacular, was more likely than Catholicism to produce literacy in that vernacular. This would imply that the relative failure of the Protestant Reformation in Ireland militated against Irish language literacy, since prayer books and a translation of the Bible into Irish were produced by the Anglican church at the same time as in Wales. Although there is some truth in this view, it exaggerates the differences between Protestant and Catholic Reformations at the popular level. Much recent writing on the subject, following Delumeau, has stressed the similarities between the two, seeing them as part of a broader movement for the reform of popular culture. This is particularly the case as regards pedagogy and reading, with an equal emphasis in all churches on the reading of the catechism, for example.[23]

This can be illustrated by the case of Brittany, where a thoroughgoing Catholic Reformation at a popular level produced print literacy in Breton, and where, like Wales, this religiously-based literacy laid the basis for a later secular printed literature. The missionary effort began about 1610, and flourished particularly after the 1640s, when it was directed by the Jesuit Julien Maunoir. Parish missions were intense and affecting, using a range of techniques and media. Large coloured images on card were used to explain and convey doctrine. These were the *taolennou*, which remained in wide use in Breton religious practice. All missions in Breton-speaking areas were conducted in Breton, and Maunoir ensured that only priests who were fluent Breton speakers took part. The reading of religious works was emphasised, and a permanent travelling salesman was employed to distribute printed material in Breton. The most popular of these were written by Maunoir himself, and his *Cantiquou Spirtuel* had nine editions in Quimper alone in the seventeenth century. These works established the norms of modern written Breton.[24]

The existence of a religious literacy in Breton created the conditions for the growth of a secular literature. The earliest example is the *Dictionnaire et Colloques François-Breton* of Guillaume Quiquer in 1626, which by 1759 had had 19 editions; it was superseded by the anonymous *Nouveau Dictionnaire et Colloques* (1717), which had a total of 35 editions in the eighteenth and nineteenth centuries. These two works were designed as much for French speakers wishing to learn Breton as for the reverse; thus there was in Brittany, at the level of print, an interaction between the two languages, and a role for Breton in print which does not seem to have existed in Ireland. Even if the main attraction of these texts was the learning of French, it is nevertheless significant that this approach to literacy in French was through a pre-existing literacy in Breton. In Ireland, print literacy in Irish was often approached through literacy in English, even for Irish speakers.[25]

By the early nineteenth century, there was a substantial market for small cheap books and ballads printed in Breton. The output of at

least one printing house in Morlaix, that of Ledan, from 1805 onwards, was mainly in Breton, containing both religious and secular
works, and the inventory of a printer in Quimper in 1777 indicates
that 40 per cent of the stock was in Breton, about 12 000 items, including about 7000 copies of small religious works, catechisms and
rosaries. Two printers in early nineteenth-century Vannes sold about
40 different small pious works in Breton, mainly translations of French
texts. Finally, a modern catalogue of broadsheet ballads printed in Breton
lists over a thousand titles, many times more than that which has survived in Irish, although, given the problem of survival rates, calculations are hazardous.[26]

Contemporary evidence for the circulation of these Breton books
can be found among the responses to the inquiry into regional languages in France conducted by the Abbé Grégoire in the early 1790s.
Some of the questions in Grégoire's survey concerned printed texts in
these languages. Most of the responses mention the paucity of such
texts in areas where regional languages were spoken. Those from Brittany, however, make it clear that such printed works were common:

'It is very possible to obtain a collection of these Breton books from
Derien, a bookseller in Quimper, who, as well as stocking them, has
a particular knowledge of the language';
'What is the merit of these works?' – '[Their merit is] that of
teaching reading in Breton';
'Are they readily available?' – 'Yes, for money'.[27]

There was a corpus of popular printed literature in Breton, therefore,
similar to the *Bibliothèque Bleue*, and containing similar texts, particularly religious and chivalric. Many of these texts, such as a version
of *Les Quatre Fils Aymon*, were in the form of rhyming plays, and
were part of a tradition of popular theatre which flourished in the nineteenth century. The printed texts, like those of the *Battle of Aughrim*
and ballad sheets, were bought and memorised by those who participated in the spectacles.[28]

The case of Scotland, while Protestant, was similar to that of Ireland and differed from those of Wales and Brittany, in that a religiously
based literacy in Gaelic was not established in the sixteenth or seventeenth centuries. It was not until the evangelical revival of the late
eighteenth and early nineteenth centuries that a body of popular printed
literature, almost exclusively religious, appeared. A series of missionary
societies, often linked to similar organisations in Ireland and Wales,
established Gaelic schools and distributed Bibles, tracts and other

literature. By the 1820s these, along with the activities of travelling Gaelic preachers, inspired a religious revival in the highlands which eventually manifested itself in the establishment of the Free Presbyterian church which broke away from the Church of Scotland in 1843. This revival produced a substantial corpus of printed sacred literature in Gaelic, particularly songs and psalms, as well as a number of short-lived periodicals. A Glasgow publisher's list of religious texts in Gaelic from 1853 featured 45 titles, of which 13 were poetry and song.[29]

THE REFORMATIONS IN IRELAND

Comparison with other similar language areas, therefore, focuses attention on the role of the Reformations in Ireland in creating literacy and a printed literature. The Protestant Reformation produced a printed catechism in Irish in 1571, a New Testament in 1602 and a Book of Common Prayer in 1608, but evangelisation, whether in Irish or English, did not make a serious impact among the population at large.

Later Protestant evangelism through Irish was concentrated in the early nineteenth century, in the activities of the Irish Society in particular. It was linked with Scottish evangelism, had a considerable pooling of resources and experience, and it produced a body of religious works in print. While Scottish evangelism drew some criticism from landlords, who thought it had potential for social unrest, in Ireland the opposition from the Catholic church was intense, and the campaigns on both sides contributed to an atmosphere of heightened sectarian tension after the 1820s. Religious literacy in Irish was subsequently viewed with suspicion by the Catholic clergy, a development recollected in the folklore of the 1930s. According to a man in his sixties in Co. Cork in 1933:

> The priests would be furious if they saw books in Irish in the house, and these would have to be hidden from them because they might speak about them from the altar.[30]

The Catholic Reformation produced a number of seventeenth-century works in Irish, printed mainly in Louvain, and which were among the most frequently transcribed texts within the Irish manuscript tradition. They were not accompanied by a comprehensive catechising and pedagogical effort, however. Such an effort did not begin until a century later.

The reasons for the relative lateness of a popular Catholic reformation in Ireland have been discussed in relation to the *Pious Miscellany*. They include unstable political conditions in the seventeenth century, the official proscription of the Catholic church from the late seventeenth century (though it was largely tolerated in practice), distance from Rome and the relative poverty of the laity. The Tridentine mission at a popular level started in the mid-eighteenth century, was at its height in the early and mid-nineteenth century, and was consolidated in the aftermath of the Great Famine of 1845–50. It began in the southeast and in towns, where the disabling conditions applied least: Munster and south Leinster contained a strong Catholic middle class which had close trading links with Catholic Europe, particularly France. It was this early phase of reform which produced the printed popular Catholic literature in Irish, which was largely published in the towns and cities of the south-east with the sponsorship of Catholic clergy. In the rest of Ireland, however, reform got under way much later. This can again be illustrated by comparison with Brittany, where Jesuit activity in the seventeenth century was based on the parish mission; in Ireland the first sustained missions in rural areas came in the 1820s, and many areas in the north had their first missions in the 1850s.

By the late eighteenth century, however, the Catholic church in most areas was functioning primarily in English. The extent to which English speaking priests ministered to Irish speaking congregations was a problem for the Catholic hierarchy in this period, whereas in Brittany, as we saw, missionary priests had to be able to speak Breton. At the parish level, one possible consequence can be seen in an episode in Carleton's 'The Poor Scholar', in which a sermon preached in English by a Catholic priest in Ulster is translated by those members of the congregation who were able to understand it. A hint of the problem can be found as early as 1736 in the introduction to Gallagher's *Sermons*, which describes the book as intended for 'as many as can speak, or tolerably pronounce, the Irish', and also in the memorial sent by Bishop O'Brien of Cloyne to the Congregation of Propaganda in 1764 seeking funds for the publication of an Irish dictionary for the use of priests: 'a good Irish dictionary, in which . . . the terms of this language would be correctly explained and in which our missionaries could find the words and explanations which they may have forgotten [i.e. while studying in Europe], or perhaps never knew.'[31]

At the level of writing and print, Ó Cuív has drawn attention to the fact that 'comparatively few official Catholic documents in Irish are known' from the eighteenth century, and Corish has noted that 'the duty of catechising children tended to devolve on the schoolmaster'.

Given that, by the nineteenth century, hedge schools were primarily an anglicising influence, it is possible that in many Irish-speaking areas, the catechism would have been learnt in English. It seems therefore that in Ireland, in contrast to Brittany, popular religious print literacy, where it existed, was being created in English rather than in Irish. According to Ó Cuív, '[it was] symptomatic of the lack of initiative in the purely religious field . . . that so many of the devotional works in Irish composed in the seventeenth and eighteenth centuries remained in manuscript throughout this period, when there must have been a great need for religious reading matter in Irish.'[32]

The case of Bishop O'Brien is instructive. He was a Gaelic scholar and a patron of poets and scribes, and while conducting an unusually early series of missions in Co. Cork in 1765–6 left copies of prayers in Irish with the priests and schoolmasters. When his successor returned to the same parishes in 1770, he found these prayers still being recited.[33] As in the case of Brittany, it seems fair to conclude that had more missionary activity in Irish taken place at such an early stage, it would undoubtedly have been effective in promoting the reading of religious material in Irish, and subsequently of secular literature. The Irish Society feared precisely such a process when they refused to print any texts other than scripture and reading primers:

> It was . . . considered that, as the love of the ancient language, and not any desire to peruse the Sacred Word, was the impelling motive which sent the peasant to our schools, he would when taught to read, naturally take up any Irish book that he could find in preference to the Bible . . .[34]

In early modern Europe, the written forms of vernacular languages were usually standardised by the circulation of early printed books, and these were frequently religious texts produced by institutional churches. The language of Luther's Bible became standard literary German, Welsh was standardised by the Bible of 1588, and Breton by Maunoir's *Cantiquou Spirtuel*. In Ireland, a virtually unchanged standard literary language had existed throughout the later Middle Ages, but declined after the seventeenth century along with the learned class and aristocracy who had cultivated it, and no replacement norm appeared for the spoken vernacular. For a printed text in Irish to circulate widely, to overcome obstacles such as regional variations in dialect and to create a new written norm, it would have required a strong institutional backing, most probably as part of a comprehensive religious reform movement.

In the event, no such backing emerged, whether Protestant or Catholic. If, as Febvre and Martin have written, 'Printing certainly exercised a far profounder influence on the development of the national languages than any other factor', its relative absence precluded the development of a strong popular literacy in Irish.[35]

10 The Ideology of Status in Ireland

On a broadly political reading of the genres of popular literature discussed above, one theme emerges from three of the genres, though of course it is not the only theme. Chivalric romance, criminal biography and the historical literature all address the question of social hierarchy and its legitimacy, and through their production and reception we can trace some patterns of hierarchy and deference in eighteenth- and early nineteenth-century Ireland. These concerned the relationships between three groups: the aristocracy and gentry; the larger tenants, particularly those of them who had lost gentry status in the seventeenth century; and the smaller tenantry and peasantry.

In their emphasis on nobility of blood, the chivalric romances in particular, and to a lesser extent the criminal biographies, embody a world-view in which status is ascribed rather than achieved, and in which personal qualities are inherited rather than learned. A nobility, in other words, not only exercises political and social power by virtue of birth and descent, but is also uniquely just, brave and virtuous for the same reason. Conversely, character defects are thought to be hereditary among the lower classes.[1] Given a popular readership, therefore, the content of popular literature has frequently been seen as a form of ideological domination or aristocratic hegemony, either inculcating an ideology of status, or acting as a brake on the transition from a society of orders, based on an ideology of status, to a society of classes. One strand of French Marxist writing on the *Bibliothèque Bleue*, including particularly Mandrou and Muchembled, has stressed its tranquilising and alienating effects, and has seen it as a force for social stability and deference during the eighteenth century. According to Mandrou:

> None of these books offers a justification, in the manner of Bossuet, of this social order [which is] silently accepted . . . like the immutable secrets of nature. The *Bibliothèque Bleue* encourages social conformity.[2]

It does this by proposing a direct diffusion of values down the social scale within the texts. According to Muchembled, 'consumption of the books is directly linked with the diffusion, albeit in a simplified form, of dominant values.'[3] As noted previously with reference to chivalric romance, this line of argument assumes a straightforward acceptance of the texts by their lower-class readers. There were other possible modes of reception, however. On the one hand, the popularity of such works in chapbook form could be attributed to the fact that such ideas existed beforehand within peasant society, rather than being instilled by the reading of the books; on the other hand, the versions of nobility contained in the texts could equally be used as ideals against which to measure and criticise the actuality.

These problems of interpretation are general. In eighteenth-century Ireland, however, there were also differences in the implications of status ideology. The aristocracy and gentry (the landed classes) contained an unusual number of recent arrivals, families who had become landed after the wars of the late sixteenth and seventeenth centuries. Many of these new owners came from gentry backgrounds in Ireland and Britain, but many did not, but had taken advantage of the opportunities arising from large-scale land forfeiture after the wars of the 1640s and more particularly of the 1690s.

Of course, status ideology everywhere had to allow for a certain amount of social mobility and assimilation. Some older noble families declined for economic or demographic reasons, while newer families purchased noble office, or were ennobled for a service to the crown or state. The trappings of nobility, such as land and a large house, could be bought, and pedigree could be acquired for the second generation through marriage, or could be fabricated. In Ireland, however, the changes in the landed class were sweeping and sudden. Moreover, many of those who had previously held the land, and who had been landed for generations, remained in their areas as smaller landowners or tenants. The logic of status would favour the dispossessed over the new owners, when those new owners were less well born. Consequently, an important support of an *ancien régime* aristocracy was lacking in Ireland when genealogy and birth could not be convincingly invoked.

The difficulties presented to an aristocracy by insecure ideological status, and the resultant anxiety, can be documented. As in England and Europe, individuals certainly felt the stigma of lack of birth and consequent non-acceptance by the status group, and attention was drawn by their enemies to their low birth in phrases such as 'son of a barber' or 'son of a tanner'.[4]

This refers to acceptance by an aristocracy itself of individual newcomers. What is more pervasive in Ireland, though impossible to measure, is a collective sense of insecurity or illegitimacy within the landed classes. Such a sense of insecurity existed within sections of the landed élite in Ireland throughout the eighteenth and nineteenth centuries, focusing on the question of legitimacy of title to land. Land obtained after confiscation was frequently lacking in supporting legal documentation such as title deeds, and ownership was therefore vulnerable to the sort of legalistic argument made in Reily's *Impartial History*.

Title to land was discussed in the debates of the Irish Parliament on a number of issues in the 1780s and 1790s, such as the regency crisis in 1788–9 and the Catholic Relief Acts in the early 1790s, and in particular over the granting of the parliamentary franchise to Catholics. Some members of Parliament, wrote the Lord Lieutenant in 1792, were worried about 'lower Catholics talk[ing] of their ancient family estates'. Perhaps the classic statements of this perception were made by John Fitzgibbon, successively Attorney-General and Lord Chancellor, who electrified the Irish House of Commons in 1789 and the Irish House of Lords in 1793 by using security of property as an argument against both the independence of the Irish Parliament and voting rights for Catholics:

> The ancient nobility of this kingdom have been hardly treated. The Act by which most of us hold our estates was an Act of violence – an Act subverting the first principles of the Common Law in England and Ireland. I speak of the Act of Settlement . . .
>
> [This act violated] the sacred and fundamental principles of the common law . . . every acre of land in this country which pays quit rent to the crown is held by title derived under the Act of Settlement . . .[5]

Ownership of land was one of the traditional signs of nobility, and if the legitimacy of that ownership was questioned, the other signs would have to be reaffirmed. These other characteristics, however, were also problematic in different ways.

The most obvious alternative would have been to emphasise blood and descent, but these were often lacking in precisely those cases where land had been acquired in the seventeenth century. Various ways around this were tried. A common plot in early nineteenth-century Anglo-Irish fiction, for example, was the legitimisation of the occupancy of a new Protestant landowner by marriage with the descendants of the original (dispossessed) Catholic landowners. Antiquarian and literary interests among landowners were also a way of establishing links with the old order and achieving a status based on antiquity of title. An extreme example was the Kilkenny landlord, Sheffield Grace, who in the 1820s commissioned a number of pseudo-seventeenth-century poems in Irish in praise of putative ancestors. These poems were passed off as genuine seventeenth-century productions and accepted as such until the mid-twentieth century.[6]

Alongside antiquity and genealogy, *ancien régime* aristocracies pointed to military service as a justification of status. Noble status was originally achieved through military exploits, and nobility involved a willingness to continue that service. This had two related aspects: on the one hand that of prowess in combat, expressed for example in the chivalric romance; and on the other, the claim to a right of ruling by military conquest. Thus, in sixteenth-century France, some sections of the nobility presented themselves as descendants of the Franks, who had conquered the kingdom, while in the seventeenth century, the older nobles stressed their military origins as *noblesse d'épée*, in contrast to more recent bureaucratic *noblesse de robe*.[7]

In Ireland, the successful conquest described in the historical chapbook literature could therefore be used to justify aristocratic status, and some sections of the Irish nobility could be seen as the last *noblesse d'épée* established in western Europe. However, the Irish landed classes do not seem to have pursued this argument with reference to the wars of the sixteenth and seventeenth centuries. There were some elite appeals to a right of possession deriving from the Norman conquest of the twelfth century, but the military dimensions of the later conquest were not invoked. Celebrations of Cromwellite or Williamite victories did not have upper-class backing or participation during the eighteenth century, and the *Battle of Aughrim*, for example, remained an exclusively popular text.

There were a number of reasons why the Irish landed classes might avoid such justifications. In the first place, to claim legitimacy by conquest is to admit the legitimacy of a reversal of conquest in the same way, and a Stuart or French invasion was a real possibility until the early nineteenth century.[8] In any case, not all the new landowners had been soldiers, and many were speculators who had bought cheap land in the aftermath of confiscation. Finally, a legal prohibition on the bearing of arms by Catholics restricted the role of many landlords as military leaders of their tenantry.

The fragility of traditional ideological support within the newer sections of the Irish landowning aristocracy affected their relations with two groups in particular. The first group consisted of the descendants of the pre-1600 landowning families, whether these were émigrés or had remained in Ireland and still owned or held land. The second was tenants and others on their estates, with whom relations depended to a large extent on deference to status.

THE 'DISPOSSESSED'

As regards the first group, notions of status were fundamental to the old Gaelic and Anglo-Irish aristocracy, as with European aristocracies in general, up to the seventeenth century. These ideas continued among their descendants, including those whose land had been confiscated. A classic statement can be found in the many genealogical tracts produced by the learned classes employed by the old elite, as pedigree was fundamental to their idea of nobility. The introduction to one such tract, compiled in 1650 and written in Irish, contains a classic statement of the ideas of status and the hereditary nature of qualities, whether good or bad:

> Everyone who is white of skin, who is bold, who is honourable . . .
> who is bountiful of clothes, wealth and gold ornaments and who is
> not afraid of battle or combat, these are the descendants of the Sons
> of Míl in Ireland [i.e. the aristocracy] . . .
>   [All who are] black-haired, vociferous, ill-doing, mean, graceless,
> disorderly, vulgar, slavish . . . these are the descendants of the Fir
> Bolg [i.e. the peasantry].[9]

Remnants of the learned class which produced this ideological justification survived in eighteenth-century Ireland, and their productions were prized by Gaelic or Old English (Anglo-Norman) families. One example was Brian Maguire, a member of one of the minor branches of the Maguires of Fermanagh, who was tenant of a substantial holding in the early eighteenth century. He commissioned a large number of manuscript transcriptions between 1712 and 1721, including the genealogical tract quoted above, various other genealogies and an 'origin tale' of his own branch of the family. The collection also included chivalric romances, whose ideology blended easily with the other texts. Maguire was therefore consolidating his social status by a straightforward assertion (or perhaps fabrication) of his pedigree.[10]

The other group which employed Gaelic genealogists in the eighteenth century were the Irish aristocratic émigrés in France, Austria and elsewhere in Europe. These lacked land, and therefore had an even greater need to demonstrate noble descent, to be eligible for office, whether civil, military or ecclesiastical, or to arrange suitable marriages. Although proofs of aristocracy were not instantly transferable from one society to another, there was nevertheless what one writer has called 'a small industry' of genealogy among the Irish abroad. This phenomenon can appear peripheral, and even comic, with an official in Morlaix in 1735 complaining that 'he had never seen Irishmen in this country who did not declare themselves gentlemen'. However, it did have implications for social hierarchies in Ireland, since an entire other aristocracy was in place outside the country, whose genealogy was potentially superior to that of many newer landed families within Ireland.[11]

Alongside genealogy and history, the principal literary survival of older Gaelic culture in the eighteenth and nineteenth centuries was poetry, and much of this poetry is also suffused with an ideology of legitimate descent. Moreover, compared to earlier centuries, many of the eighteenth-century poets bore the names of landed families, O'Sullivan or Fitzgerald for example, rather than those of the hereditary bardic families. Poem after poem, therefore, laments the passing of the 'legitimate and real' owners and criticises the newcomers, attributing the loss of patronage to the lack of pedigree of these new landowners. The poetry is also strongly Jacobite, and loyalty to the hereditary succession of the Stuarts of course shares the same view of birth and descent.

The most influential student of this poetry, Daniel Corkery, presented this ideology of status, initially aristocratic, as having been transmitted to the general population, or at least having become their property, through the gradual impoverishment of the poets. Cullen has pointed out that Corkery exaggerated the poverty of the poets and their patrons, and that the outlook and preoccupations of the poetry were essentially those of the lesser Gaelic gentry and large tenant farmers. Status ideology and an emphasis on descent would clearly appeal to families which had suffered a loss of social and economic standing. (In the same way, the renewed appeal of chivalric romance in sixteenth-century Spain has been linked to the difficulties of aristocracy.) Nevertheless, the persistence of the poetry in the oral tradition, as well as the fact that the poetry itself moved closer to folk themes, shows that it acquired firm roots in the lower social strata. The shift in format of printed chivalric romance, from expensive quarto as well as chapbook in the late seventeenth and early eighteenth centuries to exclusively chapbook by the late eighteenth, marks a similar shift in the social locus of status ideology.[12]

THE TENANTRY

The account given above of the transmission of both Gaelic poetry and printed romance in English is diffusionist, and presents aristocratic ideology as being transmitted unidirectionally, via texts, to a lower-class audience. It takes no account of the reception of the those texts, and in assuming that reception to be unproblematic, postulates a pre-disposition in the popular audience towards acceptance. Did the smaller tenants and labourers share the ideology already, and did they question the legitimacy of new landowners, making them less inclined towards deference?

For the lower classes, as much as for competing elites, some aspects of social deference certainly seem to have been more problematic in Ireland then elsewhere. For a tenantry, blood and descent seem to have been as important an ideological support of hierarchy and status as they were for the landowners. This can be underlined by a comparison with Scotland, where landlords were frequently the heads of clans and thus had blood ties with their tenants. This strengthened the landlords' hands when they wished to clear their estates and evict tenants, while at the same time making them more inclined to support their tenants during subsistence crises. Irish landlords, on the other hand, were both weaker and less benevolent.[13]

An examination of vertical ties within Irish society more generally reveals that genealogy and descent were not the only reasons why such ties might be comparatively weak. There was, for example, in the eighteenth century a cultural gap between many landlords and their smaller tenants. This was clearest in matters of language. Differences existed between elite languages and popular vernaculars in many areas of *ancien régime* Europe. The gap was wider in Ireland than elsewhere, however, since so many of the landed classes were monolingual English speakers, while many tenants were monolingual Irish speakers or else spoke little English: that is, not only was the habitual language of the elite different to that of the people, but the elite were unable to speak the popular language.

This is clear from the widespread use of interpreters in law courts until at least the mid-nineteenth century. This contrasts with areas like Languedoc, where the upper classes habitually spoke French, the people Occitan. Here, eighteenth-century courts did not need interpreters, since the magistrates understood Occitan and frequently commented on the local varieties spoken by witnesses. Given that the dispensing of justice was one of the services by which aristocracy was coming to be

defined in the eighteenth century, following in the tradition of man-
orial courts, appearance in court in Ireland would often serve to underline cultural difference as much as it would reinforce respect and
deference.[14]

If the role of magistrate was problematic as a manifestation of vertical ties, the role of military commander was even more so. Tenants
serving under aristocratic or landlord command in army or militia regi-
ments would experience a very direct form of vertical command; moreover, such command emphasised the military prowess which was such
an important manifestation of noble virtue, and which was embodied
in the chivalric romances. In eighteenth-century Ireland, because of
the legal ban on Catholics bearing arms, landlords were unable to benefit
from this particular strategy to strengthen vertical ties with many of
their tenants. Alternatively, tenants did not get to appreciate the military
qualities of their lords at first hand. As Connolly has put it, religious
disability 'debarred [tenants] from taking on as fully as they might the
role of deferential subordinates'.[15]

Circumstances therefore would lead us to expect that sections of the
tenantry would have had reservations about the legitimacy of their landlords. Instances of the perception of status as problematic can be found
in the persistence of older structures of deference. These were found
in Roscommon in the 1770s, for example, where the O'Conor family,
while still landowners, retained the aura of the greater power of their
ancestors. Arthur Young noted that Charles O'Conor of Clonalis was
treated by the common people as if he still held the ancestral O'Conor
land: 'They send him presents of cattle . . . upon various occasions.
They consider him the prince of the people involved in one common
ruin.' Similarly, Charles O'Hara, a member of one of the Gaelic families who held onto their land, was told by his tenants in 1762 that
'according to their own tradition [they] have lived under me there 500
years; 'tis their phrase.' Although the tenants were probably trying to
flatter O'Hara, the underlying idea is that his greater antiquity of status entitled him to greater respect.[16]

Sometimes the timescale of such persistence was surprisingly long.
In Kilkenny in 1746, the period and location of the activities of the
highwayman Captain Freney, an English visitor observed:

a man mounted upon a little horse, that most of the others seemed
to pay an extraordinary respect to, tho' I thought neither his figure
or dress seemed to draw it upon him . . . that person was of an ancient race . . . and though his patrimony may have been in the hands

of others for more than seven centuries.. the survivor still calls the estate his.. he enjoys it in imagination.. says, My house, my land . . . they are often allowed a cabin and a small parcel of ground rent free . . . and expect to be treated with respect by every one.

Although, as Connolly has pointed out, this sort of residual deference had 'no practical political significance', it continued to influence people's underlying attitude to landholding and status.[17]

In the later eighteenth century, as we have seen, the question of legitimacy began to focus on legal title to land. Arthur Young was told in Cork that 'a gentleman's labourer will regularly leave to his son, by will, his master's estate'. A raid on the O'Conor territory in 1786 by an armed force led by Alexander O'Conor came as a result of the apparent discovery of an old will excluding part of the estates from confiscation. O'Conor, although he 'resided in a poor cabin', 'was looked up to by the people as a prince of the royal line'.[18]

The revival of legal claim to land would still only have affected the direct descendants of landowners. By the 1790s, and certainly by the early nineteenth century, the sense of dispossession had become more general and, following the politicisation of the 1790s, more subversive. A sense of dispossession occasionally appeared among all those sharing the surname of the original holders. Col Irwin, a Sligo landlord, remembered (in the 1820s) an instance of this during the 1798 rebellion. One of Irwin's labourers had joined the French army which had landed in Mayo, and 'fought a battle with another person of his name for the lands on which I reside; he claimed them as descended from the family whom Oliver Cromwell dispossessed of them.' Their name was McSweeny, and Irwin's estate had been held by the McSweeny family, some of whom were still living in the area in the 1820s. Irwin also recollected seeing a map, owned by a man called McDermott (another dispossessed Gaelic family), an innkeeper, 'which marked out the whole forfeited properties of Connaught'. The implication is that the map represents some form of title to the land on the part of the descendants of the original holders, and that the map is a more generalised form of will. The wider social use of the concept can be seen in the comment of a traveller in the 1830s, who found, even among the poorer peasantry, 'a hankering after what they deem their rightful possessions'.[19]

The motif was later taken up and used within Catholic politics in the nineteenth century. The respect in which O'Connell was held derived much of its strength from his Gaelic gentry descent. A poem from the 1820s praising him begins with the lines:

'Sé Domhnall binn O Conaill caoin
An planda fhíor den ghaelfhuil.

[Sweet Daniel O'Connell is the true plant of Gaelic blood.]

During Tocqueville's tour of Ireland in the 1830s, he was told by a fellow passenger in a stage coach in Co. Clare that the area was originally the land of the O'Connell family, presumably an argument for the legitimacy of O'Connell's being an MP for Clare.[20]

LEGITIMACY AND CRIME

The extent to which respect for older structures survived implies a corresponding questioning of the new. The association between status and legitimacy of crime made in the criminal biography is perhaps the most potent example of this questioning, and the case of *Irish Highwaymen* shows that questioning applied to crime in general. The association of crime with status is not only made in printed popular literature, but is found within elite discourses, both English and Gaelic.

As regards elite anglophone culture, the history of the word 'tory' is a case in point. In common with terminology elsewhere in Europe, the word 'tory', 'tóraithe' meaning 'pursued', like 'bandit', signifies a condition rather than a crime, one which is not therefore wrong in itself. In British politics by the early eighteenth century it had come to describe Jacobites, adherents of an ideology which stressed the legitimate descent of the Stuarts. This double meaning is found in Begley and McCurtin's English–Irish Dictionary of 1732, which translates 'Tory' as 'Neach théid thar dlighe' [an outlaw], but 'Torys' as 'Drung dhoine do leanus go dílíos an fírlíne ríogha a gcogadh agus a síoth' [A group who faithfully support the true royal line in war and in peace].[21]

In Irish law, the term retained its original meaning until at least the late eighteenth century, although genuine tories (in the sense of bandits dislocated by the wars of the seventeenth century) had disappeared by the 1730s. The gradual elimination of an ambiguous term might be expected under such circumstances. In Italy, for example, during the French occupation of the early nineteenth century, the term 'bandit' began to be replaced by the authorities with 'brigand'. 'Brigandage', associating with other bandits, was a crime and could therefore be used to put bandits more clearly in the wrong. In contrast to Italy, therefore, an English-speaking, centralising state in Ireland which was attempting to extend the rule of law to all areas retained the Irish-derived term 'tory' which was inimical to all these purposes. The result was, as Lecky put it, that 'the tradition of the original tories . . . had a very mischievous effect in removing the stigma from agrarian crime', and possibly from other sorts of crime as well.[22]

Why was this so, and why were Freney and others in the mid-eighteenth century, ordinary housebreakers and highway robbers (albeit with some protection from sections of the gentry), referred to in the proclamations for their arrest, as 'Tories, robbers and rapparees, out in arms and on their keeping'? One reason lies in the legal provisions for the compensation of victims of robbery.

The initial legislation against tories dates from the seventeenth century, and allows for victims of tory robbery to be compensated. The compensation was to be paid by the barony or county where the robbery occurred. This was in accordance with a common law principle whereby a territory was responsible for a crime on the grounds that it sheltered the offenders. In the case of the tories, it was because they were said to be 'countenanced, harboured and concealed' by the people. One novel feature of the Act, however, was that the compensation was to be complete; for other types of robbery, the compensation was for only half the amount stolen.[23]

The provisions were generous and soon led to abuses. An Act of 1707 introduced a stricter procedure for the declaration of robberies, since 'several persons have made a trade of obtaining robbery money from the country, pretending to have been robbed'; further refinements were added in 1719. Nevertheless, the full compensation remained in force throughout the eighteenth century. It was therefore in the interest of victims of robbery to issue proclamations against tories; and to the extent that the term 'toryism' contained a legitimising principle for crime, the law itself perpetuated it.[24]

Similar legitimising can be documented in at least one case within Gaelic poetry. Dating probably from the late seventeenth century with additions in the eighteenth, it is a song in praise of a tory or rapparee, Cathal Mac Aoidh, who is presented as pursuing legitimate crime against new settlers:

> Thug siad a mbréag, ní gadaí mé féin,
> Ar son mé bheith éadrom earráideach baoth,
> 'S dá mbainfinn luach éadaigh de bhodaigh an Bhéarla,
> Cé bheadh 'na dhéidh ar Chathal Mhac Aoidh?

> [They lie, I am no robber,
> Although I am frivolous and foolish

And if I should take the price of some clothes from the
English-speaking louts
Who would blame Cathal Mac Aoidh?]

In the final verse of later versions, Mac Aoidh, though not necessarily of a landed/dispossessed family himself, is presented as being related to them, and therefore sharing their legitimacy:

Tá mo ghaol le Ó Néill, 's le Mag Uidhir ón scéith,
Is gach uaisle dá mhéid dá dtuig liom a rá,
Raghallaigh is Ruarcaigh, Mathghamhnaigh is Búrcaigh,
Gealach na gcuantaí, Cathal Mhac Aoidh.

[I am related to O'Neill and Maguire
And every noble I could mention
O'Reillys and O'Rourkes, MacMahons and Burkes
The light of the harbours, Cathal Mhac Aoidh.]

The parallel with the English language criminal biography is almost complete when Mac Aoidh is referred to as a 'captain':

Níl aon chaiptín ó Bhóinn go Doire na seol,
A scaipfeadh an t-ór le Cathal Mhac Aoidh

[There is no captain from the Boyne to Derry
Who can give out gold like Cathal Mac Aoidh.]

He is also praised, like some of the characters in *Irish Highwaymen*, for his musical accomplishments.[25]

CONSEQUENCES

The notions of status and lineage were therefore available for use as an ideological weapon against the elite in Ireland. This was not a unique phenomenon. In early modern Castile, descent and purity of blood was a preoccupation in all levels of society, since communal approval was necessary for ennoblement. Lineage therefore became 'a means by which the peasant could avenge himself on the pretensions of noble and urban wealth'. A study of the eighteenth-century gentry in Wales notes that the emergence of new gentry families, coupled with the anglicisation of older families, led to an abandonment of patronage of Welsh culture, including poetry and genealogy. 'In turn, the culture abandoned by the gentry was promoted by lower class groups, among whom it acquired plebeian and radical overtones.'[26]

More generally, ideas of reciprocal obligations within a hierarchical system underlay much popular protest in eighteenth-century Britain and Europe.[27] When elites departed from their traditional obligations, collective action by the people reminded them of their duties. It was the failure of magistrates and authorities to control food prices in poor harvest years, for example, which led to food riots. In other words, when the practice of an upper class departed from the conventions which underlay their status, they were criticised. In Ireland it was not so much the practice of the elite which did not conform to convention, but much of its personnel.

Tensions over traditional obligations typically arose when the elite no longer accepted its traditional role. This non-acceptance parallels a more general and well-documented 'withdrawal of the upper classes' from many aspects of previously shared culture. Ireland was no exception, and gentry participation in, and sponsorship of, popular activities like hurling and faction fighting declined from the eighteenth century. When this happened, the relative fragility of the ideological support of status in Ireland became clearer.[28]

The parliamentary debates referred to above indicate at least an unease among the gentry about questions of status, and at most a crisis of ideological confidence. An ideology of hierarchy was eventually articulated in Ireland in the 1780s and 1790s, in response to widespread resistance to church tithe and agitation for reform of Parliament. It made use of the justification of conquest, referring to the 1640s and 1690s, but not as a foundation myth of aristocracy. The first mature statement came in a 'Letter to the Protestants of Ireland' issued by Dublin Corporation in 1792 in opposition to the removal of Catholic civil disabilities:

> The Protestants of Ireland would not be compelled by any authority whatsoever to abandon that political situation, which their forefathers won with their swords, and which is therefore their birthright . . .

The source of military victory was not aristocratic military prowess, however, but supernatural intervention:

> . . . the question was tried upon an appeal to heaven, whether this country should become a Popish kingdom, governed by an arbitrary and unconstitutional Popish tyrant . . . or enjoy the blessings of a free Protestant government . . . The great ruler of all things decided in favour of our ancestors . . . and Ireland became a Protestant nation.[29]

The foundation and legitimisation of social and political structures in Ireland was therefore in the last analysis religious. Significantly, this statement of what came to be known as 'Protestant Ascendancy' came not from the landed classes but from an urban mercantile interest, more conscious of privileges which had a sectarian foundation.[30] The difference between hierarchy based on status and hierarchy based on religion was clear for example to Henry Grattan, landowner and MP, who supported the Catholic franchise in 1793. Refusing Catholics the right to vote, according to Grattan, produced the unnatural state of affairs whereby 'the Protestant beggar has an advantage over the Catholic proprietor'. 'Protestant Ascendancy' as an ideology was therefore more appropriate to non-aristocratic Protestants. It came to be shared, however, by many in the aristocracy.[31]

The singularity of Irish aristocracy in *ancien régime* Europe was therefore matched by the singularity of its defence. As W.J. McCormack has written, summing up a debate on the origins of the term and the concept 'Protestant Ascendancy':

> There is a fundamental difference between the general terms dealt with by . . . *Begriffsgeschichte* and the Irish notion of protestant ascendancy. In the case of 'state', 'revolution' etc. it is possible to compare a relatively large number of instances of each concept . . . With protestant ascendancy we confront the peculiar problem of a category of which there is only one instance.[32]

The shift of emphasis towards religion as the site of contest for political legitimacy after the 1790s changed the reception and interpretation of many of the motifs contained in the chapbook literature, similar to the changing perceptions of Ashton's *Battle of Aughrim*. The question of land title, for example, came to have religious dimensions as well as legal and genealogical. Protestant pamphleteers maintained that the Catholic church advocated the reclaiming of forfeited land:

> It seems to be a principle of the Popish faith, that Catholics may and ought to drive out heretics from any lands or possessions . . . on the other hand that no time can sanction the title of a heretic to lands which had ever at any time belonged to Catholics.[33]

The term 'tory' equally took on religious as well as lineage connotations in the heightened atmosphere of religious rivalry in early nineteenth-century Ulster. A sectarian fight which took place in Co. Londonderry in 1813 was described from the Protestant point of view in a ballad printed in 1815, containing the following description of the Catholic attack:

> The tory whistle, loud and shrill
> Did quick resound o'er moor and hill,
> Fall on brave boys, destroy and kill
> All Protestants in Garvagh.

That the memory of dispossession also lingered in the area is evident from the later account of the battle in the autobiography of a young onlooker. Some of the wounded, he wrote, were taken to the demesne of Lord Garvagh, where:

> the chief caretaker of the grounds was an aristocratic-looking man called Kane – a Roman Catholic, who was said to be a lineal descendant of the original owners of the estate.[34]

Most of the political motifs of Irish chivalric and bandit literature are found here: aristocracy, lineal transmission of 'superior' features, dispossession and outlawry, overlaid with a sectarian dimension which ensured the continuing relevance and attraction of that popular literature in the nineteenth century.

11 Popular Print and Popular Culture

Most studies of literacy and print culture in the historiography of eighteenth- and nineteenth-century Ireland approach them from the point of view of economic or political history. For economic history, literacy has a double significance. On the one hand, it acts as a measure of relative wealth, as an indication that people have money to invest in education and that there are returns on such an investment. On the other hand, a certain level of literacy is posited as a prerequisite for development, since it permits greater participation in a market economy as well as the diffusion of innovations. For political history, mass literacy is seen as indispensable for large-scale mobilisation which, in the form of nationalist movements, is seen to be the most important development of the period. It does this both structurally, by making possible the coordination of agents over a wide area, and ideologically, by creating an awareness of a community of interest among separate groups.

Reading, writing and publishing are therefore measured and described as structural phenomena characteristic of large regions or of Ireland as a whole. The focus is on the rise or decline of national literacy levels and the provision of schools, and on the creation of communications networks, usually corresponding to market areas. These areas come to form cultural units through a process of homogenisation due to the mass circulation of information in newspapers and other printed forms, and through attendance at the national school system. Thus, according to Cullen, 'by 1851 half the population was literate . . . [and from then on] public opinion hardened and deepened irreversibly in a remarkably homogeneous form of expression.' Organisationally, this manifested itself in the difference between the O'Connelite mass organisations of the 1820s and 1840s, which were coordinated by an educated elite, and the national agrarian agitation of the 1870s, which was initiated from below, mainly through notices in newspapers. Ideologically, the structures of communication permitted the diffusion of the successive forms of nationalism characteristic of those movements.[1]

As the case of the tract societies and the United Irishmen demonstrates, however, such diffusion was never a straightforward process.

Different groups reacted in different ways to the content of printed media, and that content was best understood by those who were already predisposed to accept it. Levels of literacy and structures of communication do not in themselves constitute a complete explanation of change, whether economic, political or cultural. Literacy and printing are not neutral technologies which are uniform in their effects, and their impact depends on how they are adopted and used by groups and by individuals.

This study has approached the reception and appropriation of print culture through some of the most frequently read popular texts. Much of what has been said about that reception has been inferential. An interpretation of *Irish Highwaymen*, for example, was suggested by a comparison with English and French criminal biography as well as with folk memory of dispossession. More generally, successful texts were those which could be adapted relatively smoothly to the conventions of oral culture, and which established themselves within specific oral practices. The romances were located in the context of the reading aloud of Irish-language manuscript romances. *The Battle of Aughrim* was performed as a folk play and a Protestant foundation ritual. The songs of the *Pious Miscellany* were absorbed into the ceremonial of the funeral wake and into other forms of domestic Catholic religious practice.

This is an argument for a degree of continuity between the printed and the oral, but it is clear that their reciprocal influence was itself a process of change. Some aspects of oral practice were gradually transformed by the penetration of texts from print, as in the case of the *Pious Miscellany*. At the same time, in the case of *James Freney* for example, the character of printed books was altered to a greater or lesser degree by their reception.

READING ALOUD

One form of transformation which applied frequently to all the texts was that they became oral recitations, performances or simply rumours, repeated to others quite independently of the printed book. The most obvious way in which this happened was through the practice of reading aloud, the classic way in which written texts entered an oral culture when a society or group was partially literate. Reading aloud, or 'collective reading', has been the subject of some recent investigation, and some of its characteristics are worth stressing.[2]

Within French historiography, much of the discussion of the reading aloud of the *Bibliothèque Bleue* has centred on whether or not it took place at the peasant *veillée*, a regular village gathering during winter nights for working and storytelling. Mandrou, Bollème and others saw the *veillée* as the central locus of group reading, but more recent writers have stressed that no description of the *veillée* specifically mentions the reading of books. Chartier considers such collective reading to be a romantic motif, 'a better indication of the nostalgia or the expectations of literate people at the end of the eighteenth century than of peasant practices'. More sceptical still is Guilcher, who doubts whether reading aloud of any kind was practised within peasant society.[3]

This debate refers principally to France between the sixteenth and the eighteenth centuries. In Ireland, gatherings at night for storytelling, known as 'áirneáil' or 'scoraíocht', were a central feature of rural life from the eighteenth to the twentieth centuries, and the principal locus of transmission of oral literature. The reading of manuscripts in Irish at these gatherings is well attested, both by observers and by the evidence of the manuscripts themselves. There seems no reason to suppose that printed books would not also have been read aloud, or that storytellers would not have taken material from them for recitation at such gatherings. In any case, what is being referred to as 'reading aloud' is the recitation of a printed text, whether the printed object itself is present or not. Material from Ó Súilleabháin's *Pious Miscellany* was sung at another of the formal occasions of recitation, the funeral wake, and the printed text may or may not have been present.[4]

Where books were present, reading aloud was usually undertaken for material and financial reasons as well as cultural ones. There were few printed texts in rural areas, and although chapbooks were not expensive, they were nevertheless a luxury for the poorer classes. Moreover, the opportunities for buying them were infrequent, a trip to a town for a fair, or the visit of a travelling pedlar. Newspapers were even more expensive, and would usually be read aloud by the large farmers, schoolteachers or priests, who were able to afford them. If the books were read at night, lighting was ineffective and expensive; and many older people, even if they were able to read, would suffer from failing eyesight and would need to be read to.

As a cultural practice, and in so far as construction or transformation of the meaning of a text is concerned, it is useful to distinguish two types of reading aloud, which can be characterised as 'vertical' and 'horizontal'.

In the vertical kind, there is a hierarchy, whether social or cultural or both, which places the reader above the listener. The better off would read to the less well off, the learned would read to the unlearned, and the literate would read to the illiterate, in classic forms of cultural mediation. One of the most frequent instances would be that of a clergy-man reading scripture aloud in church and explaining a particular bib-lical passage. Such reading aloud could sometimes amount to a form of translation. This process was described by an Anglican clergyman in the preface to an Irish-language version of the life of Christ in 1849, in which he contrasts the formal Irish contained in the seventeenth-century Irish versions of the Bible with the everyday Irish of Co. Londonderry:

> A few persons of better capacity and information (such as in their schooldays might be competent to act as teachers and monitors of classes) may learn it by a certain degree of study; but for these to render it intelligible to others to whom they may read it, they must omit, alter and paraphrase as they go along, substituting modern words for old ones, and popular for grammatical expressions.[5]

The practice of 'vertical reading' is well attested in Ireland in the late eighteenth and early nineteenth centuries, particularly for newspapers:

> The writer has often known Cox's Magazine to be read aloud to a crowd of villagers on a Sunday evening, while the people swallowed down every word, and imbibed every principle, more deeply instilled by the comments of the reader.

> The men whom you saw are poor labourers who have finished their day's work, and they are gathered together at the door of the school so that the teacher, when he has finished his lessons, can read the newspapers aloud.
> 'And who gives them this newspaper' I asked.
> 'I get it' said the priest.

> [A travelling labourer working on a large farm] was always anxious to hear the newspapers, which Mr. S— [the owner], as is not unusual in this part of Ireland, often read to the labourers of an evening, after their work was finished.[6]

In all these cases, there is a relationship of power (or at least social hierarchy) involved: texts are read to labourers and small farmers by gentlemen, teachers or priests. In terms of reception, this represents a more or less straightforward diffusion downwards. The content is chosen by the reader, not only because of literacy, but also because of the expense of newspapers.[7] Moreover, the texts would be chosen and read in such a way as to underline the reader's point of view, as when Cox's magazine was 'more deeply instilled by the comments of the reader', and the meaning of the text could be heavily influenced by that reader.

One striking feature of this first type of reading aloud is its formality and regularity. It happens 'on Sunday evening', 'after work', 'after mass'. The best-known Irish picture of reading aloud, Henry McManus's *Reading 'The Nation'*, painted in the 1840s, shows the action taking place after mass.[8] This use of fixed times suggests that the audiences were large and that the occasions were seen as important and not to be missed.

Some commentators see reading aloud as always underlining the superior prestige of the literate.[9] This view, essentially diffusionist, is also the one most frequently found in Irish historiography, particularly in discussions of popular politicisation in the 1790s, focusing on the propaganda campaign of the United Irishmen. It was not the only manifestation of the practice, however, and reading aloud could equally well take place between equals, what can be called 'horizontal' reading.

This was partly because cultural hierarchies did not always coincide with social or familial ones. In 1814, for example, a farmer named Cornelius Duggan received a threatening letter from a labourer. Duggan was unable to read, and took the letter to Thomas Bourke, a labourer in his employment, who read it to him. Likewise, in a period of expanding education, children were frequently literate when their parents were not, and could read to them. Edmund Rice in 1810 described how 'the boys [in his school in Waterford] read the library books for their parents at night and on Sundays'. It is even recommended as a practice in some popular printed texts, as in the preface to an Irish translation of *Think Well On't*, published in Clonmel in 1819:

Anois couairlim done haihaireacha agus do na mahaireacha a chuir diachuivi air a gclann (ma is sgolairiye iad) a leihead seo docheannach agus caibiodail de do leayav go minic do vuintir an tige.

[I advise fathers and mothers to make their children (if they are scholars) buy this book and frequently to read a chapter to the household.]

A similar instruction is found in a preface to some editions of the *Pious Miscellany*: 'During the long nights of winter, a hymn or song out of this litle book may be sung in every Roman Catholic family.' An extreme, but frequent, version of this phenomenon would be the case of illiterate monoglot Irish-speaking parents whose children had learnt to read English: the children would provide a simultaneous translation when reading.[10]

Moreover, it was frequently the case that the listeners were able to read themselves. Material constraints meant that in a group of literates, some or all of whom wanted to read a text, one would read it aloud to the others. Such a practice also functioned as a form of sociability, a 'group reading' similar to those practices within elite culture described by Chartier. In many areas of Ireland from about 1820, such horizontal reading probably became more frequent, as the economic downturn reduced disposable income while at the same time literacy rates continued to rise with the state funding of primary education. In areas of deindustrialisation there was a reduced demand for child labour which actually freed children to go to school. There was therefore an increasing number of readers, but they were not necessarily able to buy a correspondingly larger number of texts. The decades before the Famine were certainly a golden age for the cheapest collectively read (or sung) text, the single-sheet ballad.

These 'horizontal' forms of reading aloud probably had many interruptions, explanations, comments and criticisms, constituting a kind of communal determination of the meaning of a text. This facilitated the entry of printed texts into a communal, predominantly oral culture, in which such practices already existed. Commentary and participation were characteristic of certain oral genres, particularly the historical legend, or narratives concerning local beliefs and traditions. The following description of storytelling in Co. Londonderry in the early nineteenth century is an example:

> The manner of preserving the accuracy of tradition . . . in the winter evenings, a number of seanachies [storytellers] frequently meet together and recite alternately their traditional stories. If anyone repeats a passage, which appears to another to be incorrect, he is immediately stopped, and each gives his reason for his way of reciting the passage, and the dispute is then referred to a vote of the meeting.[11]

Given that chapbooks were frequently (and in the eighteenth century perhaps mostly) read in this way, it is not surprising that those texts which were suitable for reading aloud were popular. For narrative texts such as romances and criminal biography, this was facilitated by their episodic form, the larger narrative broken into many small sections. Listeners might come and go during the reading, and there were plenty of points at which the reading could be suspended. These texts also provided constant excitement – in a romance, armies and giants were killed on every second page. This feature in fact made them unsuited to continuous reading, and partly explains the disdain felt after the mid-eighteenth century on the part of more cultured elite readers, more accustomed to silent individual reading and a 'global' comprehension of the text.[12]

The transformations effected by this mode of transmission varied, and cannot necessarily be deduced from the text or its typographical appearance. Changes were least likely where texts were closest to an oral original; this was probably the case with a collection of international folk tales such as *The Seven Wise Masters of Rome*. On the other hand, the printed text of a romance may frequently have been used as the basis for a more improvised, oral telling of the story. In other instances, changes could be quite radical. The example in Chapter 8 of the oral retellings of the Carleton story discussed by Earls shows the written text being stripped down to its bare essentials, losing much of the author's moral intentions in the process.

Another type of transformation resulting from the episodic nature of narrative and the discontinuous style of reading meant that individual fragments of texts could survive in oral tradition. In the twentieth-century folklore collections, by far the most frequent item from *Irish Highwaymen* was a story in which Redmond O'Hanlon is outwitted by a boy whom he attempts to rob. Ó hÓgáin has pointed out that this is a standard migratory legend, which accounts for its acceptance and survival. At the same time, however, it is a very unrepresentative section of the printed life of O'Hanlon, since it is the only occasion on which he loses a confrontation.[13]

Finally, a character from a printed text could enter the oral tradition without any of his accompanying narrative. This is the case with the fairly frequent folklore concerning James Freney. Despite the popularity of his chapbook life, few of the folklore stories originated in the printed text. Where O'Hanlon's status is perhaps diminished, Freney's by contrast is enhanced, since the oral sources present him as far more of a bandit-hero than does the printed text. Any printed text therefore needs to be read and interpreted in the light of such oral preoccupations, bearing in mind that the 'psychodynamics of orality' can have a radically transforming effect on the content of such texts.[14]

THE PROPHECIES OF PASTORINI

Orality was not the only transforming aspect of the reception of printed texts. There is one well-documented case of a printed 'popular' text being appropriated and changed by the entire cosmology of Irish-language popular culture in the early nineteenth century. The text in question is the Bible, more precisely, the New Testament, which was distributed in large quantities, both in English and Irish, by evangelical and 'improving' societies from about 1800 on, along with their chapbooks.

In the 1820s, some verses from the Book of Revelation provided a strong vein of millenarianism to an agrarian protest movement of those years in the south of Ireland. Of course, Revelation is notoriously liable to different interpretations, but the use made of it by the rural lower classes in this period illustrates not only a transformation of meaning consequent on appropriation, but also the way in which the intentions of those who wrote and distributed printed material could be subverted.[15]

The protest movement in question, known as the Rockites, received enormous popular support in southern Ireland, and was directed against the tithes which a mainly Catholic population paid to the state Anglican church. The agricultural depression in the years after 1815, coupled with a series of bad harvests and a famine in 1822, made these tithes more onerous, and led to demands for their reduction or suspension. There were violent attacks on tithe collectors, on soldiers sent to enforce collection, and on those who paid tithe despite the prohibitions of the Rockites.

Sporadic agrarian protest movements were widespread in rural Ireland in the years 1760–1845, and were directed at the regulation of mainly economic issues such as rent, tithe and agricultural employment. The Rockite movement was one of the largest of these movements, lasting four or five years in perhaps ten counties, and it was remarkable among the agrarian movements for the extent to which millenarian ideas were part of its ideology. These millenarian ideas were those contained in the so-called prophecies of Pastorini, which circulated widely in pamphlet and broadsheet form in the southern parts of Ireland from about 1815. These were derived from a longer work, *The General History of the Christian Church*, which was a commentary on the Book of Revelation by Pastorini, the pen name of Charles Walmesley, an English Benedictine Bishop, which was first published in 1771.[16] The particular section which circulated in pamphlet form in Ireland concerned Chapters 4–8, describing the opening of phials by an angel prior to the Second Coming.

There are six phials in all, each of which Pastorini's exegesis equates with 300-year periods, beginning with the death of Christ. The sixth phial or period, beginning about 1525, saw the rise and then the destruction of evil forces, in which Pastorini includes Protestantism. This interpretation forecast, therefore, the destruction of Protestant churches in 1825, and was explosive in the context of a largely sectarian agitation against a Protestant established church in the early 1820s.

Until recently, accounts of Irish rural protest and revolt stressed the relative absence of prophecy and expectations of supernatural intervention, whether millenarian or messianic. This was explained by the rationality of these movements and the practicality of their immediate goals. More recently, the emphasis has changed. Apart from Donnelly's work on the 1820s, there have been treatments of the role of prophecy in the disturbances and rebellion of the 1790s, particularly in the north of Ireland, and among both Presbyterians and Catholics; and of messianic elements in Gaelic culture, particularly in Munster.[17] Pastorini, therefore, was entering a culture in which supernatural assistance or deliverance was an established motif.[18]

Pastorini's *General History* marked a significant departure, however, as it was a scholarly text from elite culture, based on one of the two classic biblical millenarian books, the Book of Revelation.[19] It is a prophecy which is based on a tortuous mathematical interpretation of a scriptural text. Prophecies of this sort had circulated in the north of Ireland in the 1790s and before, but mainly among Presbyterians, whose culture was more biblically based than that of their Catholic neighbours.[20] The prophecies of the Catholic Defenders of the 1790s were usually messianic rather than millenarian. Where they contained biblical elements, they were often parts of the Bible which had been long absorbed into Gaelic culture, such as the Book of Exodus, large parts of which were incorporated in the Gaelic Irish origin legend and in Gaelic folk-history. These presented the Irish as Israelites in Egypt, to be led out of captivity by a leader with supernatural qualities.[21]

The question is therefore why a biblically-based millenarianism, closer to conventional European forms, should have emerged with such force in Irish popular culture around 1820. There is of course the obvious fact that the interpretation of Pastorini was directed at the 1820s, and specifically at the year 1825. However, prophecies can always be adapted to suit particular dates, and this only explains the appeal of the particular arithmetic of the exegesis, leaving unanswered the question of why this form of prophecy should have emerged at that point.

More important is the distribution of Bibles by Protestant evangelical societies, coupled with the growth of literacy in those years. From the early years of the nineteenth century, thousands of Bibles, in both Irish and English, had been distributed throughout Ireland as part of a pacifying missionary effort. Although the number of conversions may not have been great, this 'second reformation' had a strong impact in many areas, not least because of its use of Irish in evangelising. According to one Catholic priest in 1824:

> I have myself been a Catholic missionary in the county of Kilkenny for some years . . . I have found Irish Bibles in many poor cabins which were there many months unknown to me or to any other priest . . . Reading a Protestant Bible without leave in Ireland renders a man more liable to ecclesiastical censures. And yet they were read with more pleasure and more frequently than Catholic prayer books because they were in Irish.[22]

Many lower-class Catholics in Munster would therefore have seen and heard the biblical texts in question for the first time in this period, and perhaps have acquired sufficient knowledge of the text to make comprehensible a relatively scholarly exegesis of a section of the Book of Revelation. The prophecy would have derived much of its force from this novelty. A similar process took place in parts of the Highlands of Scotland in the same period, following similar evangelical activity in which Bibles in English and Gaelic were distributed. A landlord who refused to negotiate rent reductions was criticised by his tenants in terms taken from the Book of Revelation. They 'began to talk of . . . their rights, as the Elect few, to possess the earth'.[23]

The timing of the popularity of Pastorini in Ireland can also be explained in the context of the messianic elements within Irish-language culture. Since the late seventeenth century at least, it had contained a motif of expectation of deliverance. In the seventeenth century, it was to come from a mythical warrior, Ball Dearg O'Donnell; in the eighteenth, it was to come from the exiled Stuarts, and later from Catholic France, which was to send military assistance; and in the early nineteenth century it was to be Napoleon, who was a frequent hero of Irish ballads. After the defeat of Napoleon in 1815, however, there was no longer a hope of deliverance coming from France. A culture so strongly permeated by expectation of deliverance needed a new source of hope, a role that was soon filled by the Biblical interpretation of Pastorini.

This final reason may seem excessively functionalist. It is striking however, that when 1825 came and went without the destruction of the Protestant Church, expectations were transferred almost immediately to Daniel O'Connell, who is presented in many ballads as Moses leading the Irish/Israelites out of captivity:

> The bondage of the Israelites our saviour He did see,
> He then commanded Moses for to go to set them free,
> And in the same we did remain suffering for our own
> Till God He sent O'Connell for to free the church of Rome.[24]

The Book of Revelation and Pastorini's exegesis were therefore absorbed into a strong, indigenous prophetic/messianic tradition, and were altered to suit that tradition. Thus, the account of Pastorini given by the contemporary Munster folk poet Tomás Ruadh Ó Súilleabháin adds the economic and military aspects which are not to be found in Pastorini's text itself, but were fundamental to the indigenous tradition:

> Go bhfuil sé scríofa i bPastoriní
> Go maithfear cíos do Ghaedhalaibh
> 's go mbeidh fairrgidhe breac le flít ag teacht
> Isteach thar phoinnte Chléire.

[It is written in Pastorini that the Irish will not have to pay rent, and that the seas will be speckled with ships coming around Cape Clear.][25]

Within this messianic tradition, the popularity of Pastorini marks a shift in style. The older prophetic tradition was embodied mainly in the Irish-language texts which circulated orally and in manuscript. Pastorini was printed, written in English, and its power depended on familiarity with the Bible, which in most cases was introduced in English. Thus Antoine Raiftearaí, a Connaught folk poet contemporary with Ó Súilleabháin, uses the English word 'Revelation' in an Irish-language poem, rather than an Irish-language equivalent.[26]

Even more clearly than the chapbooks, therefore, the case of Pastorini shows a popular culture appropriating and transforming those elements in print culture which corresponded to its own motifs. Considered in a wider context of social order and unrest, moreover, this appropriation diametrically opposes the intentions of the elite groups who circulated the texts. This is true not only of the Bible, but also of Pastorini's *General History* itself.

Pastorini, or Walmesley, born in 1722, was in his early career a Catholic Enlightenment figure who was interested in Newtonian science and published treatises on trigonometry and lunar motions. The *General History* combines a Catholic view of Revelation, stressing the

ultimate defeat of Protestantism, with a use of mathematics for ex-
egetical purposes which derives from Newton's later works. It had an
immediate success in scholarly clerical circles on the continent, being
translated into Italian, Spanish, French and German.[27]

By the 1790s, however, the *General History* was being reprinted,
with the author's approval, as an anti-revolutionary tract, and the French
Revolution was interpreted as part of the trials of the church towards
the end of the 'fifth age', which was to last from 1525 to 1825. It was
in this spirit that the initial editions of Pastorini in Ireland were published, 'undoubtedly encouraged, if not actually engineered, by the British
government', according to Scott, and with the support of the Catholic
hierarchy. Thus, the introduction to the 1805 Dublin edition states that
the French were 'guilty of attacking God's regent', and criticised the
Revolution for having attacked property. In Catholic elite culture in
Ireland, therefore, Pastorini was regarded and printed as a politically
conservative work.

From about 1815 onwards, the sections of the work dealing with the
destruction of Protestantism in the 1820s were being reprinted separately as small pamphlets and broadsheets and used in support of the
anti-tithe agitation. Given that 'Protestantism' in Ireland in the early
nineteenth century meant an entire political and social system, the prophecy had by then become radical rather than conservative – the over-
throw of Protestantism would have meant social revolution.

As for the Bible, this was distributed largely by Protestant missionary societies, and like the improving tracts, was intended both to convert and to encourage social stability. In practice, at least as far as the
Book of Revelation was concerned, the effect was entirely the opposite. In other words, the peasants and farmers of Munster in the 1820s
had appropriated scripture from a Protestant elite and an exegesis from
a Catholic elite, and used the mixture to attack the state church and
the Protestant establishment in a way which embarrassed and frightened middle- and upper-class Catholics. Pastorini was condemned by
the Catholic hierarchy and its popularity denied by Catholic political
leaders.[28]

The appropriation, as well as the strength of prophecy in popular
culture, was well understood by Bishop Doyle of Kildare, who condemned
the use of Pastorini in a pastoral letter directed at the Rockites in 1822:

> There have been to our own knowledge instances of persons neglecting
> their domestic concerns and abandoning their families to misery and
> want, through a vain hope, grounded on some supposed prophecy,

'that mighty changes were just approaching'. For more than half a century, it was predicted that George IV would not reign: and his very appearance among you was scarcely sufficient to dispel the illusion . . .

But you will tell me that your prophecy is not of this kind, that it is derived from the sacred scriptures, as they are explained in the book of Pastorini, called *The History of the Christian Church*. That book, dearest brethren, has been perverted to very different ends from those which the pious author intended.[29]

The Rockite movement was not a minor occurrence. It involved large numbers of people throughout Munster and the midlands, produced a striking level of violence during three or four years, and necessitated the deployment of over 20 000 regular army troops. Its use of Pastorini's prophecies shows how the motifs of popular culture, influenced in this case by a particular historical conjuncture, could transform the original intent of a widely circulated printed text, and make it the vehicle of quite a different ideology.

APPROACHES TO POPULAR CULTURE

The example of Pastorini and of the chapbook texts in general shows a reciprocity of influence between readers and texts. Printed books were read in 'oral' ways; English-language texts were read in the light of Irish-language preoccupations; conservative theological texts from the official church became the foundation of a radical popular millenarianism. The diversity and complexity of the resulting interpretations demonstrates the difficulties and shortcomings of a system of classification of texts such as that discussed in the introduction. By the same token, it demonstrates similar problems in applying such categories to the overall cultures of reception of those texts, and in conceptualising popular and local cultures in eighteenth- and nineteenth-century Ireland.

Studies of these cultures come in a variety of forms, and from a number of different disciplines. There are studies of particular aspects of folk or material life, based on a combination of twentieth-century fieldwork and the reports of eighteenth- and nineteenth-century ethnographers. These include topics such as farming implements, storytelling or calendar customs. Others have focused on a particular regional culture, emphasising its local specificity. Whelan, for example, has identified an area of East Munster and south Leinster characterised by continuity of settlement patterns and the consequent persistence of many older cultural forms and practices, such as the sport of hurling. There is a large and growing literature on peasant political organisation, drawing on studies of popular protest elsewhere, and viewing it as a constituent of later political movements, both parliamentary and agrarian.[30]

These and other studies have emphasised the extent to which economic and social change, usually described as 'modernisation', was reflected in cultural practices, and how elite movements for moral reform and 'improvement' of popular culture, such as the temperance crusade, worked in parallel with this wider change.[31] The most comprehensive such reform was that undertaken by the Catholic church, and this has produced a correspondingly large historiography. This literature offers a point of departure for consideration of the issue of the conceptualisation and categorisation of popular cultures.[32]

These social histories of popular Catholicism have described a broad range of the beliefs and practices which existed in eighteenth- and early nineteenth-century Ireland. As guides to people's religion as a system of belief, however, they suffer from a major, perhaps inevitable, drawback. Their focus is primarily on the institutional church and on its success in establishing or consolidating itself as a social and political force in the eighteenth and nineteenth centuries. This process provides the narrative thrust of most of the accounts. The principal disagreements have been over the precise timing of the process, whether it occurred before or after the Famine of the 1840s; and over how rapid and typical it was, whether it was a 'devotional revolution' unique to Ireland and resulting from the specific economic and political conjuncture of mid-nineteenth century Ireland, or whether it was a delayed Tridentine reform on the European model.

One of the principal aims of the Catholic church in this process was the extension of clerical control over all sources of supernatural power in society and the encouragement of regular and disciplined observance, and historians have emphasised the assaults of the clergy on unapproved beliefs and practices. Within this framework, 'popular' religion has been defined either in opposition to official religion, or residually as the non-orthodox, 'magical' or 'superstitious' beliefs of the laity.

The result of this perspective, and of the historians' necessarily heavy reliance on ecclesiastical sources, is somewhat to skew the overall picture of popular religion by treating as fundamental a distinction which probably did not exist in the mentality or culture of the laity, that between orthodox and non-orthodox beliefs. This distinction is clerical in origin, and indeed one of the first steps in religious reform was for the clergy to persuade or educate the laity to make this distinction themselves. The church's desire for reform therefore implies that the distinction did not previously exist in popular culture.[33]

Historians, then, have taken over the categories used in clerical sources, some even to the extent of using a term like 'superstition' as if it had an objective meaning, or using phrases like 'non-christian but harmless beliefs'.[34] This is not to say that they have altogether adopted the attitudes of the clergy – all are sympathetic to the non-orthodox forms of belief and practice (although there is a clear tendency to treat them in a more functionalist manner than orthodox Christianity). Nevertheless, the rigid use of these categories falsifies what was a continuous range of belief in popular culture. To write that 'the Catholic laity of the eighteenth and nineteenth centuries had little difficulty in reconciling popular magic and orthodox Catholic doctrine' or that 'superstition [was] woven into orthodox religious practice' implies that the laity were aware of the difference and that the combination of elements was a conscious act.[35]

The problems of categorisation go deeper, and can call into question the use of a category such as 'religion' itself. Creating a distinction between sacred and profane was one of the fundamental aims of both Protestant and Catholic reformations, and according to Stuart Clark, 'the distinction between "religious" and other activities often had little meaning until the the coming of reform, and then only to reformers'. It was a distinction which would still have made little sense to the eighteenth- and nineteenth-century Irish peasantry, and what strikes modern observers of so-called 'traditional celtic spirituality' most strongly, for example, is the extension of religious feeling into every area of life without exception. The same would go for most pre-modern societies: physical environment was sacred, religion was life and vice versa.[36]

The use of analogous categories underlies much of the historiography of eighteenth- and nineteenth-century Irish popular culture discussed above, and of discussions of literacy and printing. These categories derive from modernisation theory, which is probably the dominant influence on the writing of Irish cultural history of this period. (The term 'modernisation' is ubiquitous in this literature, although, like 'superstition', it is rarely given an explicit definition.) Cultural change is presented as a transition from a 'traditional' society to a 'modern' one, and these are conceptualised as ideal-type constructions, seen in terms of a specific series of polarities or dichotomies, which are considered to be roughly co-extensive. They can be set out as follows:

Oral	————	*Literate/print*
Irish language	————	*English language*
Popular/folk religion	————	*Official Catholicism*

In economic terms:

Subsistence	————	*Commercialised*

and overall:

Traditional	————	*Modern*

This scheme is usually presented as a model of cultural change, whereby rural Ireland in this period is described as shifting, more or less continuously and inevitably, from the categories on the left to those on the right. Over the long term, it is true that a process of this kind can be detected, but such an account has a number of problems as the basis of a cultural history of eighteenth- and nineteenth-century Ireland. Descriptively, as will be clear from the case of language and popular printing, it misses much of the complexity of cultural practice at any given time.

At a theoretical level, it is open to many of the criticisms made of early schemas of modernisation. It conceives change as being mainly internal to a system and proceeding smoothly, ignoring the effect of external forces. In the Irish case, there was one significant exogenous event in the form of the Great Famine of the 1840s. The Famine is incorporated into modernisation schemas in either of two ways. Sometimes it is said to have been a psychological shock, demonstrating to those who lived through it the disadvantages of traditional ways, whether of agriculture or religious belief. More usually, it is presented as a sudden alteration in the structure of rural society, decimating the labourers and smaller farmers. Since these groups were the most traditional in outlook, and since traditional culture was in decline before the Famine, the Famine is therefore said to have accelerated change, rather than initiating it, and therefore as an agent of modernisation, albeit a spectacularly destructive one.

More relevant to discussion of the late eighteenth and early nineteenth centuries are two other assumptions which early forms of modernisation theory made about cultural change.[37] The first is that tradition and modernity are two mutually exclusive categories or sets of categories, and that a growth of the 'modern' qualities automatically entails a corresponding decline of the 'traditional' ones. A standard article on the decline of Irish is devoted almost entirely to the spread of English, for example, while the growth in orthodox (Catholic) religious observance is frequently taken to necessitate a decline in folk religion, and is measured in that way.[38]

The second assumption is that the sets of oppositions or dichotomies form functionally interdependent wholes, and that therefore change in one domain entails change in the other domains. Language and religion are linked, for example, in two ways. Some of the decline in popular religious belief is attributed to the decline of Irish, since that belief would have been predominantly expressed in Irish. It has also been suggested that as Irish speaking declined, official Catholicism replaced the Irish language as the communally cohesive force in Irish society. As regards literacy, much writing on this period assumes literacy to have been acquired exclusively in English, and that language change was to a large extent a consequence of the demand for literacy.[39]

Both sorts of assumption can be seen in an analysis like that of Connolly, discussing the early nineteenth century:

> Education brought with it literacy, openness to outside influences, and the abandonment of traditional modes of thought and action . . . The process of social change can be traced in the decline of the Irish language . . .[40]

The history of popular literacy and popular culture in this period provides counter-examples to most of this analysis. As regards the first assumption, the 'zero-sum equation', Lee has recently emphasised the logical difficulties inherent in attributing the decline of Irish to the growth of English. In the domain of Catholicism, an increasing orientation of belief and practice towards parish church and clergy was not incompatible with continued adherence to other forms of religion. As the folklore about magical deeds performed by priests suggests, the increasing social prominence of the clergy was expressed partly in terms of their power over the local supernatural, that is, within the framework of traditional belief. Taylor's study of nineteenth- and twentieth-century Donegal shows a continuing and dynamic relationship between official and local or popular religion. In a telling example, he explores the different attitudes towards alcoholic priests which were held by the official church and by the priest's congregation. To the former, the priest was inefficient and embarrassing; to the latter, his perceived magical powers were held to be greater. The contrast was extreme in the case of a priest who was defrocked for excessive drinking, since the church held him to have reduced powers, while for the people they were increased as his person was no longer subject to church discipline. In other words, the greater discipline and control characteristic of a more modern church régime, instead of diminishing local beliefs, could actually provide those beliefs with a stronger focus.[41]

As regards the second assumption, it is not at all clear that the categories are interlinked in the way the model suggests. A growth in literacy was compatible with, and indeed aided by, a decline in the commercialised economy in some rural areas. The collapse of the domestic textile industry in the north and west after 1830, which removed the cash income from many families and areas, actually freed children to attend school, since their labour became less valuable in the home. In the area of literacy and print, the success of the *Pious Miscellany* as well as the frequent printings of Irish-language catechisms in early nineteenth-century Munster show that both print literacy and orthodox Catholicism existed in Irish. Moreover, folk religion continued despite language shift, and popular religious practices were still being condemned by diocesan synods in English-speaking areas in the twentieth century. Folk religion could even benefit from some aspects of modernity. The best attended pattern pilgrimage in the Leitrim–Roscommon area in the 1890s, for example, was at Lasser well, Kilronan; this was because it was near the railway and special trains were put on for it, despite its having been condemned by the Catholic clergy.[42]

In other words, 'traditional' and 'modern' features could and did coexist and even be mutually reinforcing. Cultural change, therefore, did not always follow the directions and the mechanisms assumed by the tradition/modernity model. As some critics of modernisation theories have pointed out, such distinctions were originally elaborated as typological rather than chronological. In much of the Irish historiography, tradition and modernity are treated chronologically, and in the case of the eighteenth and nineteenth centuries, are located outside the period. The result is that the culture of the period is discussed principally in terms of reference points external to it, and is characterised as being somehow inherently unsatisfactory or problematic. This is evident, for example, in the vocabulary of cognitive dissonance used by the historians of religion cited above, in the observations that 'the whole atmosphere of pre-Famine Catholicism was one of ambiguity', or that 'on account of the many transitional elements in its character, Ireland was an unstable society'.[43] It is not necessary to subscribe to a conception of culture as a single coherent unit to realise that such approaches will have difficulties doing justice to the lived experience of the period.

At the most fundamental level, the problem may be due not only to the categories used for analysis but also to the objects of analysis chosen. To categorise beliefs and practices as 'sacred' or 'profane', 'official' and 'popular', to write about 'the Irish language' or 'the English language' in the nineteenth century, is to write the history of ideas rather than culture, a history in which people become the more or less awkward carriers of these ideas. The fact that they can carry what looks to the modern eye like a collection of distinct or contradictory ideas then becomes unnecessarily problematic. As noted in the context of popular religion, the distinctions would not have made sense to the actors, and miss the coherence as well as the complexity of cultural practice at any given time.

An ethnographic approach, whether to reading or religious practice, avoids many of these difficulties. Ideally, the approach to popular literature taken in this book would be complemented by an study of a small group or even an individual, building a picture of a local print culture. This would place reading practices in the context of a whole life experience, showing how they related to other aspects of life, perhaps in ways which are not immediately apparent. This latter approach, however, while well grounded, has a reciprocal need of a wider survey of printed popular literature, both to fill the gaps in documentation which are inevitable in studies of non-elite groups in the past and in order to grasp the specificity and the typicality of local experience.

This study, therefore, is based on texts. It has attempted to show something of popular culture or cultures by exploring the ways in which those texts were produced, read, interpreted and reproduced. The process of diffusion and reception of chapbook texts is, of course, not the whole of popular culture, but it presents an opportunity to see that culture in a dynamic setting, transforming and renewing itself.

Appendix:
Editions of Texts

CHIVALRIC ROMANCE

Surviving copies of chapbooks of chivalric romance frequently lack dates, and establishing a precise bibliography is difficult. Chapmen's lists including all four titles discussed are found in:

The Trojan Wars, printed by Anne Law, Dublin, 1759.
Ascanius, or the young adventurer, printed for R.J[ackson], Dublin, 1779.

Adams lists Belfast editions and advertisements as follows:

The Seven Champions of Christendom: 1729, 1731, 1766, 1772, 1777, 1780, 1782.
Valentine and Orson: 1750, 1765, 1766, 1777, 1780, 1782, 1787.
The Seven Wise Masters: 1729, 1731, 1766, 1772, 1777.

All four titles occur in the lists of both C.M. Warren, Dublin, and J. Smyth, Belfast, in the early and mid-nineteenth century.
Other editions include:

The Seven Champions of Christendom:
Dublin, Wogan, 1801 '21st edn.' (Szoverffy)
Limerick, Goggin, 1806 (R. Herbert, *Limerick Printers*, p. 16)
Belfast, Simms and McIntyre, *c.* 1850 (National Union Cat.)

Valentine and Orson:
Clonmel, 1811 (Bradshaw, p. 824)

The Seven Wise Masters:
Dublin, A. Fox, 1814, '38th edn.' (National Union Cat.)
Dublin, C.M. Warren, 1816 (CBE)
Drogheda, Patrick Kelly, 1831 (NLI)
Dublin, C.M. Warren, '39th edn.', no date (CBE)

Don Belianis of Greece:
Dublin, 1792 (National Union Cat.)
Belfast, J. Smyth, 1831 (CBE)

CRIMINAL BIOGRAPHY

Year	Place	Location/source
Cosgrave: *Irish Highwaymen*		
1747	Dublin	BLC
'12th edn'	Dublin	NLI
c.1772	Belfast	Adams
1782	Dublin	Bradshaw
1799	Wilmington	Nat. Union
c.1800	Belfast	Bod.
1801	Dublin	Nat. Union
1831	Dublin	Linenhall
1839	Dublin	BLC
1843	Dublin	Bod.
*The Life and Adventures of James Freney**		
1754	Dublin	NLI
c.1766	Dublin	NLI
1807	Dublin	Bod.
1807	Waterford	Dix A
1814	Dublin (Fox)	BLC
1814	Dublin (Jones)	Gilbert
1827	Limerick	TCD
1835	Belfast	Adams
1861	Dublin	Day

* There is a list of printings in F. McEvoy (ed.) *The Life and Adventures of James Freney* (1988), Appendix 1, p. 61.

There are also some undated, probably mid-nineteenth-century, editions of both texts in these and other libraries.

HISTORIES

Year	Place	Printer	Location/source
H. Reily: *The Impartial History of Ireland*			
1690			Bod
1720			K; Bod.
1742			K
1749			K
1754			K; BLC
1754	Different edn		K; BLC
1762	None		K; NLI

continued

Year	Place	Printer	Location/source
1768			K
1781			K
1787	Dublin		K; BLC
1792	Dublin		TCD
1799	Dublin		K; BLC
1801	Limerick	McAuliffe	NLI; Herbert
1810	Dublin	Wogan/Larkin	FLK
1832	Dublin	Grace	CBE
1833			K
1837	Dublin		BLC
n.d.	Limerick	Goggin	NLI
n.d.	Dublin	PCD Warren	CBE

N. Crouch: *History of Ireland**

1693	London		Bod.
1731	Dublin	S. Fuller	NLI
('7th edn')			
1746	Dublin	Goulding & Jackson	
('12th edn')			
1765	Dublin	Jackson	
1811	Westminster	(Quarto)	Bod.

* It was advertised in Belfast publications of 1772, 1777, 1780 and 1782. It is impossible to say whether this refers to one or more editions.

The Siege of Londonderry

1738–9	Dublin		NLI
1739	Dublin		Bod.
1744	Belfast		Adams; Bod.; NLI
1744	Newry		Bod.
1750	Belfast		Adams
1759	Belfast		Adams; NLI
1774	Newry		Adams
1774			TCD
1777	Dublin	T. Wilkinson	NLI
1787	Strabane		Adams
1841	Dublin		Bod.

*The Battle of Aughrim**

1728	Dublin	Powell	NLI; Bod.
1756	Dublin	W. Davis	TCD
1765	Dublin		Stratman
1767	Belfast	Magee	Adams
1768	Dublin	Wilkinson	NLI
1771	Dublin	Corcoran	NLI
1777	Dublin	Wilkinson	NLI

* There was also a scholarly edition of *Aughrim* in 1841 by the Rev. John Graham.

Year	Place	Printer	Location/source
1781	Newry		Adams
1784	Dublin	Powell	CBE
1785	Strabane	Bellew	NLI
1800	Belfast		Adams
1814	Dublin	Jones	NLI
1815	Limerick		Dix B
1815	Dublin	Connolly	Linenhall
1816	Dublin	Clarke	Stratman
1819	Limerick	Goggin	Herbert
1827	Limerick	Goggin	Herbert

Londonderry and *Aughrim* together

1783 ('16th edn')	Dublin	Wogan	Stratman
1784 ('17th edn')	Dublin	Wogan	NLI
1795 ('19th edn')	Dublin	Wogan	TCD
1810	Limerick	Goggin	Herbert
1814 ('22nd edn')	Dublin		Bod.; TCD
1830	Belfast	Smyth	Biggar
1835 ('24th edn')	Belfast	Smyth	
n.d.	Dublin	C.M. Warren	
1880	Dublin	P.D.C. Warren	

Key to location/source:
Adams: J.R.R. Adams: *The Printed Word and the Common Man* (1987)
Biggar: F.J. Biggar collection, Belfast City Library
BLC: British Library catalogue
Bod.: Bodleian Library
Bradshaw: *A Catalogue of the Bradshaw Collection of Irish Books in the University Library, Cambridge* (1916)
Day: R. Day: 'A Note on Freney', *Journal of the Cork Hist. and Arch. Soc.*, 2nd Ser. XI (1906), pp. 198–200
Dix A: E.R. Dix: *Books, newspapers and pamphlets printed in Waterford 1801–1820* (1916)
Dix B: E.R. Dix: 'Printing in Limerick in the nineteenth century', *Irish Book Lover*, XVIII (1930), pp. 39–42
FLK: Franciscan Library, Killiney, Co. Dublin
Gilbert: Dublin City Library, Gilbert collection
Herbert: R. Herbert: *Limerick Printers and Printing* (Limerick 1942)
K: P. Kelly: '"A light to the blind": the voice of the dispossessed elite in the generation after the defeat at Limerick', *Irish Historical Studies*, XXIV (1985), pp. 431–62
Linenhall: Linenhall Library, Belfast

NLI: National Library of Ireland
Stratman: C.J. Stratman, *A Bibliography of Printed English Tragedy*
  (London, 1966)
Szoverffy: J. Szoverffy: 'Rí Naomh Seoirse: Chapbook and Hedge Schools',
  Éigse, IX (1958), pp. 114–28.
TCD: Trinity College Dublin

Notes

CHAPTER 1 APPROACHES AND METHODS

1. Surveys include Lebrun (1993), Barry (1995). There is a detailed bibliography of the French historiography in Dotoli (1991), pp. 325–68.
2. The most celebrated exception is the sixteenth-century Friulian miller Menocchio, whose unusual interpretations of relatively learned texts were noted in detail by the Inquisition, and which are related to a wider oral culture in Ginzburg (1980).
3. As is evident from their titles, for example Darnton (1986), Rose (1992).
4. Roche (1987), pp. 59–62; Queniart (1978), pp. 155–63; Gailey (1977).
5. Vincent (1981), Rose (1992).
6. Mokyr (1983), p. 21.
7. The literature of popular protest in Ireland is summarised in Clark and Donnelly (1983), pp. 3–35.
8. Lapoint (1992), Levack (1987), pp. 185–6; Danaher (1972).
9. Cullen (1990a), Ó Coigligh (1987), Fender (1914).
10. hÓgáin (1995), pp. 3–9.
11. These issues are discussed in Joutard (1983), Ch. IX. The most complete analysis of such a process in Ireland is Earls (1984).
12. Wright (1935), pp. 86, 92; Capp (1985), p. 206.
13. Rich (1612), p. 4.
14. Pollard (1989), p. 222; O'Sullivan (1960), p. 189.
15. The responses are discussed in Chartier (1988a), particularly. pp. 161–4.
16. Bell (1804), pp. 40–1.
17. Certeau, Julia and Revel (1986).
18. Wiseman (1855), pp. 227–9.
19. Ashton (1882), Intro., pp. v–viii.
20. [Kennedy] (1865), (1866). Kennedy, (1801–1873) is identified as the author in *The Wellesley Index to Victorian Periodicals*, Vol. IV (1987), pp. 329–30.
21. Evans (1897); [J.J. Marshall] (1910); Dix (1910). Marshall's article in fact consists of the first pages of Kennedy's article of 1866.
22. Spufford (1981), pp. 72–5.
23. Kenealy (1908), pp. 41–2.
24. Mandrou (1964); Spufford (1981).
25. Capp (1977); Bollème (1969). The *Bibliothèque Bleue* facsimile collections were published under the general editorship of Daniel Roche and include Lüsebrink (1984), Chartier (1982), Bollème and Andriès (1983), Flandrin and Hyman (1983), Farge (1982), Favre (1984).
26. Chartier (1985); Vincent (1981), (1989).
27. Muchembled (1985).
28. Lusebrink (1984), Intro.
29. Adams (1987); Phillipps (1952); Pollard (1989).

30. O'Donoghue (1896).
31. Stokes (1799), p. 41.
32. Hely Dutton (1808), pp. 236–8; Wakefield (1812), Vol. II, p. 401; O'Driscoll (1823), Vol. II, p. 80.
33. Parl 1825b, p. 44.
34. De Brún (1982–3), pp. 70–82; Parl 1825b, p. 43.
35. Parl 1809, p. 109; Colley (1992), pp. 167–8.
36. Parl 1825b, pp. 553–9.
37. Spufford (1981), Chs. VI–VIII.
38. Mandrou (1964), pp. 32–3; Martin (1978), p. 79; Morin (1974).
39. Queniart (1979a).
40. Certeau, Julia and Revel (1986), p. 129; Marais (1980), p. 87: 'All classification, although necessary, is dangerous, to the extent that it is done with reference to exterior categories, to a science formulated since the scientific revolution, to academic definitions of literary genre and to a counter-reformation Catholicism'.
41. For a similar argument, see Marais (1980), p. 86.
42. Chartier (1988b), pp. 28–32.
43. The British Library Reading Experience Database envisages the allotting of texts to two or three genres simultaneously: Eliot (1996), p. 89; the suggestion about cookery books is by Andriès, quoted in the introduction to Flandrin and Hyman (1982), p. 96. It is all the more plausible given that 'plenty', as much food as you want, is such a frequent theme in folk tales: see, for example, Weber (1981).
44. See, for example, the criteria of Marais (1986), p. 90: 'printed once or twice, temporarily popular, appearing at a certain time and becoming more or less popular, permanently popular, popular to the point of inspiring imitations.'
45. Denmead Job Book (see Ch. 2); Matthieson (1836), pp. 75–6.
46. Pollard (1973).
47. Thackeray (1902 edn), p. 402; wages from McGrath (1928) *passim*, and Dutton (1808), p. 185.
48. Mokyr (1983), Ch. 2; Mokyr and Ó Gráda (1988), pp. 209–35. 'Mass consumption' can be defined as the importation of enough of a commodity to allow 25 per cent of adults to use it once daily: Shammas (1990), p. 78.
49. Parl 1835a, pp. 635, 638; Ó Ceallaigh (1967), p. 43.
50. McGrath (1928), entry for 5/7/1827; McParlan (1802), p. 66. There are similar figures in Tighe (1802), pp. 473–84.
51. Parl 1830, p. 430.
52. Dickson (1993).
53. Tynan (1985).
54. For example, *The Schoolmaster's Assistant, being a compendium of arithmetic ... to which is added, a very necessary and useful appendix, containing a particular account of the coins, weights and measures used in Ireland*, advertised by the Quaker bookseller, Isaac Jackson in 1770.

CHAPTER 2 LITERACY AND EDUCATION

1. Houston (1988), pp. 92–6; Furet and Ozouf (1982), p. 302; Logan (1992), p. 32, pp. 239–46; Laqueur (1976), p. 255.
2. Astoul (1992).
3. Meyer (1974), pp. 336–9; Furet and Ozouf (1982), pp. 174–5; Houston, however, points out that such models were unknown in Britain: Houston (1985) p. 180; Queniart (1979b).
4. Grevet (1993), p. 448. See also Garnot (1990), p. 158, where the signature data are considered to be part of a 'historiographic illusion'.
5. Mason (1814–19), Vol. I, p. 330 (Dungiven, Co. Derry); Vol. III, pp. 625–6 (Kilkenny). For the circulation of notes see Barrow (1975), pp. 30–3; Coote (1801a), pp. 58, 97, 114, 140, etc.; Coote (1801b), p. 67.
6. Mac Síthigh (1984), p. 153.
7. Kirkham (1990), p. 87.
8. Donnelly (1980), p. 7.
9. Queniart (1984), pp. 28–9.
10. Beames (1983), pp. 75–7; examples from eighteenth-century England are given in Laqueur (1976), p. 267 and in Thompson (1975).
11. Bric (1987).
12. Bartlett (1990); Neuburg (1971), p. 105.
13. Mason (1814–19), Vol. I, p. 588; *A Short Treatise on the evils of litigation, malpractices of attorneys and lawyers etc* (1846), p. 5; McCabe (1985), p. 49.
14. Houston (1988), pp. 134–7.
15. Furet and Ozouf (1982), pp. 59–62, 167–74; Queniart (1984), pp. 25–7.
16. Akenson (1988), p. 118.
17. Kirkham (1990), pp. 81–2.
18. Furet and Ozouf (1982), pp. 166–91, 309; Laqueur (1976).
19. Cipolla (1969), p. 126; Schofield (1981), p. 203. A more extreme view is found in the comments in twentieth-century Irish censuses on reported ability to speak Irish: 'Personal judgement enters very largely ... it is quite clear from the census data that different standards of proficiency were applied by individuals at different censuses ... it is extremely doubtful if the statistics ... are of any value' (Census of Ireland 1956).
20. Logan (1992), p. 228; Graff (1987), p. 19.
21. Freeman (1957), Ch. 6; this judgement reappears in larger works of synthesis, e.g. Bowen (1981), p. 451, where Irish illiteracy in 1830 is described as 'appalling'. Cipolla's figures come from a wide range of sources, reflecting differing criteria of literacy, and need to be treated with caution. They are nevertheless suggestive. Cipolla (1969), pp. 113–14.
22. R = 0.784 and 0.362 respectively.
23. The equation is of the form FRO41 = a + bHOU41 + cPROT61, where FRO41 is the proportion of women over 5 years of age who read only in 1841, HOU41 is the proportion of houses of class 1 and 2 in 1841, and PROT61 is the proportion of female Anglicans and Presbyterians in 1861. The values are a = 17.66, b = –0.03, c = 0.40 (t-values are 8.80, –0.45 and 11.98 respectively). There were 69 baronies in Ulster in 1841. The matter is not as clear as this result might suggest, however. The 1861

census also included an analysis of the literacy profile of the different religious denominations. As in 1841, Ulster still contained a higher proportion of women RO than women RW overall, whereas in Munster, for example, the opposite was true. When broken down by religion, however, it emerges that women who could read only were predominantly Catholic. In Antrim, Armagh, Down and Londonderry, Catholic women RO outnumbered RW, while there were more Protestant women RW than RO in all four counties. In Munster, on the other hand, Catholic women were more likely to be RW than RO in all counties.

24. R = 0.806. The regression equation is READ = 19.12 + 1.56HOU, where READ is the proportion of those over 5 years of age who can read and HOU is the proportion of class 1 and 2 houses (*t*-values are 4.57 and 7.47 respectively).
25. On adult education, De Brún (1983a), p. 289; on the decline of writing ability after school, Perrot (1975), p. 308; there is a reported case from 1838 of people having lost the ability to read in Altick (1957), p. 169.
26. W. Carleton, 'The Hedge Schoolmaster and the Abduction of Mat Kavanagh', in W. Carleton, *Traits and Stories of the Irish Peasantry*, Vol. II (1831).
27. Grosperrin (1984), p. 30; Furet and Ozouf (1982), p. 247, refer to the 'invention' of the school by the village community, prior to state intervention.
28. Furet and Ozouf (1982), p. 303; Daly (1979); Hoban (1983), pp. 21–36.
29. Parl 1825b.
30. Logan (1992), pp. 37–8.
31. Corish (1981), p. 79: 'A substantial minority [of the pay schools] were de facto parish schools': Daly (1981), p. 112.
32. Newenham (1809), Appendix XXIX.
33. Grosperrin (1984), p. 36; Hoban (1983); Cullen (1990a), p. 28, also warns against an overestimation of church influence in pay schools.
34. Akenson (1970), pp. 61–8; for the debate on popular education in England see Silver (1965), Ch. 1, and Graff (1987), pp. 315–16; in France, Richter (1987), Ch. 2., Grosperrin (1984), Ch. 1.
35. Parl 1812–13, p. 331 ff.
36. Akenson (1970), p. 86.
37. Ó Canainn (1983).
38. Parl 1830, p. 425.
39. Report on the State of Popery; Corish (1981), p. 103; Newenham (1809), Appendix XXVI; Parl 1826–7, Appendix no. 22, pp. 898–999; Mooney (1990).
40. Parl 1812–13.
41. Parl 1826–7.
42. Houston (1988), pp. 49–50; for Baden, Graff (1987b), p. 289; Ó Gráda (1988), pp. 18–20.
43. Mokyr (1983), p. 184.
44. Many of the over-16s, and some of the 11–15 year-olds were probably monitors.
45. Grosperrin (1984), p. 75; Spufford (1981), Ch. 2.
46. Parl 1835a, pp. 634, 641; a similar comment on children's clothes in the south-east was made by the agricultural writer William Hickey (Martin Doyle), Parl 1830, p. 165.

47. Parl 1830, p. 426.
48. M. Daly: 'Women and work in Irish history', paper given to the Galway Labour History Group seminar, 27 March 1992.
49. Grosperrin (1984), p. 75; Daly (1979), p. 160. In Co. Kilkenny about 1800, for example, reading cost one shilling and sevenpence a quarter, writing two shillings and twopence and arithmetic three shillings and ninepence: Tighe (1802), p. 513.
50. Furet and Ozouf (1982), p. 94; Chartier, Compere and Julia (1976), p. 141.
51. O'Donoghue (1896), Vol. 1, p. 25; Parl 1825b, pp. 43, 553–9.
52 Dutton (1808), pp. 236–7; Wakefield (1812), Vol. 1, p. 400, quoting Dutton.
53. Parl 1825b, Appendix 261, pp. 820–1; De Brún (1982–3), pp. 70–82.
54. Daly (1979); Hoban (1983).
55. *Royal Commission of Inquiry into primary education in Ireland, Report*, H.C. 1870 XXVIII, Pt. 2, p. 30. I would like to thank Tadhg Foley for this reference.

CHAPTER 3   PRODUCTION AND DISTRIBUTION

1. Pollard (1989), p. viii; Wheeler (1978).
2. Mandrou (1964), pp. 36–42; Spufford (1981), Ch. IV; Quaker records, Dublin, Friends MS MM II 22. The Denmead job book is in Cork City Library.
3. Spufford (1981), pp. 111, 120; Hunter (1988) for 1681; Chester port books, P.R.O. (London) E 190 1363/1 for 1702.
4. Pollard (1989), pp. 16–17.
5. Phillipps (1952), p. 125; Wall (1958), pp. 89–109; Records of the Guild of St Luke NLI MS 12,123, p. 23.
6. Mayer (1994).
7. Eustace and Goodbody (1957), p. 42; Munter (1988), p. 145.
8. See Swanson (1985), p. 7. The phrases are from advertisements for Anne Law 1759 and Isaac Jackson c.1750.
9. Dickson (1988), pp. 67–76; Andriès (1989), p. 14.
10. Wall (1989), pp. 61–72.
11. See below, Ch. 6.
12. See below, Ch. 9.
13. Benson (1990), pp. 45–59; Corish (1985), p. 171.
14. Herbert (1942), p. 16 ff.
15. Bradshaw Catalogue no. 8494; Herbert (1942), p. 36; Adams (1987), pp. 43–6. *The Battle of Ventry* was first printed in Cork in 1819.
16. Adams (1987), pp. 138, 194–9.
17. PRONI: Down Grand Jury presentments, Lent 1814; *Catalogue of the Bradshaw Collection* (1916), no. 3754; Matthieson (1836), p. xxii.
18. Shields (1987).
19. Benson (1990), pp. 51–2.
20. The 1822 *Report on Revenue* lists 53 booksellers in 29 towns outside Dublin: Parl 1822, p. 1231.
21. Ibid., Appendix 4. Parnell was a member of the Sunday School Society for Ireland.

22. Mason (1814–19), Vol. III, pp. 627, 166.
23. Spufford (1984), p. 18; Parl, 1844, p. 377.
24. Darmon (1972), p. 97 ff.
25. Parl 1881, p. 459. I would like to thank Charles Benson for this reference.
26. Wall (1958), pp. 110–11; Darnton (1979), p. 309; *Irish Builder*, 15 April 1878.
27. Fontaine (1993), pp. 253–9.
28. Fontaine (1993), Ch. 3; Mui (1989), pp. 101–2, Map 3.
29. MacLysaght (1939), pp. 66, 125.
30. Irish Folklore Commission (IFC), MS 1483, pp. 122–61.
31. Spufford (1981), p. 111, 120; Phillipps (1952), p. 124.
32. Licence revenue from 1747 to 1789 is listed in Cavendish (1791); from 1784 to 1799 in the *Journals of the Irish House of Commons*, Vols 22–25 and XIII–XIX; from 1817 to 1823 in Parl 1824, p. 225; for 1830 and 1840 in Parl 1844.
33. There had been attempts at licence schemes in England since the middle of the sixteenth century: see Spufford (1984), p. 6.
34. Spufford (1984); Spufford (1981), Ch. V; Darmon (1972).
35. 19 G2 c.5 v.6; 25 G3 c.20 v.13.
36. It is not clear why the licensing system should have collapsed only in Ireland.
37. Mui (1989), p. 99; Lee and Schofield (1981), p. 21.
38. Shammas (1990), pp. 236–8; Daultrey, Dickson and Ó Gráda (1981), pp. 601–28.
39. Shammas (1990), p. 238.
40. Customs officials in the early nineteenth century were certainly worried about the smuggling of whiskey out of Ireland and cotton goods in by pedlars coming from Scotland. (PRONI: T1095/2/25 Customs letter book 1786–1822.)
41. The census of 1841 adopted a system of classifying occupations different to those of 1831 and 1851. People were asked to describe their occupations themselves rather than choosing from categories set out by the census commissioners. The result lists 38 pedlars in King's County, six in Co. Galway, two in Co. Derry and Drogheda, one in Cos Meath and Cavan, and none at all in the rest of the country.
42. The accounts are for Athlone 1788–9 and Mallow 1788–9. In Athlone 70 out of 83 licences were taken between March and June; in Mallow 8 out of 10. PRO (Ireland) Revenue Exchequer 2B/105/9, 2B/105/22.)
43. Fontaine (1993), Ch. VII; Mui (1989), p. 98; Barbier (1985), p. 251; Darmon (1972), pp. 50–5; Ó Gráda (1973).
44. [D. Defoe] (1727), pp. 26–7; *Dublin Journal*, 3–6 January 1729–30. For similar complaints in eighteenth-century France, see Sauvy (1984), p. 431.
45. Parl 1810a, Appendix A, Letter from P. Colquhoun and Charles Poole. Pedlars in Armagh told a folklore collector in the 1950s that they had always dressed as sailors and pretended that they were carrying contraband, as this made their wares more saleable (IFC MS 1483, p. 122 ff).
46. McNally (1812), Vol. 3 pp. 402–4; the appeal to shopkeepers in the *Dublin Journal* referred to 'their dexterity in disposing of unaccustomed goods'.

47. SPOI Rebellion Papers 620/35/87; ibid. 620/29/8. See also Donnelly (1980), p. 16.
48. Chartier (1987), pp. 265, 333; Du Sorbier (1983), Ch. 3; Spufford (1984), p. 8.
49. IFC MS 54, p. 323.
50. Chartier (1987), p. 333.
51. McKendrick, Brewer and Plumb (1982), p. 87; Mui (1989), pp. 73–97.
52. *Tipperary Free Press*, 14 November 1827; 17 November 1827; Fontaine (1993), pp. 210–11.
53. IFC MS 107, p. 514; other examples of pedlars referred to by name are MS 259 (Co. Waterford), pp. 134–5, MS 485 (Co. Galway), p. 217; a horror story with a pedlar as hero/victim is found in MS 159 (Co. Galway), pp. 426–8 and MS 733 (Co. Kerry), pp. 442–5.

CHAPTER 4   CHIVALRIC ROMANCES

1. Simons (1992), p. 132.
2. Gibson (1949), pp. 55–6; Spufford (1981), p. 233.
3. Spufford (1981), p. 74.
4. Burke (1978), p. 278; *British Library Catalogue*; the preface to *Don Belianis* is reproduced in Gibson (1949), pp. 95–7.
5. Murphy (1961), p. 44; Andriès (1989), p. 122.
6. Schmitt (1983), p. 39ff.
7. Chartier (1988), pp. 18–19; Darnton (1986).
8. Murphy (1961), pp. 30–37.
9. Bruford (1968), Ch. 6, quote on p. 56.
10. Bruford (1968), p. 50; Hollo (1996), pp. 57–71; Szoverffy (1958); Ó Cillín (1926).
11. Bruford (1968), p. 48; Andriès (1978), pp. 51–66.
12. Chartier (1985), pp. 85–6; Simons (1992), pp. 131–2.
13. Murphy (1961), p. 47; Bruford (1968), p. 61.
14. Ó Cillín (1926).
15. Spufford (1981), p. 249; Mandrou (1964), 1985 edn p. 151.
16. Spufford (1981), pp. 249–50; Adams (1987), pp. 53–9.
17. Ordnance Survey Letters, Co. Derry.
18. As R.O. Jones puts it, in discussing the popularity of the romance in sixteenth-century Spain, 'to call them "escapist" is to give no answer worth considering': Jones (1971), p. 54.
19. Muchembled (1985), pp. 291–2.
20. '*Valentine and Orson*' and 'J. Shirley' in the *National Union Catalogue*; examples of juvenile readers of romance in the eighteenth century are given in Simons (1992).
21. Bell (1804), pp. 40–1.
22. Bercé (1987), Ch. 1.

CHAPTER 5   CRIMINAL BIOGRAPHY

1. For Guilleri, Chartier (1987)
2. Hobsbawm (1959) and (1969); Blok (1972); Crawford (1982).
3. Chartier (1987); Du Sorbier (1983), Ch. 3; Aydelotte (1913).
4. Parker (1967), Chs 4 and 5, quote on p. 100; Sieber (1977), Ch. 3; Du Sorbier (1983), Ch. 1; Du Sorbier (1986); Head and Kirkman: *The English Rogue* (New York, 1928 edn), pp. 30–4, 220–7.
5. Sharpe (1985); Lusebrink (1982).
6. Linebaugh (1977); Harris (1982).
7. *The Last Speech of J[onathan] W[ild] the notorious thief taker* (Dublin, 1725); Bleackley and Ellis (1933), p. 128; *Authentic memoir of the remarkable and surprising exploits of Mandrin, Captain-General of the French Smugglers*... (Dublin, 1755); two single-sheet last speeches are reproduced in MacLysaght (1939), Appendix H.
8. *The Last speech and dying Words of Elinor Sils*... (Dublin, 1725).
9. I used Smith in a slightly censored reprint: Hayward (1926); some of the lives from Johnson's *General History* are found, also censored, in Rayner and Crook (1926).
10. Faller (1987), Ch. 6.
11. Earls (1988).
12. Hayton (1988).
13. *The Life and Glorious Actions of the most Heroic and Magnanimous Jonathan Wild, Generalissimo of the prig forces in Great Britain and Ireland*. ... (London, 1725), p. 4.
14. Lusebrink (1984), pp. 21, 40.
15. Connolly (1987), p. 43; McMahon (1980–1); Hobsbawm (1969), pp. 42–3.
16. *Count Hanlan's Downfall or a true and exact account of the killing of that archtraytor and tory Redmond O Hanlan*. ... (Dublin, 1681).
17. Dublin, 1682.
18. There may have been intermediate versions, but I have seen no references that would point to their existence.
19. This is close to another of Hobsbawm's criteria of social banditry: 'A man becomes a bandit because he does something which is not regarded as criminal by his local conventions but is so regarded by the state or by local rulers' (Hobsbawm, 1959, p. 15).
20. Prendergast (1887), p. 79.
21. *The Irish Freebooter or Surprising adventures of Captain Redmond O'Hanlon*. ... (London, 1819).
22. D'Alton (1847); Brennan (1990), pp. 161–96.
23. Cullen (1990b).
24. Linebaugh (1977), pp. 257, 264; Humphreys (1940), p. 384; McEvoy (1988), p. ii.
25. Earls (1990).
26. De Brún (1982–3); *First Report of the Commissioners for Irish Education Inquiry*, H.C. 1825 XII, Appendix 261; Crofton Croker (1824), p. 55.
27. *Journal of the Kilkenny and South–East Ireland Archaeological Society*, N. Ser. Vol. I (1856–7), pp. 59–60; there is a copy of the broadside in TCD 189 t. 1., no. 262.

28. Ó Foghludha (1905), p. 53; *Belfast News-Letter*, 28 December 1790, quoted in Adams (1987), p. 91; Knott (1836), p. 16; *Dublin Penny Journal*, 3 May 1834; Ó Laoghaire (1916), pp. 130–6.

CHAPTER 6   TIME, RITUAL AND HISTORY

1. Mandrou (1964), pp. 146–9; Bollème (1969); Capp (1979).
2. Maiello (1994), pp. 131–47.
3. Cressy (1989); Hutton (1994); Colley (1992), pp. 20–2.
4. Barnard (1991).
5. McGovern (1994). I would like to thank Prof. D.G. Boyce for this reference.
6. Kelly (1985), p. 432.
7. Fagan (1986), Ch. 10: 'Cornelius Nary, controversial divine'.
8. Hill (1988), p. 116.
9. Hill (1988).
10. Ó Coigligh (1987), pp. 137–48; a similar contemporary historical poem from Munster, sharing Raiftearaí's time scale and also acknowledging Keating, is 'Sighle Ní Ghadhra', in Fender (1914), pp. 89–92.
11. Ó Donnchadh (n.d.), p. 377.
12. Barnard (1993).
13. McGovern (1994), Ch. 2.
14. Greene and Clark (1993); Clark (1965), pp. 282, 292–347; personal communication from Dr Chris Wheatley.
15. *Ireland's Mirror: or, a chronicle of the times*, Vol. I (Dublin, 1804), p. 279. I am grateful to Chris Wheatley for this reference; O'Donoghue (1896), Vol. I, pp. 25–8.
16. Shields (1990).
17. Hewitt (1974).
18. O'Donoghue (1896), Vol. I, pp. 25–8.
19. Sibbett (1914–5), pp. 151–7, 194; Adams (1988).
20. Hill (1984–5); Hill (1993); McGovern (1994), pp. 70–2. The other principal studies of modern Orange ritual are Loftus (1990) and (1993); on the early history of the Orange order, the standard works, Senior (1966) and Gibbon (1975), concentrate on economic and social context, and have little to say about symbolism or ritual.
21. *Belfast Newsletter*, 15 July 1796, 14 July 1797; *Dublin Journal*, 13 July 1799, where both battles are mentioned, 19 July 1800.
22. Mason (1814–19), Vol. II, p. 459.
23. Connerton (1989), pp. 65–7.
24. Dagnall (1991), p. 26.
25. *Freeman's Journal*, 13 July 1799; Colley (1992), p. 21.
26. Quoted in Gregg (1840).
27. *Ireland's Mirror*, Vol. II (1805), pp. 138–9.
28. Mason (1814–19), Vol. I, p. 594.
29. Connolly (1983); Parl 1835b, p. 40.

CHAPTER 7 THE CATHOLIC REFORMATION

1. Delumeau (1977); Larkin (1972); Miller (1975); Connolly (1982); Hynes (1978).
2. Connolly (1982), pp. 60–5, 79–80; Coombes (1981), pp. 45–6.
3. Hynes (1978); Whelan (1988).
4. There is a bibliography for the period until 1800 in Green (1995); some of the eighteenth- and nineteenth-century catechisms are discussed in Tynan (1985).
5. *Sixteen Sermons*, Dublin, W. Powell 1835, translated by J. Byrne. For the individual sermons Matthieson (1836), p. 58.
6. Gallagher, intro.; Luckett (1981), p. 83.
7. On the printing of psalm books in England, Watt (1991), pp. 55–67.
8. Launay (1993); Andriès (1989), pp. 79–83; Queniart (1991); Delumeau (1977), p. 191; Croix (1981), Vol. II, p. 1203.
9. Ní Riain (1993).
10. Rees (1987), pp. 57–61; McLeod (1975).
11. Launay (1993), pp. 382–92; MacLean (1915), p. 35.
12. Meek (1989a) and (1989b).
13. *Dain Spioradail le Dughall Bochanan* (1946 edn); MacInnes (1951), pp. 280–1; Buchanan's diary is printed in McBean (1919).
14. *Duan Iosa*, for example, occurs in RIA MS 304 (Dungarvan, Co. Waterford, 1765–7), RIA MS 780 (Co. Kerry, 1779) and Brit. Mus. MS Egerton 160 (Co. Limerick or Clare, 1781); *Duan Mhuire* occurs in RIA MS 109 (Co. Waterford, 1767–9); and both in RIA MS 413 (Lismore, Co. Waterford, 1772–80).
15. John Rylands Library, Manchester, Irish MS 64. I would like to thank Pádraig De Brún for pointing this manuscript out to me.
16. The most recent biographical accounts are Ó Fiannachta (1982), pp. 184–96, and De Paor (1995), both based principally on the internal evidence of the poetry. Modern editions of the poetry are Ua Duinnín (1903) and Ó Fodhlugha (1929).
17. Whelan (1988); Corish (1985), p. 170.
18. Venard (1979), p. 150.
19. Langlois (1974), p. 532; Connolly (1982), pp. 92–3. More generally, however, the situation in Ireland contrasts with that of France, where in the late eighteenth century many confraternities were in decline – see Delumeau (1977), p. 220; Venard (1979), pp. 149–50.
20. Keenan (1983), p. 139; Corish (1985), p. 133.
21. Ó Dúshláine (1987), pp. 133–79.
22. See, e.g., O'Rahilly (1951), foreword: '[The poets] attribute the sufferings of the people to their own sins'.
23. Gallagher: *Sixteen Irish Sermons*, no. 2, 'On the Last Judgement'.
24. Connolly (1982), p. 230.
25. This concept was most fully developed in the religious poetry of Aonghus Fionn Ó Dálaigh at the beginning of the seventeenth century: see McKenna (1919), p. ix, 'Christ demands from us on the last day the éiric of his wounds.'
26. Pointed out by Ó Fodhlugha (1929), p. 147.

27. Connolly (1982), p. 141.
28. Connolly (1982), p. 137.
29. Ó Súilleabháin (1967); Mason (1814–19), Vol. I, p. 596.
30. Fawcett (1971), p. 84.
31. Coleman (1924); Clare: Gunn (1984), pp. 5–6; Meath: RIA MS 1075; Donegal: *Cuimhne Coluimcille* (1898), p. 34; Galway: Mac Giollarnath (1941).
32. White and Lawrence (1993).

CHAPTER 8 'IMPROVING AND PRACTICAL LITERATURE'

1. Burke (1978); Porter (1982), Ch. 7: 'Changing experiences'; Hayton (1995).
2. *Northern Star*, 7–11 January 1792, 8–11 February 1792, 30 May 1792.
3. Quoted in V. Kinane: 'Literary food' for the American Market: Patrick Byrne's exports to Mathew Carey' (unpublished paper 1993). I am grateful to Mr Kinane for permission to quote this paper.
4. Magee (1796), p. 71.
5. Donnelly (1980); Curtin (1990); Dunne (1990); Whelan (1993).
6. O'Day (1982), Ch. 13; Porter (1982), Ch. 7.
7. Passmore (1970), Ch. 8; Horne (1978), Ch. 1; Neuberg (1971); the same debate in eighteenth-century France is dealt with in Chisick (1981) and Richter (1987), Ch. 2.
8. Archer and Vaughan (1971), Ch. 4.
9. *Mr. Orde's Plan* (1787), pp. 13–14; McDowell (1979), pp. 92–3.
10. Roberts (1834), Vol. II, p. 458.
11. Roberts (1834), Vol. II, p. 379.
12. Pedersen (1986).
13. Association for Discountenancing Vice (ADV), 1806 report, p. 6. In 1796, the Association had 482 members, of whom 268 were clergymen, nearly all Anglican, including three archbishops and 11 bishops: Magee (1796), Appendix.
14. Graves (1794), Appendix.
15. Roberts (1834), Vol. II, p. 432.
16. ADV, 1806 report, pp. 6, 38.
17. ADV, 1806 report, p. 12; ADV, 1820 general report, p. cxii. ADV, 1829 report, pp. 118–19.
18. Jones (1952), pp. 145–9.
19. Parl 1813–14, p. 331.
20. Beddoes (1813).
21. Akenson (1970), pp. 85–5; Bowen (1978).
22. Trench to Leadbeater, May 1813: Leadbeater (1862), Vol. II, p. 251; ibid., p. 258.
23. Leadbeater (1813), p. vi.
24. Ibid., p. vi.
25. On the Kildare Place Society, see Adams (1987), pp. 98–107; Goldstrom (1972), pp. 59–61; Hislop (1990).
26. Parl 1825b, p. 43; ibid., appendix 203, p. 445.
27. Kildare Place Society Book Sub–Committee (KPSBS), no. 1.

28. Ibid., nos 4, 6, 9.
29. Ibid., no. 9.
30. Ibid., nos 12, 52.
31. The emphasis on 'useful knowledge' was very much a characteristic of contemporary philanthropic societies in England, the classic example being the Society for the Diffusion of Useful Knowledge, founded in 1827.
32. Crofton Croker (1825–8), 'The Harvest Dinner'.
33. *First Report of the Catholic Book Society* (1828); Feeney (1982); Wall (1964).
34. Black (1960), p. 86.
35. Archer and Vaughan (1971), p. 68; Dewar (1812), p. 87; Walker (1825), p. 29; the editor and translator James Hardiman parodied this attitude in his collection of Irish songs of 1831: 'To the fascinating influence of these [love] songs have been attributed many of the early marriages and much of the 'superabundant' population of our country. This, no doubt, will be deemed a new discovery in the science of political economy, and as such is respectfully offered to the grave consideration of the Malthuses ... of our day' (Hardiman, 1831), Vol. I, p. 202).
36. Goldstrom (1966); Akenson (1981), pp. 177–9.
37. Doyle (1833), pp. 20, 42, 75.
38. Feeney (1982), p. 6.
39. ADV, 1806 report, p. 33.
40. Doyle (1833), p. 55.
41. Roberts (1834), Vol. II, p. 458.
42. De Brún (1983a), p. 309, n.176.
43. Whateley (1835).
44. *First Report of the Catholic Book Society* (1828), p. 13.
45. Dickson and Pollard (1973).
46. The memorial plaque to Watson in Mary Street church, Dublin, gives him the sole credit for the idea of the ADV.
47. In the 1820s Watson made £1900 profit from his activities for the association: 1825 report, pp. 35, 382.
48. M.G. Jones (1952), p. 144; for Watson, see Bradshaw (1916), p. 292.
49. ADV, 1806 report, pp. 22–3; Moore (1904), p. 253.
50. Jones (1952), p. 148; Smith (1986), p. 96; Hurst (1969), p. 15: 'an enlightened member of a ruling class who wished it to deserve its power and privileges through devotion to what she considered its obvious duties towards the rest of the community.'
51. Quoted in Brown (1981), p. 69.
52. Neuberg (1977), p. 264.
53. *The Nation* 23 March 1844, 17 August 1844, 4 January 1845; *Galway Vindicator*, 19 February 1945 (all in NLI MS 3978). The links between temperance and nationalism are shown in Kearney (1979).
54. Leadbeater (1862), Vol. II, pp. 172, 192.
55. Carleton (1845).
56. Adams (1987), p. 101; Houston (1988), pp. 213–18.
57. Bell (1987).
58. Barrett (1977); Kearney (1979).
59. Quoted in *Cork Constitution*, 29 August 1867 (in NLI MS 407).

60. Leadbeater (1862), Vol. II, p. 189.
61. De Brún (1983b). The correspondent is answering the question 'Do you conceive the Irish-speaking population clearly comprehend the religious books which are read to them in the Irish language ...?'
62. Earls (1984).

CHAPTER 9 LANGUAGES AND LITERARY

1. Maps in Fitzgerald (1984) and Freeman (1957); Logan (1992), pp. 239–44; Furet and Ozouf (1982), Ch. 7.
2. Ó Murchú (1986).
3. Cullen (1981), p. 132; Furet and Ozouf (1982), p. 297.
4. Daly (1990); Ó Gráda (1973); Devine (1994), pp. 116–17.
5. Withers (1988), pp. 146–9.
6. Quoted in Queniart (1984); Furet and Ozouf (1982), p. 298; Logan (1992), pp. 65, 237.
7. Ó Cuív (1986), p. 381.
8. Ó Conchúir (1982); Cullen (1990a).
9. De Brún (1983a), p. 322.
10. Adams (1987).
11. Tynan (1985), Ch. 5: Wall (1969); McKenna (1991).
12. De Brún (1983a), p. 308.; Ó hAilín (1968).
13. The earlier Protestant texts were in Roman type, but after 1820, Gaelic type predominates.
14. Gallagher (1736); *Cheithre Sholeirseadha de'n Eagnuidheacht Chríostuidhe etc.* (Waterford, 1820).
15. 1858 edn, O'Daly, Dublin, introduction.
16. Another example is *The Spiritual Rose, or method of saying the rosaries ... rendered into Irish*, printed in Monaghan in 1825.
17. Tynan (1985), pp. 47–8.; TCD 189 t 2 no. 48. The 1722 catechism is discussed in Williams (1986). For phonetic script in manuscripts, Cullen (1990a), p. 32; Ó Muraíle (1983), p. 56.
18. Wall (1958), p. 93.
19. Ó Tuathail (1939). A similar observation was made about Maghera, Co. Derry, in 1814: Mason (1814–19), Vol. I, p. 592.
20. Cullen (1990a), pp. 39–40.
21. Vray (1993), pp. 228–36.
22. Durkacz (1983), pp. 34, 37; Jenkins (1987), pp. 204–11, 369; Rees (1987) lists 5656 items, in Welsh and English, but does not give the totals for each language. It appears that over half were in Welsh. Dix and Ó Casaide (1905) list 156 items printed in Irish by 1820.
23. Delumeau (1977).
24. Croix (1980), Vol. 2, pp. 1209–30; Sauvy (1984), pp. 430–33; Queniart (1985); Desgraves (1984), pp. 62–73. For the images, Sauvy (1989).
25. Desgraves, (1984), pp. 62–73; Le Menn (1980).
26. Le Menn (1985); Le Flocc'h and Le Menn (1985); Langlois (1974), pp. 427–32.
27. Gazier (1880), pp. 282, 632, 638–47.

28. Le Menn (1983), pp. 428–50; Guilcher (1990), p. 153.
29. Durkacz (1983), pp. 108–33; the list is that of Neil Campbell, Glasgow, printed in *Tri Laoidhean le Donnachadh Mac Dhugaill* (1853).
30. Keenan (1983), p. 157; Connolly (1982), p. 60; Neville (1993), p. 27.
31. Connolly (1982), p. 80; Carleton (1889), p. 10.; Gallagher (1736), Intro.; F.M. Jones (1952). The most comprehensive discussion of the relationship between the Catholic church and Irish is in Ó Tuathaigh (1986).
32. Ó Cuív (1986), p. 380; Corish (1981), p. 109.
33. Coombes (1981), pp. 85–8.
34. *Christian Examiner*, September 1833, quoted in De Brún (1983a), p. 309.
35. Febvre and Martin (1976), pp. 319–20.

CHAPTER 10   THE IDEOLOGY OF STATUS IN IRELAND

1. Turner (1988); Jouanna (1977); Goubert (1973), pp. 153–67.
2. Mandrou (1964), 1985 edn, pp. 178–9; Muchembled (1985), pp. 288–93.
3. Muchembled (1990), p. 145.
4. Beckett (1986), pp. 93–5; Connolly (1992), p. 65.
5. McCormack (1985), p.70; Boyce (1982), p. 127; *The Parliamentary Register* IX (Dublin, 1790), pp. 129–30.
6. Nic Eoin (1990), p. 478.
7. Jouanna (1977), Ch. IX.
8. This argument was put to me by Tom Bartlett.
9. O'Raithbheartaigh (1932), pp. 21–2.
10. Cunningham and Gillespie (1988).
11. Ó Catháin (1987); Meyer (1972), p. 1024 ff.
12. Corkery (1924), Ch. VI; Ó Cuív (1986), pp. 374–423; Cullen (1969); Ó hOgáin (1990), pp. 2–3.
13. Devine (1988).
14. Connolly (1992), pp. 130–1: Castan (1974), pp. 16–17, 115.
15. Connolly (1992), p. 143.
16. Cullen (1969), p. 25; Bartlett (1982).
17. [Chetwood] (1746), pp. 147–8; Connolly (1988); the most comprehensive treatment is Whelan (1995).
18. Cullen (1969), p. 25; Wilde (1852), pp. 101–2.
19. Parl 1825a, pp. 696, 698; Ó Tuathaigh (1972), p. 1.
20. Fender (1914), p. 95; Tocqueville (1953), p. 174.
21. Ó Beaglaoich and McCurtin (1732).
22. Davis (1988), pp. 74–5; Connolly (1987), p. 45; Lecky (1892), Vol. I, p. 355.
23. An Act for the better suppressing Tories, Robbers and Rapparees, 7 Will. III c. 21; for half compensation, 10, 11 Ch. I; on the principle of collective and territorial responsibility see Radzinowicz (1956), pp. 163–7.
24. 6 Anne c. 11 (1707); 6 G I c. 12; the legislation was renewed for 21 years as late as 1755, 29 G II c. 8. For one example of fraud, see *The Trial and Conviction of Patrick Hurley* (London and Dublin, 1701): Hurley claimed to have been robbed of 1200 pounds.
25. Ó Buachalla (1976), p. 46. See also Ó Fiaich (1973), pp. 93 and 146.

Although it is probably by a northern poet, the earliest version is in a manuscript written in Kerry in 1701. The printed versions are from mid-nineteenth century manuscripts.

26. Thompson (1991); Jenkins (1983), p. 194.
27. The classic exposition is Thompson (1971).
28. Burke (1978), pp. 270–81; Whelan (1993).
29. 'Letter to the Protestants of Ireland', printed in Gilbert (1909), pp. 284–7.
30. The precise origins of the term 'Protestant Ascendancy' have been the subject of debate over the last ten years, largely centring on whether the appearance of the term in speeches and pamphlets of the 1780s signified the full elaboration of the concept. From the point of view of the history of traditional ideologies discussed here, McCormack's designation of the Corporation Address of 1792 as the first full appearance of the concept is most convincing. The most recent summing up of the debate is McCormack (1993).
31. *A full and accurate report of the debates in the Parliament of Ireland in the session 1793 . . .* (Dublin, 1793), p. 240.
32. McCormack (1993), p. 141.
33. *Orange Vindicated in a reply to Theobald McKenna* (Dublin, 1799), p. 17. The same point had been made by Fitzgibbon in the debates on the 1793 Catholic Relief Bill.
34. McClelland (1973). The ballad was originally printed in *The Orange Miscellany* (Huddersfield, 1815). The Kanes (Ó Catháin) had in fact been a Gaelic landed family in the area.

CHAPTER 11 POPULAR PRINT AND POPULAR CULTURE

1. Cullen (1981), p. 238; Clark (1979), pp. 122–5, 252–5; Lee (1980); Hoppen (1984), pp. 456–60.
2. Chartier (1989); Schenda (1984); Nelson (1976–7); Chartier and Roche (1984), pp. 420–2; the phrase 'collective reading' is used in Richter (1987), pp. 12–13.
3. Mandrou (1964), p. 22; criticisms include Chartier (1988a) particularly pp. 164–7, Lyons (1986), and Guilcher (1990).
4. Ó Duilearga (1942); Ó Duilearga (1945); Bruford (1968), pp. 56–7.
5. Ó Tuathail (1939).
6. Mason (1814–19), Vol. III, pp. 639–40; Tocqueville (1959), p. 167; [Whitty] (1825).
7. There are other examples in Donnelly (1980) and Connolly (1986), p. 19; for the price of newspapers in the 1820s, see Inglis (1952), p. 9.
8. Reproduced in Sheehy (1980), p. 35.
9. Schenda (1984).
10. HO 100/180/125 – I am grateful to Tom Bartlett for this reference; Logan (1992), p. 103; [R. Challoner trans. P. Denn], *Machtnuig go Maith Air* (Clonmel, 1819). For the *Pious Miscellany* see Chapter 6.
11. Mason (1814–19), Vol. I, p. 318. For the manuscripts, Bruford (1968), p. 50.
12. Chartier characterises the implicit reading of the *Bibliothèque Bleue* as 'linear and not at all global' (1985), p. 86.

13. Ó hOgáin (1985), pp. 184–5.
14. The phrase is from Ong (1982).
15. The role of prophecy in the protest of the 1820s is described by Donnelly (1983).
16. Scott (1985).
17. Particularly Ó Farrell (1976).
18. Donnelly (1980); Miller (1978), pp. 66–90; Bartlett (1985); Adams (1987), pp. 86–90; Ó Buachalla (1983).
19. The other being the Book of Daniel: see Cohn (1957), pp. 19–29.
20. Miller (1978), p. 82.
21. MacAlister (1938–56).
22. DeBrún, 'The Irish Society's Bible Teachers' (1983a), p. 294.
23. Quoted in Saunders (1950), pp. 261–3.
24. Quoted in O'Ferrall (1985), p. 263.
25. Fender (1914), p. 95.
26. Ó Coigligh (1987), pp. 147–8.
27. Scott (1985).
28. See Donnelly (1983), pp. 107–10.
29. *A Pastoral Address to the Deluded and Illegal Association of Ribbonmen*, quoted in Read (ed.), *The Cabinet of Irish Literature* (1902 edn), pp. 76–80.
30. Danaher (1972); Whelan (1988) and (1993). The literature on popular protest is large: for summaries, see Clark and Donnelly (1983), pp. 25–35, and Fitzpatrick (1985).
31. Kearney (1979); Malcolm (1983).
32. There is a summary of this literature in Connolly (1985), pp. 49–60. The principal works are Larkin (1972), Miller (1975), Hynes (1978), Corish (1981), Connolly (1982), Keenan (1983), McGrath (1990), Mooney (1990) and Inglis (1987), Chs 6 and 7, an overview which follows Elias.
33. Davis (1974) and Chartier (1984).
34. Mooney (1990), p. 189; Keenan (1983), p. 22; 'superstition' has 16 entries in the index of Corish (1981) but is nowhere defined in the text; for the changing definitions of superstition, see Monter (1983), Ch. 7.
35. Connolly (1982), p. 111, Keenan (1983), p. 113; a partial exception is the folklorist Diarmuid Ó Giolláin (1990), who emphasises 'a continuum of the sacred from official religion to folk-religion'. However, he goes on to develop a Gramscian notion of conflict between the two which is structurally not far removed from the historians' presentation: 'Unofficial world views ... are *always* in opposition to the official worldview' (p. 68 – my emphasis).
36. Clark (1985), p. 63; Carmichael (1900), with a selection in De Waal (1988), p. 5: 'Religion permeated everything they did. They made no distinction between the secular and the sacred.'
37. Tipps (1973); So (1990), pp. 33–6. I am grateful to Tony Varley for these references.
38. Wall (1969); Connolly (1982), p. 278; for criticism of similar 'dualisms' in the historiography of nineteenth-century rural France, Sahlins (1994), pp. 129–34.

39. Mooney (1990), pp. 189, 208–10; Larkin (1972), pp. 649–50; Ni Dhonnchadha (1991); Cullen (1981), pp. 131–2.
40. Connolly (1985), p. 25.
41. Lee (1985), pp. 662–6; Kennedy (1979); Taylor (1990).
42. Duncan (1894), p. 194. A fuller argument for the fundamental continuity of traditional and modern is made in Horton (1982).
43. Smith (1973), p. 66; Hoppen (1984), p. 216; Cullen (1981), p. 22.

Bibliography

PRIMARY SOURCES

Manuscripts

Dublin
National Library:
  Ms 407: Scrapbook of Mrs William Hickey
  Ms 3978: Scrapbook of John O'Daly
  Ms 12 123: Records of the Guild of St Luke
  Ordinance Survey Letters (manuscripts in the Royal Irish Academy, transcripts in the National Library)

National Archives:
  Rebellion Papers
  Revenue Exchequer 2B/105/9, 2B/105/22

Representative Church Body [Church of Ireland] Library:
  Kildare Place Society Book Sub-Committee Ms

Religious Society of Friends Archives:
  Ms MM II: Inventory of Samuel Fuller

Dublin City Library, Gilbert Collection:
  Robinson Manuscripts

Department of Irish Folklore, University College Dublin:
  Irish Folklore Commission Manuscripts

Belfast
Public Record Office of Northern Ireland:
  T1095/2/25 Customs letter book 1786–1822
  Grand Jury Presentments, Co. Down 1816

Cork
City Library:
  Job book of Henry Denmead 1813–17

London
Public Record Office:
  CUST I/40: Commissioners of Excise (Ireland), minute book 1746
  E 190 1363/1: Chester port books, 1701

Manchester
John Rylands Library:
Irish MS 64 (Microfilm in National Library of Ireland)

Editions of Texts

J. Ashton (1882) *Chap-books of the Eighteenth Century* London
G. Bollème and L. Andriès (1983) *Les Contes Bleues* Paris
R. Chartier (1982) *Figures de la Gueuserie* Paris
A. Carmichael (1900) *Carmina Gadelica: hymns and incantations . . . collected in the Highlands and Islands of Scotland . . .* 5 vols Edinburgh
M. De Paor (1995) *Tadhg Gaelach Ó Súilleabháin* Dublin
Dain Spioradail le Dughall Bochanan (Glasgow 1946)
A. Farge (1982) *Le Miroir des Femmes* Paris
R. Favre (1984) *La Fin Dernière* Paris
S. Fender (1914) *The songs of Tomás Ruadh Ó Súilleabháin* Dublin
J.T. Gilbert (1909) *Calendar of the Ancient Records of Dublin* Vol. XIV Dublin
M. Gunn (1984) *A Chomharsain Éistigí agus amhráin eile as Co. an Chláir* Dublin
A. Hayward (1926) *A Complete History of the Lives and Robberies of the Most Notorious Highwaymen, by Alexander Smith* London
D. Hyde (1906) *Amhráin Diadha Chúige Chonnacht: The Religious Songs of Connaught* Dublin
H.-J. Lüsebrink (1984) *Histoires Curieuses et Véritables de Cartouche et Mandrin* Paris
R.A.S. MacAlister (1938–56) *Lebor Gabala Erenn: The Book of the Taking of Ireland* 5 vols Dublin
L. McBean (1919) *Buchanan, the Sacred Bard of the Scottish Highlands* London
F. McEvoy (1988) *The Life and Adventures of James Freney* Kilkenny
S. Mac Giollarnath (1941) *Annála Beaga ó Iorrus Aithneach* Dublin
M. McGrath (1936–7) *Cinnlae Amhlaoidh Uí Shúilleabháin/The Diary of Humphrey O'Sullivan* 4 vols London
T. Mac Síthigh (1984) *Paróiste an Fheirtéaraigh* Dublin
L. McKenna (1919) *Dánta do chum Aonghus Fionn O Dálaigh* Dublin
B. Ó Buachalla (1976) *Nua Dhuanaire* Dublin
C. Ó Coigligh (1987) *Raiftearaí: Amhráin agus Dánta* Dublin
T. Ó Donnchadh (n.d.) *An Leabhar Muimhneach* Dublin
T. Ó Fiaich (1973) *Art Mac Cumhaigh: Dánta* Dublin
R. Ó Foghludha (1905) *Amhráin Phiarais Mhic Gearailt* Dublin
R. Ó Foghludha (1929) *Tadhg Gaelach* Dublin
R. Ó Fodhludha (1941) *Dánta Diaga Phádraig Din* Dublin
Cecile O'Rahilly (1951) *Five Seventeenth-century Political Poems* Dublin
T. Ó Raithbheartaigh (1932) *Genealogical Tracts* Dublin
S. Ó Tuama and T. Kinsella (1981) *An Duanaire 1600–1900: Poems of the Dispossessed* Mountrath, Co. Laois
J.L. Rayner and G.T. Crook (1926) *The Complete Newgate Calendar* London
P. Rawlings (1992) *Drunks, Whores and Idle Apprentices: criminal biographies of the eighteenth century* London

'Report on the State of Popery, Ireland, 1731' *Archivium Hibernicum* I–IV (1912–15)

J. Szoverffy (1958) 'Rí Naomh Seoirse: Chapbooks and Hedge Schools' *Éigse* IX p. 114–28.

E. De Waal (1988) *The Celtic Vision: Prayers and Blessings from the Outer Hebrides* London

P. Ua Duinnín (1903) *Amhráin Thaidhg Ghaedhalaigh Uí Shúilleabháin* Dublin

Official Publications

Proclamations, Ireland at large, 1744–1753

Journals of the Irish House of Commons

The Parliamentary Register IX (Dublin, 1790)

Report of the Commissioners of Irish Education Enquiry 1791 (Printed in H.C. 1857–8 XXII pt. 3, pp. 341–79)

A full and accurate report of the debates in the Parliament of Ireland in the session 1793 . . . (Dublin, 1793)

Parl 1809: *Third Report from the Commissioners of the Board of Education in Ireland,* H.C. 1809 VII

Parl 1810a: *Twenty-eighth Report from the Select Committee on Finance: Police* H.C. 1810 IV

Parl 1810b: *Ninth Report from the Commissioners of the Board of Education in Ireland,* H.C. 1810 X

Parl 1812–13: *Fourteenth Report from the Commissioners of the Board of Education in Ireland,* H.C. 1812–13 VI

Parl 1822: *Third Report of the Commission of Inquiry into the Collection and Management of Revenue in Ireland* H.C. 1822 XII

Parl 1824: *An Account of the Number of Licences granted to Hawkers and Pedlars in the last 7 years* H.C. 1824 XVIII

Parl 1825a: *Report from the Select Committee on the State of Ireland* H.C. 1825 VIII

Parl 1825b: *First Report of the Commissioners of Irish Education Inquiry* H.C. 1825 XII

Parl 1826–7: *Second Report of the Commissioners of Irish Education Inquiry* H.C. 1826–7 XII

Parl 1830: *Report on the state of the poor in Ireland* H.C. 1830 VII

Parl 1835a: *First Report . . . into the condition of the poorer classes in Ireland* H.C. 1835 XXXII

Parl 1835b: *Report from the Select Committee . . . [on] Orange Lodges,* HC 1835 XV

Parl 1844: *Return of the number of Hawkers Licenced in each of the years 1800, 1810, 1820, 1830, 1840 and 1843* H.C. 1844 XXXII

Parl 1881: *Eighth Report of the Royal Commission on Historical Manuscripts* Appendix – Part 1 (Section II) (1881)

Newspapers and Periodicals

Belfast Newsletter
Dublin Courant
Dublin Journal
Dublin Penny Journal
Faulkner's Dublin Journal
Freeman's Journal
The Irish Builder
Northern Star
Tipperary Free Press

Printed Books Pre-1800

Authentic memoir of the remarkable and surprising exploits of Mandrin, Captain-General of the French Smugglers... (Dublin, 1755)
H. Cavendish (1791) *A Statement of the Public Accounts of Ireland* London
[W.R. Chetwood] (1746) *A Tour Through Ireland* London
A Compleat and true account of all the robberies committed by James Carrick, John Mulhoni and their accomplices in Dublin, Cork, Limerick, Waterford and other places in Ireland. To which is added, A true copy of his dying words etc. written by James Carrick (London, 1722)
Count Hanlan's Downfall or a true and exact account of the killing of that archtraytor and tory Redmond O'Hanlan by Art O'Hanlan one of his own party, on the 25th day of April 1681... (Dublin, 1681)
[D. Defoe] (1727) *A Brief State of the Inland or Home Trade* London
J. Gallagher (1736) *Sixteen Irish Sermons, in an easy and familiar stile* Dublin
R. Graves (1794) *A Sermon Preached Before the Members of the Association for Discountenancing Vice* Dublin
The Irish Rogue or the comical history of the lives and actions of Teague O'Divelly from his birth to this present year 1690 (London, 1690)
The Last speech and dying Words of Elinor Sils... (Dublin, 1725)
The last speech, confession and dying words of Jonathan Wild, the notorious thief taker and keeper of Newgate in London (Dublin, 1725)
The Last Speech of J[onathan] W[ild] the notorious thief taker (Dublin, 1725)
The Life and Actions of Lewis Dominique Cartouche who was broken alive upon the wheel at Paris November 28 1721... (London, 1722)
The Life and Death of the Incomparable and indefatigable TORY Redmond O'Hanlyn, commonly called Count Hanlyn (Dublin, 1682)
The Life and Glorious Actions of the most Heroic and Magnanimous Jonathan Wild, Generalissimo of the prig forces in Great Britain and Ireland... (London, 1725)
The Life of Nicholas Mooney, alias Jackson, alias The Black Knight, a notorious highwayman and street robber, who was executed at Bristol on Friday April 24th 1752... *with an account of his sincere repentance, taken from his first confinement to his execution* (London, 1752)
The Life of Nicholas Mooney, alias Jackson, born at Regar near Rathfarnham in the county of Dublin, wherein is contained an account of his parentage

*and education . . . the many robberies he committed in and about London . . .
condemned and executed there Friday April 24th 1752* (Dublin, 1752)

W. Magee (1796) *A Sermon Preached before the Members of the Association
for Discountenancing Vice* Dublin

H. More (1788) *Thoughts on the Importance of the Manners of the Great to
General Society* 4th edn Dublin

C. Ó Beaglaoich and H. McCurtin (1732) *Foclóir Béarla Gaoidheilge/English
Irish Dictionary* Paris

Orange Vindicated in a reply to Theobald McKenna (Dublin, 1799)

Mr. Orde's Plan for an Improved System of Education in Ireland (Dublin,
1787)

*Particulars of the very singular and remarkable trials, convictions and es-
capes of John Shepherd . . .* (Dublin, 1786)

B. Rich (1612) *A true and kind excuse written in defence of that book entitled
A New Description of Ireland* London

*Some account of the life and death of Nicholas Mooney . . . sold at the Rev.
Mr. Wesley's preaching houses in town and country* (London, 1776)

W. Stokes (1799) *Projects for Re-establishing the Internal Peace and Tranquility
of Ireland* Dublin

*Thoughts on National Education in six letters printed in the Dublin Evening
Post in October and September 1795* (n.p., n.d. c.1795)

The Trial and Conviction of Patrick Hurley (London and Dublin, 1701)

Printed Books 1800–1900

*The Battle of Ventry Harbour which took place in the fourth century and
which continued without intermission for 366 days* (Cork, 1824)

*The Battle of Ventry Harbour which took place in the fourth century and
which continued without intermission for 366 days* (Limerick, 1835)

T. Beddoes (1813) *Hints to Husbandmen by the late Doctor Beddoes, reprinted at the suggestion of Charles Sneyd Edgeworth* Dublin [orig. *Good
advice for the husbandman in harvest*, London, 1808]

R. Bell (1804) *A description of the condition and manners . . . of the peasantry of Ireland as they were between the years 1780 and 1790* London

R. Bellew (1808) *Thoughts and suggestions on the means apparently necessary to be adopted by the legislature towards improving the condition of
the Irish peasantry* London

W. Carleton (1830) 'The Hedge Schoolmaster and the Abduction of Mat
Kavanagh', in W. Carleton, *Traits and Stories of the Irish Peasantry* Vol.
II Dublin

W. Carleton (1845) *Parra Sastha or The History of Paddy-go-easy and his
wife Nancy* Dublin

W. Carleton (1889) 'The Poor Scholar', in W.B. Yeats (ed.), *Stories from
Carleton* London

[R. Challoner trans. P. Denn]: *Machtnuig go Maith Air* (Clonmel, 1819)

Cheithre Soleirseadha de'n Eagnuidheacht Chriostuidhe etc. (Waterford, 1820)

C. Coote (1801a) *A Statistical Survey of King's County* Dublin

C. Coote (1801b) *A Statistical Survey of Queen's County* Dublin

T. Crofton Croker (1824) *Researches in the South of Ireland* London

T. Crofton Croker (1825–8) *Fairy Legends and Traditions of the South of Ireland* London

Cuimhne Coluimcille or The Gartan Festival, being a record of the celebration held at Gartan on the 9th of June 1897 (Dublin, 1898)

J. D'Alton (1847) *Memoir of the family of French* Dublin

D. Dewar (1812) *Observations on the Character, Customs and Superstitions of the Irish and some of the causes which have retarded the moral and political improvement of Ireland* London

M. Doyle [W. Hickey] (1831) *Irish Cottagers* Dublin

M. Doyle [W. Hickey] (1833) *Hints Addressed to the Small Holders and Peasantry of Ireland on Subjects Connected with Health, Temperance, Morals etc.* Dublin

M. Doyle [W. Hickey] (1834) *Hints on Emigration to Upper Canada* Dublin, 3rd edn

M. Doyle [W. Hickey] (1835) *An Address to the Landlords of Ireland on subjects connected with the melioration of the lower classes* Dublin, 2nd edn

L. Duncan (1894) 'Further Notes from Co. Leitrim', *Folklore* V pp. 177–209

H. Dutton (1808) *Statistical Survey of Co. Clare* Dublin

An Essay on the Present State of Manners and Education among the Lower Class of the People of Ireland and the Means of Improving Them London (3rd edn 1805)

E. Evans (1897) *Historical and Bibliographical account of Almanacs, Directories, etc. published in Ireland from the Sixteenth Century . . .* Dublin

First Report of the Catholic Book Society (Dublin, 1828)

J. Gallagher, trans. J. Byrne (1835) *Sixteen Sermons* Dublin

A. Gazier (ed.) (1880) *Lettres à Grégoire sur les Patois de France* Paris

J. Hardiman (1831) *Irish Minstrelsy or Bardic Remains of Ireland* Dublin

Hints on the Formation of Lending Libraries in Ireland (Dublin, 1824)

The Irish Freebooter or Surprising adventures of Captain Redmond O'Hanlon . . . (London, 1819)

[P. Kennedy] (1865) 'Folk Books of France', *Dublin University Magazine* Nov. 1865, pp. 516–33

[P. Kennedy] (1866) 'Irish Folk Books of the last century', *Dublin University Magazine*, May 1866, pp. 532–43

M.J. Knott (1836) *Two Months at Kilkee* Dublin

M. Leadbeater (1811–13) *Cottage Dialogues among the Irish Peasantry* Dublin

M. Leadbeater (1813) *The Landlord's Friend* Dublin

M. Leadbeater (1822) *Cottage Biography, being a collection of lives of the Irish peasantry* Dublin

M. Leadbeater (1862) *The Leadbeater Papers* Dublin

W. Lecky (1892) *A History of Ireland in the Eighteenth Century* London

Leonard McNally (1812) *The Justice of the Peace in Ireland* Dublin

W. Shaw Mason (1814–19) *A Statistical Account or Parochial Survey of Ireland* Dublin

G. Matthieson (1836) *Journal of a tour in Ireland in 1835* London

C. Moreau (1827) *The Past and Present Statistical State of Ireland* London

T. Newenham (1809) *A View of the Natural, Political and Commercial Circumstances of Ireland* London

D.J. O'Donoghue (1896) *The Life of William Carleton, being his autobiography and letters etc.* London

[J. O'Driscoll] (1820) *Thoughts and Suggestions on the Education of the Peasantry of Ireland* 2nd edn Cork

J. O'Driscoll (1823) *Views of Ireland: Moral, Political and religious* London

J.P. Prendergast (1868) *The Tory War in Ulster* Dublin

J.P. Prendergast (1887) *Ireland from Restoration to Revolution* London

W. Roberts (1834) *Memoirs and Correspondence of Hannah More* London

*A Short Treatise on the evils of litigation, malpractices of attorneys and law-
yers etc.* (Dublin, 1846)

*The Surprising Life and adventures of the gentleman robber Redmond O'Hanlon,
generally called the Captain General of the Irish robbers . . .* (Glasgow n.d.
c.1850)

E. Wakefield (1812) *An Account of Ireland, Statistical and Political* London

J.S. Walker (1825) *An Essay on the Education of the People* London

J.E. Walsh (1847) *Sketches of Ireland Sixty Years Ago* Dublin

R. Whateley, trans. T Connellan (1835) *Reidhleighin air Ghnothuibh Cearba*
Dublin

[M.J. Whitty] (1825) *Captain Rock in London or The Chieftain's Weekly Gazette*
London

W.R. Wilde (1852) *Irish Popular Superstitions* Dublin

N. Wiseman (1855) 'Home Education of the Poor', in *Lectures in connection
with the Educational Exhibition of the Society of Arts, Manufactures and
Commerce, delivered at St. Martin's Hall, Long Acre* London

SECONDARY SOURCES

Ireland

J.R.R. Adams (1987) *The Printed Word and the Common Man: Popular Culture in Ulster 1700–1900* Belfast

J.R.R. Adams (1988) 'Some aspects of the influence of printed material on
everyday life in eighteenth-century Ulster', in A. Gailey (ed.), *The Uses of
Tradition: Essays presented to G.B. Thompson* pp. 111–122 Belfast

D.H. Akenson (1970) *The Irish Education Experiment: The National System
of Education in the Nineteenth Century* London

D.H. Akenson (1981) *A Protestant in Purgatory: Richard Whately, Archbishop
of Dublin* Hamden, Conn.

D.H. Akenson (1988) *Small Differences: Irish Catholics and Irish Protestants:
An International Perspective* Kingston, Ontario

T.C. Barnard (1991) 'The uses of 23 October 1641 and Irish Protestant celebrations', *English Historical Review* CVI pp. 889–920.

T.C. Barnard (1993) '1641: A Bibliographical Essay', in B Mac Cuarta (ed.),
Ulster 1641: Aspects of the rising pp. 173–86 Belfast

J.R. Barrett (1977) 'Why Paddy drank: the social importance of whiskey in
pre-Famine Ireland', *Journal of Popular Culture XII* pp. 155–66

G.L. Barrow (1975) *The Emergence of the Irish Banking System 1820–45* Dublin

T. Bartlett (1982) 'The O'Haras of Annaghmore c.1600–c.1800: Survival and

Revival', *Irish Economic and Social History* IX pp. 34–52

T. Bartlett (1985) 'Defenders and Defenderism in 1795', *Irish Historical Studies* XXIV pp. 373–394

T. Bartlett (1990) 'Militarisation and politicisation in Ireland (1780–1820)', in *Culture et Pratiques Politiques en France et en Irlande XVIe–XVIIIe Siècle* pp. 125–36 Paris

M. Beames (1983) *Peasants and Power: The Whiteboy movements and their control in pre-Famine Ireland* Brighton

J. Bell (1987) 'The improvement of Irish farming techniques since 1750', in P. O'Flanagan et al. (eds), *Rural Ireland 1600–1900: Modernisation and Change* pp. 24–41 Cork

C. Benson (1990) 'Printers and Booksellers in Dublin 1800–1850', in R. Myers and M. Harris (eds), *Spreading The Word: Distribution Networks of Print 1550–1850* pp. 45–59 Winchester

R.D.C. Black (1960) *Economic Thought and the Irish Question, 1817–1870* Cambridge

D. Bowen (1978) *The Protestant Crusade in Ireland 1800–1870* Dublin

Bradshaw (1916) *A Catalogue of the Bradshaw Collection of Irish Books in the University Library, Cambridge* Cambridge

M. Brennan (1990) 'The changing composition of Kilkenny's landholders 1641–1700', in W. Nolan and K. Whelan (eds), *Kilkenny: History and Society* pp. 161–96 Dublin

M.J. Bric (1987) 'Priests, parsons and politics: the Rightboy protest in county Cork, 1785–1788', in C.H.E. Philpin (ed.), *Nationalism and Popular Protest in Ireland* pp. 163–90 Cambridge

A. Bruford (1968) *Gaelic Folktales and Medieval Romances* Dublin

Catalogue of Manuscripts in the Royal Irish Academy (Dublin, 1926–)

S. Clark (1979) *Social Origins of the Irish Land War* Princeton

S. Clark and J. S. Donnelly Jr. (1983) *Irish Peasants: Violence and Political Unrest* Dublin

W.S. Clark (1965) *The Irish Stage in the Country towns 1720–1800* Oxford

J. Coleman (1924) 'John O'Daly', *The Irish Book Lover* (May 1924) pp. 65–7

S.J. Connolly (1982) *Priests and People in Pre-famine Ireland* Dublin

S.J. Connolly (1983) 'The "blessed turf": cholera and popular panic in Ireland, June 1832', *Irish Historical Studies* XXIII pp. 214–32

S.J. Connolly (1985) 'Popular culture in pre-famine Ireland', *Canadian Journal of Irish Studies* XII pp. 12–28

S.J. Connolly (1987) 'Violence and order in the eighteenth century', in P. Flanagan et al. (eds), *Rural Ireland 1600–1900: Modernisation and change* pp. 42–61 Cork

S.J. Connolly (1988) 'Albion's Fatal Twigs: Justice and law in the eighteenth century', in R. Mitchison and P. Roebuck (eds), *Economy and Society in Scotland and Ireland 1500–1939* pp. 117–25 Edinburgh

S.J. Connolly (1992) *Religion, Law and Power: The Making of Protestant Ireland 1660–1760* Oxford

J. Coombes (1981) *A Bishop of Penal Times: John O'Brien, Bishop of Cloyne and Ross 1701–1769* Cork

P. Corish (1981) *The Catholic Community in the Seventeenth and Eighteenth Centuries* Dublin

P. Corish (1985) *The Irish Catholic Experience: A Historical Survey* Dublin

D. Corkery (1924) *The Hidden Ireland: a study of Gaelic Munster in the eighteenth century* Dublin

W.H. Crawford (1982) 'The Ulster Irish in the eighteenth century', *Ulster Folklife* XXVIII pp. 24–32

L.M. Cullen (1969) 'The Hidden Ireland: reassessment of a concept', *Studia Hibernica* IX

L.M. Cullen (1981) *The Emergence of Modern Ireland, 1600–1900* London

L.M. Cullen (1990a) 'Patrons, teachers and literacy in Irish', in M. Daly and D. Dickson (eds), *The Origins of Popular Literacy in Ireland: Language Change and Educational Development 1700–1920* pp. 15–44 Dublin

L.M. Cullen (1990b) 'The social and economic evolution of Kilkenny in the seventeenth and eighteenth centuries' in W. Nolan and K. Whelan (eds), *Kilkenny: History and Society* pp. 273–88 Dublin

B. Cunningham and R. Gillespie (1988) 'The purposes of patronage: Brian Maguire of Knockninny and his manuscripts', *Clogher Record* XIII pp. 38–49

N. Curtin (1990) 'Symbols and rituals of United Irish mobilisation' in H. Gough and D. Dickson (eds), *Ireland and the French Revolution* pp. 68–82 Dublin

M. Daly (1979) 'The Development of the National School system, 1831–40', in A. Cosgrove and D. McCartney (eds), *Studies in Irish History presented to R. Dudley Edwards* pp. 150–63 Dublin

M. Daly (1981) *A Social and Economic History of Ireland since 1800* Dublin

M. Daly (1990) 'Literacy and language change in the late nineteenth and early twentieth centuries', in M. Daly and D. Dickson (eds), *The Origins of Popular Literacy in Ireland: Language Change and Educational Development 1700–1920* pp. 153–66 Dublin

K. Danaher (1972) *The Year in Ireland* Cork

S. Daultrey, D. Dickson and C. Ó Gráda (1981) 'Eighteenth-century Irish population: new perspectives from old sources', *Journal of Economic History* XLI pp. 601–28

P. de Brún (1982–3) 'Some documents concerning Valentia Erasmus Smith School, 1776–95', *Journal of the Kerry Historical and Archaeological Society* XV–XVI pp. 70–82.

P. de Brún (1983a) 'The Irish Society's Bible Teachers 1818–1827', *Éigse* XIX pp. 281–332

P. de Brún (1983b) 'Scriptural instruction in Irish: a controversy of 1830–31', in P. de Brún et al. (eds), *Folia Gadelica: Essays presented to R.A. Breatnach* pp. 134–59 Cork

T.M. Devine (1988) 'Unrest and stability in rural Ireland and Scotland, 1760–1840', in R. Mitchison and P. Roebuck (eds), *Economy and Society in Ireland and Scotland, 1500–1939* pp. 126–39 Edinburgh

D. Dickson (1988) 'Capital and Country 1600–1800', in A. Cosgrove (ed.), *Dublin Through the Ages* pp. 67–76 Dublin

D. Dickson (1993) 'Paine and Ireland' in D. Dickson et al. (eds), *The United Irishmen: Republicanism, Radicalism and Rebellion* pp. 135–50 Dublin

D. Dickson and M. Pollard (1973) 'Henry Denmead and the printing of Alexander's "Glanmire"', *Journal of the Cork Historical and Archaeological Society* LXXVIII pp. 134–42

[E.R. Dix] (1910) 'Irish chap books, song books and ballads', *Irish Book Lover* II October 1910 pp. 33–5

E.R. Dix and S. Ó Casaide (1905) *A List of the Books, Pamphlets etc. printed wholly or partly in Irish . . . to 1820* Dublin

E.R. Dix (1930) 'Printing in Limerick in the nineteenth century', *Irish Book Lover* XVIII pp. 39–42

J.S. Donnelly (1980) 'Propagating the cause of the United Irishmen', *Studies* LXIX pp. 5–23

J.S. Donnelly (1983) 'Pastorini and Captain Rock: Millenarianism and sectarianism in the Rockite movement of 1821–4', in S. Clark and J.S. Donnelly Jr. (eds), *Irish Peasants: Violence and Political Unrest* pp. 102–39 Dublin

T. Dunne (1990) 'Popular ballads, revolutionary rhetoric and politicisation', in H. Gough and D. Dickson (eds), *Ireland and the French Revolution* pp. 139–55 Dublin

B. Earls (1984) 'A note on *Seanchas Amhlaoibh Í Luinse*', *Béaloideas: The Journal of the Folklore Society of Ireland* LII pp. 9–34

B. Earls (1988) 'Bulls, Blunders and Bloothers: An examination of the Irish bull', *Béaloideas: The Journal of the Folklore Society of Ireland* LVI pp. 1–92

B. Earls (1990) 'Mere Irish and Fior Ghael' [review article], *Revue Belge de Philologie et d'Histoire* LXVIII pp. 739–51

P.B. Eustace and O.C. Goodbody (eds) (1957) *Quaker records, Dublin: Abstracts of Wills* Dublin

P. Fagan (1986) *The Second City: Portrait of Dublin 1700–1760* Dublin

G. Fitzgerald (1984) 'Estimates for baronies of minimum level of Irish speaking amongst successive decennial cohorts', *Proceedings of the Royal Irish Academy* LXXXIV pp. 117–55

D. Fitzpatrick (1985) 'Unrest in rural Ireland', *Irish Economic and Social History* XII pp. 98–105

T.W. Freeman (1957) *Pre-Famine Ireland: An Historical Geography* Manchester

A. Gailey (1977) 'The Ballyhagan Inventories 1716–1740', *Ulster Folklife* XV pp. 36–64

P. Gibbon (1975) *The Origins of Ulster Unionism* Manchester

J.M. Goldstrom (1966) 'Richard Whately and political economy in school books, 1833–80', *Irish Historical Studies* XV pp. 131–46

J.M. Goldstrom (1972) *The Social Content of Education 1808–1870: A Study of the Working Class School Reader in England and Ireland* Shannon

I. Green (1995) '"The necessary knowledge of the principles of religion": catechisms and catechising in Ireland, c.1560–1800', in A. Ford, J. McGuire and K. Milne (eds), *As by Law Established: The Church of Ireland since the Reformation* pp. 67–88 Dublin

J.C. Greene and G. Clark (1993) *The Dublin Stage 1720–45: A calendar of plays, entertainments and afterpieces* London

D. Hayton (1995) 'Charity schools and the enterprise of religious and social reformation, 1690–1730', in A. Ford et al. (eds), *As by Law Established: The Church of Ireland since the Reformation* pp. 166–86 Dublin

D. Hayton (1988) 'From Barbarian to Burlesque: English images of the Irish c.1660–1750', *Irish Economic and Social History* XV pp. 5–31

R. Herbert (1942) *Limerick Printers and Printing* Limerick

236   *Bibliography*

J. Hewitt (1974) *Rhyming Weavers and other country poets of Antrim and Down* Belfast

J. Hill (1984–5) 'National festivals, the state and Protestant Ascendancy in Ireland, 1790–1829', *Irish Historical Studies* XXIV pp. 30–51

J. Hill (1988) 'Popery and Protestantism, Civil and Religious Liberty: the disputed lessons of Irish history 1690–1812', *Past and Present* No. 118 pp. 96–129.

J. Hill (1993) '1641 and the quest for Catholic Emancipation, 1691–1829', in B. Mac Cuarta (ed.), *Ulster 1641: Aspects of the Rising* pp. 159–72 Belfast

J. Hoban (1983) 'The survival of the hedge schools – a local study', *Irish Educational Studies* III No. 2 pp. 21–36

K. Hollo (1996) '*Eachtra Ridire na Leomhan* ina comhthéacs Eorpach', in M. Ní Dhonnchadha (ed.), *Nua-Léamha: Gnéithe de chultúr, stair agus polaitíocht na hÉireann c.1600–c.1900* pp. 57–71 Dublin

R.J. Hunter (1988) 'Chester and the Irish Book Trade, 1681', *Irish Economic and Social History* XV pp. 89–93

M. Hurst (1969) *Maria Edgeworth and the Public Scene* London

E. Hynes (1978) 'The Great Hunger and Irish Catholicism', *Societas* VIII pp. 137–56.

B. Inglis (1952) 'O'Connell and the Irish Press', *Irish Historical Studies* VIII pp. 1–27

T. Inglis (1987) *Moral Monopoly: The Catholic Church in Modern Irish Society* Dublin

F.M. Jones (1952) 'The Congregation of Propaganda and the publication of Dr. O'Brien's Irish Dictionary, 1768', *Irish Ecclesiastical Record* LXXVII pp. 29–37

H.F. Kearney (1979) 'Father Matthew: Apostle of modernisation', in A. Cosgrove and D. McCartney (eds), *Studies in Irish History presented to R. Dudley Edwards* pp. 164–75 Dublin

D. Keenan (1983) *The Catholic Church in Nineteenth Century Ireland: A Sociological Study* Dublin

P. Kelly (1985) '"A light to the blind": the voice of the dispossessed élite in the generation after the defeat at Limerick', *Irish Historical Studies* XXIV pp. 431–62.

A. Kenealy (ed.) (1908) *The Memoirs of Edward Vaughan Kenealy LLD* London

L. Kennedy (1979) 'Profane images in the Irish popular consciousness', *Oral History* VII pp. 42–7

G. Kirkham (1990) 'Literacy in North–West Ulster 1680–1860', in M. Daly and D. Dickson (eds), *The Origins of Popular Literacy in Ireland: Language Change and Educational Development 1700–1920* pp. 73–96 Dublin

E. Lapoint (1992) 'Irish immunity to witch-hunting', *Éire-Ireland* XXVII pp. 76–92

E. Larkin (1972) 'The Devotional Revolution in Ireland, 1850–1875', *American Historical Review* LXXVII pp. 625–52

J. Lee (1980) 'Patterns of rural unrest in nineteenth century Ireland: a preliminary survey', in L.M. Cullen and F. Furet (eds), *Irlande et France 17e–20e siècle: pour une histoire rurale comparée* pp. 223–37 Paris

J. Lee (1985) *Ireland 1912–1985: Politics and Society* Cambridge

B. Loftus (1990) *Mirrors: William III and Mother Ireland* Dundrum, Co. Down

B. Loftus (1993) *Mirrors: Orange and Green* Dundrum, Co. Down

D. McCabe (1985) 'Magistrates, peasants and the Petty Sessions courts: Mayo 1823–50', *Cathair na Mart* V pp. 45–53

A. McClelland (1973) 'The Battle of Garvagh', *Ulster Folklife* XIX pp. 41–55

W.J. McCormack (1985) *Ascendancy and tradition in Anglo-Irish Literary History 1789–1939* Oxford

W.J. McCormack (1993) *The Dublin Paper War of 1786–1788: A bibliographical and critical inquiry* Dublin

R.B. McDowell (1979) *Ireland in the Age of Imperialism and Revolution* Oxford

T. McGrath (1990) 'The Tridentine evolution of modern Irish Catholicism: a re-examination of the 'Devotional Revolution' thesis', in R. Ó Muirí (ed.), *Irish Church History Today* pp. 84–99 Armagh

M. McKenna (1991) 'A textual history of *The Spiritual Rose*', *Clogher Record* XIV pp. 52–73

E. MacLysaght (1939) *Irish Life in the Seventeenth Century* Dublin

K. McMahon (1980–1) 'The O'Hanlon Letter', *Seanchas Ard Mhacha* X pp. 37–41

E. Malcolm (1983) 'Popular recreation in nineteenth century Ireland' in O. McDonagh, W.F. Mandle and P. Travers (eds), *Irish Culture and Nationalism 1750–1950* pp. 40–55 Dublin

[J.J. Marshall] (1910) 'Irish chap books', *Irish Book Lover* I July 1910 pp. 157–9

D. Miller (1975) 'Irish Catholicism and the Great Famine', *Journal of Social History* IX pp. 81–98

D. Miller (1978) 'Presbyterianism and "Modernisation" in Ulster', *Past and Present* 80 pp. 66–90

J. Mokyr (1983) *Why Ireland Starved: a quantitative and analytical history of the Irish economy 1800–1850* London

J. Mokyr and C. Ó Gráda (1988) 'Poor and getting poorer? Living standards in Ireland before the Famine', *Economic History Review* 2nd ser. XLI pp. 209–35

D. Mooney (1990) 'Popular religion and clerical influence in pre-famine Meath', in R.V. Comerford et al. (eds), *Religion, Conflict and Co-existence in Ireland* pp. 188–218 Dublin

H.K. Moore (1904) *An Unwritten Chapter in the History of Irish Education: being the history of... the Kildare Place Society* London

R. Munter (1988) *A Dictionary of the Print Trade in Ireland 1550–1775* New York

G. Murphy (1961) *The Ossianic Lore and Romantic Tales of Medieval Ireland* Dublin

G. Neville (1993) '"He spoke to me in English; I answered him in Irish": Language shift in the folklore archives' in J. Brihault (ed.), *L'Irlande et ses Langues: Colloque de Rennes 1992* pp. 19–32 Rennes

M. Nic Eoin (1990) 'Irish language and literature in County Kilkenny in the nineteenth century' in W. Nolan and K. Whelan (eds), *Kilkenny: History and Society* pp. 465–80 Dublin

M. Ni Dhonnchadha (1991) 'Neamhlitearthacht agus Gaeilge: Eagna na staraithe?' *Comhar* L (2) pp. 22–5

N. Ní Riain (1993) 'The nature and classification of religious songs in Irish', in *Irish Musical Studies* Vol. 2 pp. 190–253

B. Ó Buachalla (1983) 'An Mheisiasacht agus an Aisling', in P. de Brun et al. (eds), *Folia Gadelica: Essays Presented to R.A. Breatnach* pp. 72–87 Cork

S. Ó Canainn (1983) 'The Education Inquiry 1824–1826 in its social and political context', *Irish Educational Studies* III No. 2 pp. 1–20

D. Ó Catháin (1987) 'Dermot O'Connor, translator of Keating', *Eighteenth-century Ireland* II pp. 67–87

B. Ó Conchúir (1982) *Scríobhaithe Chorcaí 1700–1850* Dublin

B. Ó Cuív (1986) 'Irish language and literature, 1691–1845', in T.W. Moody and W.E. Vaughan (eds), *A New History of Ireland* Vol. IV pp. 374–423 Oxford

[S. Ó Duilearga] J.H. Delargy (1942) 'Irish stories and storytellers', *Studies* XXXI pp. 31–46.

[S. Ó Duilearga] J.H. Delargy (1945) 'The Gaelic Storyteller', *Proceeding of the British Academy* XXXI pp. 2–46

T. Ó Dúshláine (1987) *An Eoraip agus Litríocht na Gaeilge 1600–1650: Gnéithe den Bharócachas Eorpach i Litríocht na Gaeilge* Dublin

P. O'Farrell (1976) 'Millenialism, Messianism and Utopianism in Irish History', *Anglo-Irish Studies* II pp. 45–68

F. O'Ferrall (1985) *Catholic Emancipation: Daniel O'Connell and the birth of Irish democracy* Dublin

P. Ó Fiannachta (1982) 'Tadhg Gaelach 1715–1795', in Ó Fiannachta, *Léas eile ar ár litríocht* pp. 184–96 Dublin

D. Ó Giolláin (1990) 'Perspectives in the study of folk-religion', *Ulster Folklife* XXXVI pp. 66–73

C. Ó Gráda (1973) 'Seasonal migration and post-Famine adjustment in the west of Ireland', *Studia Hibernica* XIII pp. 48–76

C. Ó Gráda (1988) *Ireland Before and After the Famine: explorations in economic history* Manchester

T. Ó hAilín (1968) 'The Irish Society agus Tadhg Ó Coinnialláin', *Studia Hibernica* VIII pp. 60–78

D. Ó hÓgáin (1985) *The Hero in Irish Folk History* Dublin

D. Ó hÓgáin (1990) 'Folklore and Literature: 1700–1850', in M. Daly and D. Dickson (eds), *The Origins of Popular Literacy in Ireland* pp. 1–13 Dublin

P. Ó Laoghaire (1916) *Mo Scéal Féin* Dublin

N. Ó Muraíle (1983) 'Staid na Gaeilge i gConnachta in aimsir Sheáin mhic Éil', in A Ní Chanainn (ed.), *Leon an Iarthair: Aistí ar Sheán Mac Éil* pp. 37–66 Dublin

M. Ó Murchú (1986) 'The retreat from Irish: the statistical analysis and other aspects', in J. Dooge (ed.), *Ireland in the Contemporary World: Essays in honour of Garret Fitzgerald* pp. 112–21 Dublin

S. Ó Súilleabháin (1967) *Irish Wake Amusements* Cork

D. O'Sullivan (1960) *Songs of the Irish* Dublin

G. Ó Tuathaigh (1972) *Ireland Before the Famine* Dublin

G. Ó Tuathaigh (1986) 'An chléir Chaitliceach, an léann dúchais agus an cultúr in Éirinn, 1750–1850', in P Ó Fiannachta (ed.), *Léachtaí Cholmcille* XVI pp. 110–39

E. Ó Tuathail (1939) 'A rare Ulster booklet', *The Irish Book Lover* (Sept. 1939) pp. 122–7

M. Pollard (1973) '"Borrowed Twelve Cuts": a Cork printer lends and borrows', *Long Room* VIII pp. 19–28

M. Pollard (1989) *Dublin's Trade in Books 1550–1800* Oxford

H. Senior (1966) *Orangeism in Ireland and Britain 1795–1836* London

J. Sheehy (1980) *The Rediscovery of Ireland's Past: The Celtic Revival 1830–1930* London

H. Shields (1987) 'Popular broadsides in the library of the RSAI', *Ulster Folklife* 33 pp. 1–25

H. Shields (1990) 'Printed aids to folk singing 1700–1900', in M. Daly and D. Dickson (eds), *The Origins of Popular Literacy in Ireland* pp. 139–52 Dublin

E.M. Sibbett (1914–15) *Orangeism in Ireland and Throughout the Empire* Belfast

L. Taylor (1990) 'Stories of power, powerful stories: the drunken priest in Donegal', in E. Badone (ed.), *Religious Orthodoxy and Popular Faith in European Society* pp. 163–85 Princeton, NJ

M. Tynan (1985) *Catholic Instruction in Ireland 1720–1950: the O'Reilly–Dunlevy Catechetical Tradition* Dublin

S. Ua Casaide (1911) 'Some editions of O'Sullivan's Miscellany', *Waterford and South–East of Ireland Archaeological Society Journal* XIV pp. 113–22

R Uí Ógáin (1995) *Immortal Dan: Daniel O'Connell in Irish Folk Tradition* Dublin

M. Wall (1989) 'The Catholics of the Towns and the Quarterage Dispute in Eighteenth Century Ireland', in G. O'Brien (ed.), *Catholic Ireland in the Eighteenth century: The Collected Essays of Maureen Wall* pp. 61–72 Dublin

T. Wall (1958) *At the Sign of Dr. Hay's Head: . . . the hazards and fortunes of Catholic printers and publishers from the later penal times to the present day* Dublin

T. Wall (1964) 'The Catholic Book Society and the Irish Catholic Magazine', *Irish Ecclesiastical Record* CI pp. 289–303

W. Wheeler (1978) 'The Spread of Provincial Printing in Ireland up to 1850', *Irish Booklore* IV pp. 7–19

K. Whelan (1988) 'The Regional Impact of Irish Catholicism 1700–1850', in W.J. Smyth and K. Whelan (eds), *Common Ground: Essays in the Historical Geography of Ireland presented to T. Jones Hughes* pp. 253–77 Cork

K. Whelan (1993) 'The United Irishmen, the enlightenment and popular culture', in D. Dickson et al. (eds), *The United Irishmen: Republicanism, Radicalism and Rebellion* pp. 269–96 Dublin

K. Whelan (1993) 'The geography of hurling', *History Ireland* I pp. 25–8

K. Whelan (1995) 'An underground gentry? Catholic middlemen in eighteenth century Ireland', *Eighteenth-Century Ireland* X pp. 7–68

H. White and N. Lawrence (1993) 'Towards a history of the Cecilian movement in Ireland', in *Irish Musical Studies* Vol. 2 pp. 78–107

N.J.A. Williams (1986) 'Thomas Wilson, Francis Hutchinson agus litriú na Gaeilge', *Eighteenth-century Ireland* I pp. 204–7

Britain and Europe

R.D. Altick (1957) *The English Common Reader* Chicago

L. Andriès (1978) 'La Bibliothèque Bleue: les réécritures de "Robert le Diable"', *Littérature* XXX pp. 51–66.

L. Andriès (1989) *La Bibliothèque Bleue au 18e siècle: Une tradition éditoriale* Oxford

M.S. Archer and M. Vaughan (1971) *Social Conflict and Educational Change in England and France 1789–1848* Cambridge

G. Astoul (1992) 'L'Alphabetisation en Haut-Languedoc au XVIIIe siècle. Les aléas de la méthode Maggiolo dans le diocèse de Montauban', *Annales Du Midi* Vol. 104 pp. 175–94

F. Aydelotte (1913) *Elizabethan Rogues and Vagabonds* London

F. Barbier (1985) 'Libraires et colporteurs', in *Histoire de l'Édition Française Vol. 3: Le Temps des Éditeurs* pp. 229–59 Paris

J. Barry (1995) 'Literacy and literature in popular culture: reading and writing in historical perspective', in T. Harris (ed.), *Popular Culture in England, c.1500–1850* pp. 69–94 London

J.V. Beckett (1986) *The Aristocracy in England 1660–1914* Oxford

Y.-M. Bercé (1987) *Revolt and Revolution in Early Modern Europe* Manchester

H. Bleackley and S.M. Ellis (1933) *Notable British Trials: Jack Sheppard* London

A. Blok (1972) 'The Peasant and the Bandit: Social banditry reconsidered', *Comparative Studies in Society and History* XIV pp. 494–503

G. Bollème (1969) *Les Almanachs Populaires aux XVIIe et XVIIIe Siècles* Paris

J. Bowen (1981) *A History of Western Education Vol. III: The Modern West* London

P. Burke (1978) *Popular Culture in Early Modern Europe* London

B. Capp (1977) *Astrology and the Popular Press* London

B. Capp (1985) 'Popular Literature', in B. Reay (ed.), *Popular Culture in Seventeenth Century England* pp. 198–243 London

Y. Castan (1974) *Honnêteté et Relations Sociales en Languedoc* Paris

M. de Certeau, D. Julia and J. Revel (1986) 'The Beauty of the Dead: Nisard', in M. de Certeau, *Heterologies: Discourse on the other* pp. 119–36 Manchester

R. Chartier (1984) 'Culture as appropriation: popular cultural uses in early modern France', in S. Kaplan (ed.), *Understanding Popular Culture: Europe from the Middle Ages to the Nineteenth Century* pp. 229–55 Berlin

R. Chartier (1985) 'Du livre au lire', in R. Chartier (ed.), *Pratiques de la Lecture* pp. 62–88 Paris

R. Chartier (1987) 'The literature of roguery in the *Bibliothèque Bleue*', in R. Chartier, *The Cultural Uses of Print in Early Modern France* pp. 265–342 Princeton, NJ

R. Chartier (1988a) 'Figures of the 'other': Peasant reading in the Age of the Enlightenment', in R. Chartier, *Cultural History: Between practices and representations* pp. 151–71 Cambridge

R. Chartier (1988b) *Frenchness in the History of the Book: From the History of Publishing to the History of Reading* Worcester, Mass.

R. Chartier (1989) 'Leisure and Sociability: reading aloud in early modern

Europe', in S. Zimmermann and R. Weissman (eds), *Urban Life in the Renaissance* pp. 103–20 London

R. Chartier and D. Roche (1984) 'Les Pratiques Urbaines de l'Imprimé', in H.J. Martin and R. Chartier (eds), *Histoire de l'Édition Française Vol. 2: Le Livre Triomphant 1660–1830* pp. 403–29 Paris

R. Chartier, M. Compere and D. Julia (1976) *L'Education en France du XVIe Siècle au XVIIIe Siècle* Paris

C. Cipolla (1969) *Literacy and Development in the West* Harmondsworth

S. Clark (1985) 'French historians and early modern popular culture', *Past and Present* No. 100 pp. 62–99

N. Cohn (1957) *The Pursuit of the Millenium* London

L. Colley (1992) *Britons: Forging the Nation 1707–1837* London

D. Cressy (1989) *Bonfires and Bells: National memory and the Protestant calendar in Elizabethan and Stuart England* London

A. Croix (1981) *La Bretagne aux 16e et 17e Siècles: La Vie, la Mort, la Foi* Paris

H. Dagnall (1991) *'Give us back our eleven days': an account of the change from the old style to the new style calendar in Great Britain in 1752* London

J.-J. Darmon (1972) *Le Colportage de Librairie sous le Second Empire: Grands Colporteurs et Culture Populaire* Paris

R. Darnton (1979) *The Business of Enlightenment: A Publishing History of the Encyclopédie* Cambridge, Mass.

R. Darnton (1986) 'First Steps towards a history of reading', *Australian Journal of French Studies* 33(1) pp. 5–30

J.A. Davis (1988) *Conflict and Control: Law and order in nineteenth century Italy* Basingstoke

N.Z. Davis (1974) 'Some tasks and themes in the study of popular religion', in H. Oberman and C. Trinkhaus (eds), *The Pursuit of Holiness in Late Medieval and Renaissance Religion* pp. 307–14 Leiden

J. Delumeau (1977) *Catholicism Between Luther and Voltaire: a new view of the Counter-Reformation* London

J.-L. Desgraves (1984) *Répertoire Bibliographique des Livres Imprimés en France au 17e Siècle* Vol. 11 Baden-Baden

T. Devine (1994) *Clanship to Crofter's War: the social transformation of the Scottish Highlands* Manchester

G. Dotoli (1991) *Letteratura per il Popolo in Francia (1600–1750)* Bari

V. Durkacz (1983) *The Decline of the Celtic Languages* Edinburgh

F. Du Sorbier (1983) *Récits de Gueuserie et Biographies Criminelles de Head à Defoe* Nancy

F. Du Sorbier (1986) 'La Biographie Criminelle Anglaise: Formes narratives et circuits de diffusion', *Dix-huitieme Siècle* No. 18 pp. 155–68

G. Duval (1986) *Littérature de Colportage et Imaginaire Collectif en Angleterre à l'Époque des Dicey (1720–v.1800)* Bordeaux

S. Eliot (1996) 'The Reading Experience Database: problems and possibilities', *Publishing History* XXXIX pp. 87–100

C. Emsley (1987) *Crime and Society in England 1750–1900* London

L.B. Faller (1987) *Turned to Account: The Forms and Functions of Criminal Biography in Late Seventeenth- and Early Eighteenth-Century England* Cambridge

A. Fawcett (1971) *The Cambuslang Revival: the Scottish evangelical revival of the eighteenth century* London

L. Febvre and H.-J. Martin (1976) *The Coming of the Book* London

L. Fontaine (1993) *Histoire du Colportage en Europe (XVe–XIXe siècle)* Paris

F. Furet and J. Ozouf (1982) *Reading and Writing: Literacy in France from Calvin to Jules Ferry* Cambridge

B. Garnot (1990) *Le Peuple au Siècle des Lumières: Échec d'un dressage culturel* Paris

S. Gibson (1949) *A Bibliography of Francis Kirkman, with his prefaces, dedications and commendations (1652–80)* Oxford

C. Ginzburg (1980) *The Cheese and the Worms: The cosmos of a sixteenth-century miller* New York

P. Goubert (1973) *The Ancien Régime: French Society 1600–1750* London

H. Graff (1987a) *Labyrinths of Literacy: Reflections on literacy past and present* London

H. Graff (1987b) *The Legacies of Literacy: Continuities and contradictions in western culture and society* Bloomington

R. Grevet (1993) 'Alphabétisation et instruction des populations rurales du nord de la France (milieu XVIIIe–début XIXe siècle) *Annales de Bretagne et des Pays de l'Ouest* C pp. 441–52

B. Grosperrin (1984) *Les Petites Écoles sous l'Ancien Régime* Rennes

Y. Guilcher (1990) 'A-t-on lu à la veillée paysanne traditionelle?' in *Tradition et Histoire dans la Culture Populaire* pp. 143–59 Grenoble

M. Harris (1982) 'Trials and Criminal Biographies: A case study in distribution', in R. Myers and M. Harris (eds), *Sale and Distribution of Books from 1700* pp. 1–36 Oxford

E.J. Hobsbawm (1959) *Primitive Rebels* Manchester

E.J. Hobsbawm (1969) *Bandits* London

T.A. Horne (1978) *The Social Thought of Bernard Mandeville* London

R. Horton (1982) 'Tradition and modernity revisited', in S. Lukes and Hollis (eds), *Rationality and Relativism* pp. 201–60 Oxford

R.A. Houston (1985) *Scottish Literacy and the Scottish Identity* Cambridge

R.A. Houston (1988) *Literacy in Early Modern Europe: Culture and Education 1500–1800* London

A.L. Humphreys (1940) 'The highwayman and his chapbook', *Notes and Queries* Vol. 178 pp. 308–12, 326–30, 347–50, 368–72, 383–6, 402–4

R. Hutton (1994) *The Rise and Fall of Merry England: The ritual year 1400–1700* Oxford

G. Jenkins (1987) *The Foundations of Modern Wales 1642–1789* Oxford

P. Jenkins (1983) *The Making of a Ruling Class: the Glamorgan Gentry 1640–1790* Cambridge

M.G. Jones (1938) *The Charity School Movement: a study of eighteenth-century puritanism in action* Cambridge

M.G. Jones (1952) *Hannah More* Cambridge

R.O. Jones (1971) *The Golden Age (A Literary History of Spain* Vol. II) London

A. Jouanna (1977) *Ordre Social: Mythes et Hierarchies dans la France du XVIe siècle* Paris

P. Joutard (1983) *Ces Voix qui Nous Viennent du Passé* Paris

W.C. Lane (ed.) (1905) *A Catalogue of English and American Chapbooks and Broadside Ballads in Harvard College Library* Cambridge, Mass.

C. Langlois (1974) *Un Diocèse Breton au 19e siècle: Le Diocèse de Vannes, 1800–30* Paris

T. Laqueur (1976) 'The Cultural Origins of Popular Literacy in England 1500–1850', *Oxford Review of Education* II pp. 255–75

D. Launay (1993) *La Musique Réligieuse en France du Concile de Trent à 1804* Paris

F. Lebrun (1993) 'La culture populaire et la Bibliothèque Bleue trente ans apres Robert Mandrou', *Annales de Bretagne et des Pays de l'Ouest* C pp. 453–8

R.D. Lee and R. Schofield (1981) 'British population in the eighteenth century', in R. Floud and D. McCloskey (eds), *The Economic History of Britain since 1700: Vol I. 1700–1860* pp. 17–35 Cambridge

J.-L. Le Flocc'h and G. Le Menn (1985) 'L'Imprimerie-Librairie Blot à Quimper en 1777', *Mémoires de la Société Historique et Archaeologique de Bretagne* Vol. 62 pp. 157–78

G. Le Menn (1980) 'L'Apparition des Colloques et la réimplantation de l'Imprimerie en Basse-Bretagne', *Études Celtiques* No. 17 pp. 269–74

G. Le Menn (1983) 'Du theatre savant au theatre populaire en Basse-Bretagne. Histoire et themes', in *Langue et Littérature Orales dans l'Ouest de la France* pp. 428–50 Angers

G. Le Menn (1985) 'Une Bibliothèque Bleue en Langue Bretonne', *Annales de Bretagne et des Pays de l'Ouest* Vol. 92 pp. 229–40

B. Levack (1987) *The Witch-hunt in Early Modern Europe* London

P. Linebaugh (1977) 'The Ordinary of Newgate and his *Account*', in J.S. Cockburn (ed.), *Crime in England 1550–1800* pp. 246 69 London

R. Luckett (1981) 'Bishop Challoner: the Devotional Writer', in E. Duffy (ed.), *Challoner and his Church* London

H.-J. Lusebrink (1982) 'La Letteratura del Patibolo: Continuità e transformazioni tra '600 e '800', *Quaderni Storici* 49 pp. 285–301

M. Lyons (1986) 'Oral culture and rural community in nineteenth-century France: the *veillée d'hiver*', *Australian Journal of French Studies* 23 pp. 102–14

J. MacInnes (1951) *The Evangelical Movement in the Highlands of Scotland 1688–1800* Aberdeen

N. McKendrick, J. Brewer and J.H. Plumb (1982) *The Birth of a Consumer Society: The Commercialisation of Eighteenth-century England* London

D. MacLean (1915) *Typographia Scoto-Gadelica or books printed in the Gaelic of Scotland from the year 1567 to the year 1914* Edinburgh

M. McLeod (1975) Notes to *Gaelic Psalms from Lewis* Tangent Records TNGM 120

F. Maiello (1994) *Storia del Calendario: La misurazione del tempo, 1450–1800* Torino

R. Mandrou (1964) *De la Culture Populaire aux 17e et 18e siècles: La Bibliothèque Bleue de Troyes* Paris

J.-L. Marais (1980) 'Littérature et culture "populaires" aux XVIIe et XVIIIe siècles. Réponses et questions', *Annales de Bretagne et des Pays de l'Ouest* Vol. 87 pp. 65–105

H.-J. Martin (1978) 'The *Bibliothèque Bleue*: Literature for the masses in the Ancien Régime', *Publishing History* III pp. 70–102

R. Mayer (1994) 'Nathaniel Crouch, bookseller and historian: popular historiography and cultural power in late seventeenth-century England' *Eighteenth-Century Studies* XXVII pp. 391–419.

D. Meek (1989) 'Ath-sgrudadh: Dughall Bochanan', *Gairm: An Raitheachan Gaidhlig* No. 147 pp. 269–80, No. 148 pp. 319–31

J. Meyer (1972) *La Noblesse Bretonne au XVIIIe Siècle* Paris

J. Meyer (1974) 'Alphabétisation, lecture et écriture: Essai sur l'instruction populaire en Bretagne du XVe au XIXe siècle', in *Histoire de l'Enseignement de 1610 à nos jours: Actes du 95e Congres National des Sociétés Savantes* pp. 333–53 Paris

E.W. Monter (1983) *Ritual, Myth and Magic in Early Modern Europe* Brighton

A. Morin (1974) *Catalogue Descriptif de la Bibliothèque Bleue de Troyes* Geneva

R. Muchembled (1985) *Popular Culture and Elite Culture in France* Baton Rouge, La.

R. Muchembled (1990) *Société et Mentalités dans la France Moderne XVIe–XVIIIe siècle* Paris

H. & L. Mui (1989) *Shops and Shopkeeping in Eighteenth-century England* London

W. Nelson (1976–7) 'From "Listen Lordings" to "Dear Reader"', *University of Toronto Quarterly* XLVI pp. 110–24

V. Neuburg (1971) *Popular Education in Eighteenth-Century England* London

V. Neuberg (1977) *Popular Literature: A History and Guide* London

R. O'Day (1982) *Education and Society 1500–1800: The social foundations of education in early modern Britain* London

W.J. Ong (1982) *Orality and Literacy* London

A.A. Parker (1967) *Literature and the Delinquent: The Picaresque Novel in Spain and Europe 1599–1753* Edinburgh

J. Passmore (1970) *The Perfectibility of Man* London

S. Pedersen (1986) 'Hannah More meets simple Simon: Tracts, chapbooks and popular culture in late eighteenth century England', *Journal of British Studies* XXV pp. 84–113

J.-C. Perrot (1975) *Genèse d'une Ville Moderne: Caen au XVIIIe Siècle* Paris

R. Porter (1982) *English Society in the Eighteenth Century* London

J. Queniart (1978) *Culture et Société Urbaines dans la France de l'Ouest au XVIIIe siècle* Paris

J. Queniart (1979a) 'L'Utilisation des inventaires en histoire socio-culturelle', in B. Vogler (ed.), *Les Actes Notariés: Source d'histoire sociale XVIe–XIXe siècles* pp. 241–55 Strasbourg

J. Queniart (1979b) 'Les apprentissages scolaires élémentaires au XVIIIe siècle: faut-il réformer Maggiolo?' *Revue d'Histoire Moderne et Contemporaine* XXIV pp. 3–37

J. Queniart (1984) 'De l'Oral à l'Écrit', *Histoire de l'Éducation* XXI pp. 28–9

J. Queniart (1985) 'Livre et Lecture en Bretagne', *Mémoires de la Société Historique et Archaeologique de Bretagne* Vol. 62 pp. 287–300

J. Queniart (1991) 'Contenus et pratiques du livre de cantiques dans la France Catholique', in H.E. Bodeker, G. Chaix and P. Veit (eds), *Le Livre Religieux et ses Pratiques* pp. 252–65 Gottingen

M. Quinlan (1941) *Victorian Prelude: A history of English manners 1780–1830* New York

L. Radzinowicz (1956) *A History of English Criminal Law and its Administration from 1750* Vol. II London

B. Reay (1983) 'Popular literature in seventeenth-century England' [Review article], *Journal of Peasant Studies* X pp. 243–9

E. Rees (1987) *Libri Walliae: A Catalogue of Welsh Books and Books Printed in Wales 1546–1820*, 2 vols Aberystwyth

N. Richter (1987) *La Lecture et ses Institutions: La Lecture Populaire 1700–1918* Le Mans

D. Roche (1987) *The People of Paris: an essay in popular culture in the eighteenth century* Leamington Spa

J. Rose (1992) 'Re-reading the English Common Reader: a preface to the history of audiences', *Journal of the History of Ideas* LIII pp. 47–70

P. Sahlins (1994) *Forest Rites: the War of the Demoiselles in nineteenth-century France* Cambridge, Mass.

L.J. Saunders (1950) *Scottish Democracy 1815–1840* Edinburgh

A. Sauvy (1984) 'Le Livre aux champs', in *Histoire de l'Édition Française Vol. 2: Le Livre Triomphant 1660–1830* pp. 430–45 Paris

A. Sauvy (1989) *Le Miroir du Coeur: Quatre siècles d'images savantes et populaires* Paris

R. Schenda (1984) 'Canali et processi di circolazione della letteratura scritta e semiorale tra gli strati subalterni Europei nel '700 et '800', in G. Cerina et al. (eds), *Oralità e Scrittura nel Sistema Letterario: Atti del Covegno, Cagliari, 14–16 Aprile 1980* pp. 49–61 Cagliari

J.-C. Schmitt (1983) *The Holy Greyhound: Guinefort, healer of children since the thirteenth century* Cambridge

R. Schofield (1981) 'Dimensions of illiteracy in England 1750–1850', in H. Graff (ed.), *Literacy and Social Development in the West* pp. 201–13 Cambridge

G. Scott (1985) '"The times are fast approaching": Bishop Charles Walmesley as prophet', *Journal of Ecclesiastical History* XXXVI pp. 590–604

C. Shammas (1990) *The Pre-industrial Consumer in Britain and America* Oxford

J.A. Sharpe (1985) '"Last Dying Speeches": Religion, Ideology and Public Execution in Seventeenth-Century England', *Past and Present* No. 107 pp. 144–67

H. Sieber (1977) *The Picaresque* London

H. Silver (1965) *The Concept of Popular Education: A study of ideas and social movements in the early nineteenth century* London

J. Simons (1992) 'Romance in the Eighteenth Century Chapbook', in J. Simons (ed.), *From Medieval to Medievalism* pp. 122–43 Basingstoke

A. Smith (1973) *The Concept of Social Change* London

O. Smith (1986) *The Politics of Language 1791–1819* Oxford

A. So (1990) *Social Change and Development: Modernisation, dependence and world system theories* London

M. Spufford (1981) *Small Books and Pleasant Histories: Popular fiction and its readership in seventeenth-century England* Cambridge

M. Spufford (1984) *The Great Reclothing of Rural England: Petty chapmen and their wares in the seventeenth century* London

E.P. Thompson (1971) 'The Moral Economy of the English Crowd in the Eighteenth Century', *Past and Present* 50 pp. 76–136

E.P. Thompson (1975) 'The Crime of Anonymity', in D. Hay et al. (eds),

Albion's Fatal Tree: Crime and Society in Eighteenth-century England
pp. 255– 344 London

I.A.A. Thompson (1991) 'Hidalgo and *pechero*: the language of "estates" and
"classes" in early-modern Castile', in P. Corfield (ed.), *Language, History
and Class* Oxford

D. C. Tipps (1973) 'Modernisation theory and the comparative study of societies: a critical perspective', *Comparative Studies in Society and History*
XV pp. 199–226

A. de Tocqueville (1959) *Journeys to England and Ireland* London

B.S. Turner (1988) *Status* Milton Keynes

M. Venard (1979) 'Popular Religion in the Eighteenth Century', in W.J. Callahan
and D. Higgs (eds), *Church and Society in Catholic Europe in the Eighteenth Century* Cambridge

D. Vincent (1981) *Bread, Knowledge and Freedom: a study of nineteenth
century working-class autobiography* London

D. Vincent (1989) *Literacy and Popular Culture in England 1750–1914* Cambridge

N. Vray (1993) *Protestants de l'Ouest: Bretagne, Normandie, Poitou 1519–
1907* Rennes

T. Watt (1991) *Cheap Print and Popular Piety 1550–1640* Cambridge

E. Weber (1981) 'The reality of folktales', *Journal of the History of Ideas*
XLII pp. 93–113

C. Withers (1988) *Gaelic Scotland: The transformation of a culture region*
London

L.B. Wright (1935) *Middle Class Culture in Elizabethan England*

Unpublished Theses

M. Feeney (1982) 'Print for the People: the growth in popular writing and
reading facilities in Ireland', MLitt Trinity College Dublin

H. Hislop (1990) 'The Kildare Place Society 1811–31: an Irish experiment in
popular education', PhD Trinity College Dublin

J. Logan (1992) 'Schooling and the promotion of literacy in nineteenth-century Ireland', PhD University College Cork

M. McGovern (1994) 'The Siege Myth: The Siege of Derry in Ulster Protestant political culture, 1689–1939', PhD University of Liverpool

S. Ó Canainn (1979) 'Relations between the Catholic Church and the state
with regard to education in Ireland 1795–1825', MEd Trinity College Dublin

J.W. Phillipps (1952) 'A Bibliographical Inquiry into Printing and Bookselling
in Dublin 1670–1800', PhD Trinity College Dublin

P.M. Swanson (1985) 'Popular Literature in the eighteenth century: The Dicey
Chapbooks', PhD Northwestern University, Evanston, Ill.

Index